Blessed is the match that is consumed
in kindling flame.
Blessed is the flame that burns
in the secret fastness of the heart.
Blessed is the heart with strength to stop
its beating for honor's sake.
Blessed is the match that is consumed
in kindling flame.

From the Hebrew of HANNA SENESCH

All the verse translations in
BLESSED IS THE MATCH
are by the author

Marie Syrkin
BLESSED IS THE MATCH
The Story of Jewish Resistance

Philadelphia / 5736–1976
The Jewish Publication Society of America

Contents

Introduction

IN THE FALL OF 1945, immediately upon the conclusion of World War II, I left for Palestine on the S.S. *Gripsholm,* the first ship from New York to sail for the Middle East with civilians since the outbreak of hostilities in 1939. My purpose was to interview survivors of the death camps and participants in Jewish resistance, who at that time were to be found primarily in Palestine. *Blessed Is the Match,* published in 1947, was the result of that voyage.

Since the appearance of this book, among the first on the subject, a huge literature on all aspects of the Holocaust has arisen. The memoirs of survivors have been supplemented by major historical studies, which, like Raul Hilberg's monumental *The Destruction of European Jewry* and Lucy Dawidowicz's much later *The War against the Jews, 1933–1945,* have availed themselves fully of the mass of written evidence and archival material provided by the Nuremberg Trials and other Jewish and German sources. The great ghetto diaries of Emanuel Ringelblum and of Chaim Kaplan have been literally unearthed and published. In Jerusalem, Yad Vashem bulges with countless still unpublished memoirs of survivors of the various ghettos and concentration camps. Nor despite Adorno's stern dictum—to write poetry after Auschwitz is "barbaric"—have poets and novelists been mute. And sociologists have systematically dissected the psyche of the victims.

In 1946 none of the subsequently disclosed documentary

material was available. To establish the chronology of events and to seek to discover the design in the Nazi extermination program from often contradictory facts I had to rely primarily on the immediate memories, not recollected in tranquillity, of the sufferers. To piece together the nature and scope of the varied attempts at rescue and resistance I had the advantage of meeting some of the chief, if for the most part unsuccessful, would-be saviors. Yet with the full advantage of our present knowledge, there is little that I would omit in the narrative as gathered in firsthand encounters with the chief actors, though much that I would add. The testimony of the witnesses given freshly after the event proved to be essentially accurate and forms a significant historic record.

But there is in my opinion another compelling reason for the reissue of *Blessed Is the Match* after thirty years. Those who recounted their experiences did so in innocence and I wrote in innocence. By this I mean that our emotions were pure; we could still feel horror, and we judged with absolute clarity as to who were the guilty and who the sufferers. The murky metaphysics of later decades, in which the "guilt" or complicity of the victim became a kind of extenuation of the criminal, had not as yet evolved. The systematic denigration of the tormented with a consequent implicit rehabilitation of the tormentor was not under way. The symbiosis of the sufferer with the perpetrator of the suffering was a refinement of perception to be evolved by future analysts, and the confusion of roles fashionable in some contemporary writing about the Holocaust was wholly absent.

All the dark notes were sounded: I was told of the ambiguous function of the Jewish councils, the brutality of the Jewish ghetto police, the savage shifts for survival in the concentration camps, and of Jewish collaborators with the Germans. But the overriding theme was Nazi bestiality not Jewish degradation, Jewish valor not Jewish weakness. The victim was a martyr sanctified by his suffering, and his sins, if any, were part of his martyrdom. So, at any rate, did those whose wounds were still raw speak to me in 1945 and 1946. The simple woman who said, "Understand it humanly," was wiser as well as more compassionate than many a more sophisticated future student of the Nazi era.

In part IV, chapter 3, I mention the secret archive gathered by Emanuel Ringelblum and hidden for some later historian. Ringelblum's Yiddish *Notes from the Warsaw Ghetto* were found in a milk can dug up in the ruins of the Warsaw ghetto in 1950. In 1965 Chaim Kaplan's Hebrew diary, discovered by Abraham I. Katsh, was published in English under the title of *Scroll of Agony*. It is startling to see how the testimony of both men, disciplined scholars of note, supports the witness of the untutored men and women to whom I spoke. The secular historian, trained in political thought and action, and the Orthodox Hebrew scholar go through the same baffled progression from initial hopefulness to hopelessness as does the most ignorant ghetto inhabitant. The initial conviction that neither man nor God will permit the carnage to go on gives way finally to a despairing sense of abandonment by both man and God. Each diarist gives terrifying glimpses of what David Rousset has named *l'univers concentrationnaire*. In one of Ringelblum's early entries he records that an eight-year-old child starts screaming, "I want to steal, I want to rob, I want to eat, I want to be a German," and he notes that at the madhouse Jewish lunatics praise Hitler and give the Nazi salute.

As a religious man Kaplan is engaged in a direct theodicy. During the first Hanukkah of the war Kaplan writes: "A simple old woman asks me each day: 'Why is the world silent? Does Israel have no God!' I wished to comfort her in her agony so I lit four Hanukkah candles. And as I kindled the lights I felt they were as humiliated as I." Later he would permit himself the Job-like outcry: "But He who sits in heaven laughs."

Both writers are unsparing in their criticism of the spiritual decline of the ghetto in its extremity, the moral failure of the "criminal Jewish police" and of the "criminal Jewish council," yet the very vehemence of their condemnation indicates how high and uncompromising are their demands on their fellow Jews. Nothing more eloquently brings home Jewish helplessness in the Nazi charnel house than the self-accusations of its bravest spirits. Those who venture to pass judgment on the conduct of European Jewry must marvel more at the degree of fortitude and mutual compassion than at the number of the weak and corruptible. The writers, despite their fury at what has been debased, never lose sight of the truth that the fallen are part of the Jewish tragedy and fellow victims.

This sense of partnership, which in some instances brutalized and in others ennobled, which created heroes and sinners as well as a mass of totally defenseless beings prostrate before the Nazi juggernaut, was communicated to me vividly by those to whom I spoke. The facts were stark and self-evident. Only later would the behavior of European Jewry in its ultimate agony become the subject for psychoanalytic probing, as though the inability of enfeebled, starving men, women, and children to resist armed storm troopers was a mystery to be unraveled by the techniques of social science. Hardly a week passes in which we do not read of sizable groups of adults cowed by one hijacker. And we ask no embarrassing questions about the failure of the crew or passengers to leap at the thug with the bomb. The crew does not wish to endanger the passengers, and the passengers hope to be ransomed. Yet many still presume to censure the behavior of the wholly helpless caught in the Nazi vise.

Even those who escaped incarceration in the ghetto through their own efforts and ingenuity are not freed of blame. In *The Informed Heart* Bruno Bettelheim criticizes the parents of Anne Frank for their attempt to hide. Had they tried to escape to the free world or sought to fight the Germans they might have survived. They should have had a gun to repulse the police; and Anne should have been sent to live with a Dutch family as their child. Passivity and a desire to continue life "as usual," as well as an inability to face the reality of Auschwitz (Oswiecim), doomed the Franks.

These ex post facto strictures seem beside the point. The Franks fled to Holland from Germany in 1933. Had they been blessed with foreknowledge they would have tried to leave the European continent, but though energetic enough to leave Germany they had no prescience of future developments. A glance at a photograph of the dark-haired, dark-eyed Anne dispels the notion that she could have been successfully concealed by a Dutch family as one of their own. Aryan-looking small children could occasionally be concealed in remote villages, but not a thirteen-year-old girl unlike her blond Dutch counterparts. Had the family acquired a pistol it would probably have resulted in the immediate execution of the group, including the one survivor, the father. Perhaps this would have been a more valiant course; it was hardly a prescription for rescue from the death camp.

Perhaps the most widely argued evaluation of Jew and German during the Hitler era appeared in Hannah Arendt's *Eichmann in Jerusalem*. In 1960 Adolf Eichmann (whose negotiations with Joel Brandt are reported by me as told by Brandt in 1946), a key figure in the Nazi extermination program, head of the Gestapo's Jewish Department, and a convicted war criminal, was tracked down by Israeli volunteers in his hiding place in Argentina and taken to Israel to stand trial. In her widely publicized report of the trial Arendt developed two theses, which her considerable reputation as scholar and social philosopher endowed with a ready authority.

The first was the guilt of Jewish leaders and organizations in what befell European Jewry. The crux of her charge, in view of its continued reverberations, merits quotation. Granting that the Jews had no country, government, or arms, she writes: "But the whole truth was that there existed Jewish community organizations and Jewish party and welfare associations on both the local and international level. Wherever Jews lived, there were recognized Jewish leaders and these leaders, almost without exception, cooperated in one way or another, for one reason or another, with the Nazis. The whole truth was that if the Jewish people had really been unorganized and leaderless there would have been chaos and plenty of misery but the total number of victims would hardly have been between five and six million." The corollary of this outrageous indictment was an implicit extenuation of Eichmann as a "little man" who, robotlike, followed his *Führer*'s bidding.

The furor that followed these pronouncements is now history, but their influence is far from spent. By shifting the burden of guilt, Arendt initiated a trend of self-accusation among Jews, with an accompanying tendency to de-emphasize the culpability of the Nazi henchmen. Since my interviews not only with Joel Brandt but with numerous other "leaders" and representatives of the excoriated "Jewish organizations" bore witness to the heroism and ingenuity with which these groups and individuals sought—ineffectually—to rescue Jews and to organize resistance, the relevance to the argument of such early testimony is apparent.

The Jewish councils had the unhappy task of selecting the order in which ghetto dwellers would be dispatched for "resettlement" to unknown destinations. Elaborate studies of the functioning of Jewish councils in various ghettos indicate how detested were some of the council heads, such as Rumkowski of Lodz and Gens of Vilna. And it is clear that even less venal figures sought to defer the expulsion of their own families as long as possible. Yet however heavy the sins of the councils in their efforts to win temporary advantages for themselves, surely only those certain that they would have first chosen death for their own wives and children are in a position to judge them. In every process of "selection," whether in the ghettos or the camps, life for one meant death for another. In a sense everyone who escaped from Hitler, as in all escapes from disaster where the possibilities of rescue are limited, saved himself at the expense of another, if only by taking a place in an immigration quota. Paradoxically, many a survivor interviewed understood the natural, if unadmirable, desire to protect one's immediate kin more readily than many an untried moralist. The reduction of human beings to the level of zoological necessity was part of the Nazi master plan; that it succeeded in some instances is hardly surprising.

One concept in Hannah Arendt's study of the Holocaust

still enjoys wide acceptance and currency: "the banality of evil." This facile phrase was the logical outcome of the thesis that the Eichmanns who executed Hitler's orders, no matter how atrocious, were in reality commonplace men, with no special impulse toward evil, who would presumably just as readily have performed acts of goodness if bidden to do so. In this view Eichmann and his fellows were cogs in a huge machine; they performed their jobs with meticulous care and without any special hate of the Jews. They were not monsters even though their deeds were monstrous. Eichmann's uncontested zeal in shipping Jews to the death chambers even after Himmler, as German defeat appeared inevitable, ordered Eichmann to stop the transports is offered as an example of the latter's extreme conscientiousness, which led him to disregard the orders of a superior because of a high sense of duty to the law of Hitler. These intellectual acrobatics, offered to explain the murderous initiative of an Eichmann in abetting the Final Solution, are worth noting because they extend to the entire Nazi hierarchy and its minions, stopping short presumably only at the figure of Hitler.

Yet Hitler, too, has been described by intimates as commonplace in conversation and demeanor. Albert Speer's recollections of Hitler and his cronies diverting themselves at Berchtesgaden reflect a cultivated gentleman's bored distaste for dull and vulgar men.

But the issue is not the intellectual attainments or exceptional gifts of the Nazi executioners, great and small. However ordinary they may have been by some criteria, in one respect they were extraordinary: they achieved evil on so vast a scale that they succeeded in making evil a commonplace of existence. In their single-minded dedication to the extermination of the Jews, wherever they could be found, Hitler and his accomplices were anything but banal; they were zealots. Their historic distinction is that they succeeded in making evil banal—a quite different matter. Through them the gas chamber and the mass death factory entered the imagination of mankind with incalculable results, and they added a new word to the vocabulary. "Genocide" was introduced into the language by a Jew, Raphael Lemkin, in response to the Nazi experience. Such tenacity of purpose sprang from an impulse too exceptional to be glossed over by phrases like the "banality of evil." The men and women whom I met saw nothing banal in their torturers and nothing banal in what they had suffered. And certainly the Eichmann who declared bluntly to Brandt, *"Ware für Blut; Blut für Ware* [Goods for blood; blood for goods]," was no meek robot.

So much for the sophisticated reassessments of guilt and innocence, which would have seemed incredible in 1945. Another significant aspect of the Holocaust about which new information has become known is the degree of resistance within the death camps and ghettos. Though the revolt of the Warsaw ghetto, because of its scope, rightly remains the most celebrated, records of organized resistance in Lodz, Grodno, and Bialystok have come to light. In the death camps of Treblinka, Sobibor, in Poniatow and Trabnik, similar attempts took place. In each instance ringleaders were readily overpowered and shot down, but in each instance one or two escaped to tell their story—a story that merely confirms how little individual valor availed in the foredoomed struggle.

In *The Destruction of the European Jews* Raul Hilberg comments on the "compliance" of Jews even when standing before a mass grave into which each would shortly fall. He reports a "typical" scene as told by a German eyewitness: "The father was holding the hand of a boy about ten years old and was speaking to him softly; the boy was fighting his tears. The father pointed to the sky, stroked his head, and seemed to explain something to him."

"Compliance" seems a curious term for the scene depicted. Supposing the father had sprung at the SS men lined up behind him with their guns at the ready. Would the hopeless attempt have helped his child, or did the father, seeking to make his child's last hour more endurable by some promise of divine redemption, perform a heroic act of grace?

Another element in the reconsideration of the Holocaust

that should be noted is an ever-growing indignation at the failure of the Allies to intervene in behalf of the Jews of Europe. Criticism of the great democracies for not having taken specific measures to impede the extermination program increases with time. In *When Six Million Died,* published in 1967, Arthur D. Morse, using previously unpublished documents, exposes in appalling detail the refusal of the United States and Great Britain to consider any of the proposals to ransom Jews—proposals that kept reappearing throughout 1944. The same arguments that were responsible for the dismissal of Joel Brandt's attempt were raised in regard to other offers.

Suggestions by the Jewish Agency and representatives of the War Refugee Board that the crematoriums of Auschwitz and Birkenau be destroyed by direct bombing were dismissed by the War Department as impracticable. Carefully worked out proposals for the bombing of the railway lines that led to Auschwitz met the same fate. Chaim Weizmann was informed that the suggestions had been turned down "because of the great technical difficulties involved." Soviet Russia appears to have been particularly averse to any deflection of arms from the war effort. A further suggestion by Chaim Weizmann that not only a token handful of Palestinian parachutists be dropped in Hungary but that a force of hundreds of Palestinian Jews be parachuted behind the enemy lines was rejected by the British. The rationale for these denials was formulated crisply by U.S. Assistant Secretary of War John McCloy: "The positive solution to this problem is the earliest possible victory over Germany." By then, of course, it was too late.

These specious and callous arguments, which ring so hollow now, were accepted by most American Jews during the war years. The terrifying advance of Hitler, the need to marshal every resource to defeat the Nazis, powerfully roused American Jewry. In their emotional response anguish for European Jewry was a major component, but few were in a position either to know of or to dispute the practicability of military measures. American Jews, contrary to later accusations, were neither passive nor indifferent, though in the light of contemporary activism and protest movements American Jewry appears to have been strangely apathetic. Why did they not rush out into the streets in the style of a later generation to demand the admission of European Jews regardless of quotas or to clamor for the adoption of measures calculated to save them? The reason is that they were not a later generation. Furthermore, they were ignorant of the various rescue possibilities being secretly discussed, and, above all, in a war in which victory too long hung in the balance, they were fully committed to the proposition that the defeat of Hitler was the prime objective.

The total horror of the extermination program was not brought home till Eisenhower's troops entered Germany. Before the war and throughout the war American Jews used the methods they had always employed—intervention in Washington through their spokesmen and protests in the press and at mass meetings. It should be noted for the record that to publicize the extermination program Jewish organizations had to *purchase* advertising space in the *New York Times*. I know; I wrote some of the copy. The world was grossly unconcerned, and governments were hostile to any move that might antagonize public opinion—like the question of immigration quotas—or anger the Soviet Union; American Jews, without benefit of foresight, were ignorant and impotent; and, though deeply involved emotionally, they could take no independent action during wartime. The inevitable restrictions of the period should be remembered.

Finally, one omission in my account should be rectified. In my description of what befell Jews in Western Europe I singled out Holland for the help that the Jewish underground received from non-Jews. However, I failed to mention the extraordinary role of Denmark in saving Jews from the Nazis. When I gathered my material there were no Danish Jews in Palestine for me to meet. At any rate, none were called to my attention. The details of Denmark's heroic refusal to allow her Jewish citizens to be deported by the Germans came to light later.

At the time of the German occupation about eight thousand Jews lived in Denmark, where the Germans, who viewed the Danes as fellow Aryans, were less savage in their rule than in Eastern Europe. Yet despite Nazi blandishments and attempts at persuasion, the Danes refused to enact anti-Jewish legislation, expropriate Jewish property, or dismiss Jews from positions in the government. This recalcitrance led to a German decision to deport the Danish Jews to the death camps. The operation was to take place on October 1, 1943. However, Danish Social Democratic leaders learned of the proposed roundup and secretly alerted the Danish population. All Danish Jews were hidden, and in the course of one night were ferried to Sweden with the agreement of the Swedish government. The success of this rescue operation depended on the complete cooperation of the Danish people. This was given. The Germans managed to discover only four hundred Jews, whom they sent to Theresienstadt.

Even the fate of these four hundred Danish Jews continued to disturb the Danish government. The Danes repeatedly asked permission to inspect this camp, which the Germans used as a showplace. The persistent concern of the Danes for their Jewish citizens bore fruit even in Theresienstadt. No Danish Jews were deported to Auschwitz. The Danes wrote one of the few bright pages in the history of the Holocaust, and their achievement has not gone unhonored either in Israel or elsewhere. They are among the "righteous gentiles" for whom a special grove blooms in Jerusalem.

On the other hand, the measure of collaboration in the Nazi persecution not only of the Vichy government but of the French population in general has received increased emphasis with the passage of time. Major documentary films devoted to the reconstruction of French attitudes toward the occupation have served to put the issue in sharp focus.

In a sense this may be viewed as part of the troubled and continuing assessment of the Nazi era. The disenchantment and profound pessimism—God died in Auschwitz—as to the nature of man and society that mark so many intellectual currents of our time are the consequences of the profound spiritual upheaval that the reality of the Holocaust set in motion. Ironically, those in 1945 who believed the Holocaust to be unique not only in the suffering endured but in the character of its perpetrators had a more hopeful view of humanity.

Marie Syrkin
September 1976

I. Ud

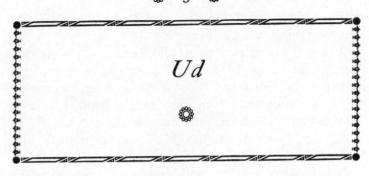

Ud

IN DAPHNE I met Ud. Daphne is a Jewish agricultural settlement in upper Galilee; Ud is a baby. The queer monosyllable by which he is known was not bestowed capriciously; nor is it a pet-name. *Ud* is a Hebrew word which means "the last brand," the ember plucked from the burning.

The boy and girl who were the parents of Ud had escaped from the Warsaw ghetto, after taking part in its last stand. Together they reached Palestine and in that land their son was born. They named him Ud. When I saw him he was a jolly, chubby baby of ten months, and he gurgled as happily as any baby with a less tragic and significant name. But the sign was upon him. Perhaps as he grew older he would resent his parents' dramatic choice, as children always resent the peculiar or the passionate in regard to themselves. No doubt child psychologists would seriously question the wisdom of involving a young life from the outset in the catastrophe from which his parents had miraculously escaped. However that might be, there he was, and I wondered if his mother, as she caressingly called his name — "Ud, Ud" — was aware each time of its terrible meaning and history.

I thought of still another child, born seven years earlier, in the fall of 1938. His mother had been one of a group of Jews driven out of the Sudeten area in one of the first of such expulsions. Because the family had been unable to get admission into any border town, the child's birthplace was a ditch. His mother named him Niemand, the German for "nobody."

The incident made something of an impression at the time. This was before the Nazi slaughterhouses had, among their other victims, destroyed the capacity for fellow feeling. We could still sense the anguish of this nativity, the terror of this Jewish mother's annunciation that the man-child she had borne was No One. In the years that have passed, I have often wondered about the fate of Niemand. Did he live? Did he escape the gas chambers? It is unlikely. There were so many ways for him to die; at any rate, I have not read his name among the few rescued. But he is unforgettable, as Ud is unforgettable.

From the German *Niemand* to the Hebrew *Ud* — there is the core of the calamity that befell my people. The symbolically named babies stand at either end of the great carnage, framing it with an artistic completeness which suggests a considered plan rather than the accident of a mother's despair or hope: Niemand, the prophetic name presaging the immense annihilation, and Ud, the small remnant!

It was no chance that I met Ud in Palestine. There he was bound to be. It was the only place where he could have been born. True, other men and women who escaped from the ghettos have begotten and given

4

birth to children in Europe and America, but the particular child, Ud, the last ember of a people, could only flicker to life in the place where I found him.

We spent the evening together, the parents of Ud and I. They spoke to me of Warsaw and of Lodz — life in the ghetto, resistance and escape. I asked about the heroes of that struggle — familiar names by now — Zivia, Frumke, Tosia, Yitzhak. The father rose. In the corner, on a small table were some photographs. "This is Zivia," he said, "and this is Frumke." I had seen their pictures in the Jewish press, but these were the original photographs, smuggled out of Poland, precious pictures of comrades carried even in flight. I looked at the sensitive young faces, one living and one dead. The snapshots stood casually on the table, and one knew that they were viewed as the simple pictures of friends, not the portraits of already semi-legendary figures. This was the household of Ud, the family that had waged the battle and made his eventual being possible. And it was a part of the logic of events that I, an American Jewess, should encounter this group in a remote agricultural settlement among the Galilean hills.

Renya, who had played a big part in the ghetto in Bendin, came into the room. (Her remarkable account of her experiences has appeared in Hebrew.) A pretty, blond girl, very "Aryan" looking, no German or Pole was likely to suspect her of being a Jewess. That was why she had been able to transport weapons from ghetto to ghetto as long as the ghettos existed, and why she had been able to escape.

Renya bent down and played with Ud. And when Hannah came in — Hannah, who had also been in Bendin, though she had taken a less prominent part than

Renya in the resistance — her first impulse too was to play with Ud. How young and lovely were these fair-haired girls! That was all part of the business of being an undiscovered messenger among the imprisoned Jewries of Poland. But Renya's grey eyes were harder, and Hannah's blue eyes sadder than those of young girls should be.

We talked all evening of how men kill and how men and children die.

I asked the questions that tormented me, and they asked the questions that tormented them. For when I wondered why six million Jews had let themselves be led to the slaughter, they demanded, "Why did you let them be led?" And when I asked, "Did they not know where the train went?" they answered me at length, but they also returned to the stern question, "Did *you* not know?"

Of the various answers I shall write later. For in my search for answers the journey to Daphne was only one. A few hours' ride away, in the valley of Esdraelon, or in Beisan, or at the base of the Judean hills, I was to meet partisans who had fought in Vilna, and Palestinian parachutists who had invaded the fortress of Europe, as well as those who had just come from Buchenwald. Each had a piece of the story and a part of the answer. And then, in Tel Aviv, over a cup of coffee, I was to speak to the man who had organized grandiose rescue schemes in Hungary; and later in Jerusalem I was to hear from the spinners themselves how the threads of salvation were spun in Geneva and in Istanbul.

But in the meantime I was in Daphne with Ud — for whom the ghetto fighters had gone down with their flaming walls, for whom the partisans had fought in the

Lithuanian woods, for whom lithe young men and girls of Palestine had leapt in parachutes into the dark lands of the Nazi, for whom the best brains and bravest hearts had plotted to outwit and outplot the murderer.

The night in Daphne was not peaceful. After Ud had been put to bed in his crib in the children's house, the men of the settlement stood watch till dawn. Word had come that a tribe of Druse Arabs in the neighborhood was threatening trouble. The sheik's son had not returned at nightfall and rumor had it that he had last been seen in Daphne. Later it was disclosed that the youth had been sampling the cafés of Tel Aviv; but till morning those on the watch tower could spy groups of Druses gathering below the bridge. So the young men, among them Ud's father, did not sleep that night, though the day's work in the fields had been hard. Fortunately, news of the Arab's whereabouts reached the tribe when dawn came, and the band dispersed. But there had been little rest.

Ud's mother looked fresh and cheerful in the morning, and she laughed when I asked, "Weren't you afraid?" Perhaps she remembered the roundup in a square in Slovakia for deportation to Warsaw which she had described to me the night before, or perhaps she thought of the bunker in which she had crouched when the shelling of the ghetto walls took place. At any rate she was gay and sure, and I did not dare ask her directly about Ud. What about him? But she read my mind and my misgivings.

"This is our place," she said looking at the patches of fresh green among the stretches of bare desert which is Daphne. "This is what we dreamt of in Poland. It gave us the strength to survive."

7

She looked with love at the little, barrack-like, one-room dwellings, at the tents, at the few acres of ploughed fields which made up the settlement. In the older settlements, comfort and beauty have already been wrested from the wilderness. There are long alleys of cypress and eucalyptus trees; bushes of roses and oleander. But here the fight with the desert had just begun; the oasis had to be created foot by foot.

I asked her why they had not chosen the easier life of the established settlements, why, after Warsaw and Bendin, they had entered the further fight with sand and stone and border tribes.

"We want to go on," she said; and then she laughed again and said, "Come, I will show you *Gan Eden.*"

Gan Eden means Garden of Eden in Hebrew. It was very hot, and I was tired after the agitating night. Even *Gan Eden* had no charms for me; but she insisted. We walked across a wide field in the blazing sun till we reached a tiny brook, or rather a rivulet. At any rate, it was flowing water in the midst of a cluster of bushes. A tree grew in the middle of the rivulet, a large, shady oak with no doubt a longer history than most of the trees one sees in Palestine. It had not been planted and tended by one of the settlers. A rickety, wooden table and wooden chair had been placed directly in the water under the wide branches, and with one leap over a rock one could sit in the shade with a trickle of water at one's feet. It didn't look like much to me; but Ud's mother, though she was undoubtedly familiar with the great rivers and forests of Central Europe, exclaimed with rapture, "Do you see why we call it *Gan Eden!*" I couldn't see but I could understand — here was a bit of greenery, and shade and coolness, which the land had given. It did not have to be wrested from the earth or created, as everything else in the waste which they were reclaiming.

And it was home. That was why the young parents of Ud were again courting danger, why they were even chancing the safety of Ud himself. They were sure that the continent from which they had escaped held nothing save the memory of death for them and the outlook for further death. The rickety table under the oak was the last fortress worth defending, the fields of Daphne the only dwelling worth building. It was *Gan Eden*.

II. The Parachutists from Palestine

1

The Mission

❀

WHY do I begin with the parachutists? Were I to trace the story of Jewish resistance and rescue chronologically, I would have to use a different order. I would have to begin with the gradual development of an underground movement in the ghettos and concentration camps of Europe. Then I would describe the attempts at rescue directed from the neutral centers of Portugal, Switzerland and Istanbul. This would be followed naturally by an account of the partisans, the Maquis, and of the ghetto revolts. Only at the end would I reach the small band of parachutists from Palestine who leapt down into the Nazi-held Balkans in order to bring help to the surviving Jews of Europe. Such a plan would no doubt be logical as well as chronological. I would follow the order of events as they occurred, and it would have the strict sequence of the calendar to recommend it.

Nevertheless, I feel that the instinct which impels me to begin the story backwards is not wholly irrational. It has its own logic which merits examination. In the first place, I must make an admission. I share the reader's reluctance to enter the ghetto gate. "People are fed up on atrocities!"— True, but that is not the chief reason why men turn away from narratives of the Nazi horror. They turn away not because they are satiated or indifferent, but because it is too hard to behold the spectacle which unfolds as soon as one dares lift the curtain be it ever so uncertainly or slightly. One needs strength to walk in and look about. Sometimes one has to borrow this strength. It is not to be had from the sufferers, no matter how heroic. I have spoken face to face with girls who fought on the ghetto barricades and in the Vilna woods, and always the sense of personal shame and of guilt before the victim overpowered every other feeling. To seek inspiration from them smacked of indecency, as though one were to watch a pyre which consumed living flesh and blood, and gloat at the splendor of the blaze.

But the young parachutists who jumped from the skies and afterwards told me their stories in the settlements of Palestine — towards them, and their lost comrades, one could indulge in the luxury of admiration. From them one could presume to take the resolution without which it is impossible to enter the charnel-house of European Jewry. The vitality of their adventure, even when it ended in death, helped one to approach the ashes of six million murdered human beings.

There is also a less personal reason for my choice of method. The story can be told from within and from without. The narratives of those who have escaped have begun to appear in all the languages of the world. These accounts have the virtue of having been composed by those best qualified to make the report and draw up the indictment — the victims themselves. But there is

14

another story too which must be told — the story of those who tried to answer the desperate cry for help. This story, despite its slight success, is part of the whole. It, too, belongs to the account, and it is reasonable and fitting that it begin with those who made the boldest, as well as the most obviously picturesque, effort to save their doomed brothers.

Till August, 1942, no one in the outside world knew what was happening to the Jews of Europe. The continent was hermetically sealed and information as to the functioning of the Nazi extermination program was not allowed to escape. On August 16, 1942, a group of Polish women who had been exchanged for German war prisoners arrived in Palestine. These were the first witnesses who brought word of the slaughterhouses established in Poland and occupied Russia by the Germans. Though their stories received little publicity in the general press, because they were viewed as too sensational to merit credence, the alarm had been given. Plans for bringing help began to take shape wherever there were free Jewish communities. Most of these plans resolved themselves into protest meetings, "to arouse the conscience of the world," and into collections of money. In America, in England, Jews composed well-documented pamphlets and uttered impassioned pleas in a desperate effort to secure some action which would stop the carnage or, at any rate, make possible the rescue of those still not in the immediate zone of slaughter. We know how little these attempts availed.

There was one Jewish community, however, which did not content itself with appeals and mass-meetings. That was the 600,000 Jews of Palestine. The *Yishuv*, as

15

the Jewish community of Palestine calls itself, determined that, whatever the obstacles, the perishing Jews of Europe had to be reached. This effort, which began in 1942 and assumed many forms, reached its climax in the venture of the parachutists. One of the individuals responsible for this plan, asked me, an American Jew, "Why were American Jews so passive in contrast with the small community of Palestine?" And when I had no good answer to give him, he answered his own question:

"Because, small though we are, we have the habit of thinking as a nation. We have the impulse to act independently. We could not sit by and do nothing while the murder went on, day in, day out. We had to do something ourselves."

First, of course, went the *shlichim*. *Shaliach* is a Hebrew word meaning "one who is sent." It can be translated as delegate, or messenger; but these are pale substitutes for the true sense. The one who is sent has a mission, and it is this quality of mission which an adequate translation must convey.

Throughout the war responsible individuals in Palestine kept drawing up concrete plans for organizing Jewish resistance in Europe. As late as February, 1944, about a million and a quarter Jews still remained alive in Bulgaria, Rumania, Hungary and Slovakia. Had these Jews been provided with equipment and help, they might have been able to turn out a considerable force of guerilla fighters.

It was proposed that a sizable number of Palestinians be sent — as *shlichim* — to organize Jewish resistance throughout the Balkans, to aid in the enlistment of Jews and non-Jews in the partisan armies, and to establish

16

centers of rescue from which they could plan the escape of refugees from occupied territories into partisan territory, from where means could be found to evacuate them to safety. According to the Jewish Agency such a scheme had several features to recommend it: it would have saved thousands of Jews otherwise doomed to be murdered; it had immediate military value; and it would have interfered with the enemy's communications. It was not so much a question of saving the Jews of the Balkans, as of giving them a chance to save themselves and, in so doing, of contributing to the defeat of the enemy. Young male Jews had been herded by the Germans into forced labor units. They were working at strategically important places. Their armed rebellion might constitute a serious threat in the back of the German forces facing the Russians in the East.

The nucleus of an underground already existed in each of the Balkan countries. Considering its limited means and isolation, it functioned amazingly well. If these attempts had been supported and coordinated, the Jews of the Balkans might have had the opportunity of rising against their oppressors. Specific points where the parachutists should be dropped, in order to turn victims into fighters, were suggested.

For, as the German armies advanced and extended their radius of authority, it became clear that efforts to penetrate from without by land had to be supplemented by a bold attempt to land within the fortress itself. This could only be done from the air. For a while, the notion of a secret landing in the Balkans from a submarine was entertained but was dismissed as impracticable. Only the sky remained. Parachutists could be dropped into enemy territory. If they landed successfully, they could establish contact with the local underground movements and devise methods of organizing resistance and rescue.

The conception was brilliant and daring. Obviously, however, it could not be carried out by the Jews of Palestine alone. There was a war going on in which they were partners. Whatever was done had to be undertaken with the approval and cooperation of the British military. Parachutists needed planes in addition to courage. Above all, they needed the permission of the British before they could proceed.

The attempt to persuade the British authorities of the feasibility of such a plan began early in 1943. The British had to be convinced that the general war effort would be aided by the venture. Their concern in the fate of the Jews of Europe was secondary. Unless they could be made to see the value of the scheme from the military point of view, little heed was likely to be given to the plea that the Jews of Europe needed immediate help. Fortunately, however, there were many sound reasons for using Palestinians as parachutists. Many of the young men and women of Palestine had originally come from the Balkans. They knew the Rumanian, Bulgarian, Hungarian or Croatian languages thoroughly, depending on their country of origin. They were familiar with the territory and local conditions. They were obviously ideal people for securing information, for establishing contacts with underground movements and partisans, and for assisting the escape of prisoners of war.

These qualifications were urged by the Palestinians as arguments for accepting their services. Furthermore, they made no secret of the fact that in the course of their activities they would seek to rescue the Jews of Europe

18

wherever and however possible. The mission was to be twofold.

The British Intelligence, who had to approve the proposal, at first hesitated to use the Palestinians. Throughout the negotiations, snags would arise, not military, but political in character. The Palestinians believed that the delays were due to an unwillingness to permit the Jews of Palestine to display so much initiative. Whatever the reasons for British reluctance, it was overcome by compelling military considerations. In 1943, the oil fields of Ploesti in Rumania had been bombarded by the Allies with enormous attendant losses. An extremely large number of American aviators had been downed. These results had been unexpected. Apparently, there had been a breakdown in the intelligence service which should have given adequate warning of the type of defense that might be encountered at Ploesti.

In view of this situation, it was decided to use the Palestinian volunteers. They would be given training as parachutists and dropped in the Balkans as developments would require. The first group entered training early in 1943. That was the official beginning of this new and dramatic venture.

It should be borne in mind that the first objective of the parachutists was to carry out the military tasks to which they had been assigned. Only after their purely military missions had been accomplished, or in order to further these missions, were they free to act in behalf of the salvation of European Jewry. This was a strict agreement strictly honored by those who entered this perilous field of action. On this understanding the Haganah (Jewish Defense Organization of Palestine) furnished volunteers.

Who were these parachutists? In the course of the war, any number of Jewish boys served as aviators and parachutists in all the Allied armies. They fought well in the air forces of the United States, Great Britain and Russia. No special distinction attaches to this fact, and there is no more call to admire an American or Russian parachutist who is a Jew than one of any other origin. The role of the Palestinian parachutists, however, was a more complex and difficult one. They had a twofold mission, either part of which was peculiarly dangerous and responsible. The individuals chosen for this task had to be far above the average in physical valor, in initiative and in mentality, since the particular types needed required a linguistic background and intellectual equipment which was not easy to find. They had to be spies and heroes, fliers and secret agents; in addition, they had to be saviors — impelled by a special passion to aid their people.

This passion explains the aura which surrounds the parachutists in the popular imagination. One strong element in the catastrophe which struck the Jews of the world was their bewildering sense of impotence before the mounting evil. The trance-like helplessness, the passivity of the increasingly less innocent bystanders, were as much a part of the calamity as the slaughter itself. Any group which seemed able to shake off the monstrous spell binding both sufferer and spectator had a positive achievement to its credit by virtue of that alone. Even if the venture should not succeed, the mere motion of breaking the bonds of lethargy and terror was a gesture of liberation not only for the actors but for the witnesses. That is why it is impossible to measure the contribution of the parachutists or of any other Jewish resistance groups in purely statistical terms. Whether they lost or won, they helped check the invading paralysis of mind and will.

All the parachutists were members of collective settlements — young men and women who by conviction and training were accustomed to practising the ideals they professed. They had led the arduous, ascetic existence of the pioneer. Having shown themselves capable of the heralded "return" to Zion, they were now the natural candidates for the secret return into the European inferno.

Of the thirty-two parachutists who set out, twenty-five per cent were lost. Those who returned have long histories of imprisonment, torture and injury to relate. It would be too ambitious and lengthy a task to seek to reconstruct the experience of each of the parachutists who went on this mission. I shall content myself with telling something of the parachutists whom I myself met. It would be inaccurate to describe their stories as "typical." In adventures of this kind, nothing is "typical"— each deed is *sui generis* — but, at any rate, their histories indicate the scope and magnificence of the attempt. And, of course, no account of the parachutists can begin without the story of Hanna Senesch, the young girl parachutist who was captured in her native Hungary, shortly after her descent into the Balkans, and who now lies buried there.

2

"Blessed is the Match"

❀

HANNA SENESCH has become a national heroine of Palestine and hers was the name which I heard most frequently upon my arrival. I heard men say, "At last the Jews have a Joan of Arc." In their youth, their sense of dedication to their people's cause, and their death there is a certain resemblance. But there is little purpose in pressing the analogy too far. Joan of Arc led the armies of France to victory. Hanna Senesch accomplished little in terms of the number of individuals rescued. And one cannot be an unsuccessful Joan of Arc. The great miracle of the Maid of Orleans lay in what she did, not only in how she did it. It is beside the point to speculate on whether in a more brutal and sophisticated age even a second Joan could have done more than try and fail.

Hanna Senesch was no Joan of Arc. She did not conquer the enemy, nor did she save the Jews of Europe. I stress the obvious not because I believe that the legend of the young and charming Hungarian girl, who so valiantly sacrificed her life, should be kept within rational limits. The romantic enthusiasm aroused by this girl's history is natural enough. I mention what Hanna did not do and could not do, to underscore the point that even if Hanna had been the equal of Joan in vision and power, she would have been essentially helpless, for she was the heroine of a people without armies to be led and without a land on which to lead them. Hanna, with all her valor and rich intelligence, hurtling herself down in a British uniform to a hostile land, was a part of the general Jewish tragedy. She had the hero's equipment, temperament and purpose, but she was bound to fail when viewed against the background of the Jewish drama. However, the attempt to breach the fortress of the foe was more than a glorious gesture. It indicated a new approach to the Nazi terror — a readiness to take independent action which, had it been repeated on a larger scale, might have effected a substantial improvement in the situation.

How much this readiness was treasured has already been indicated. That the chief measure of worship has been accorded to one of the least successful of the parachutists reveals the deep wound in the Jewish spirit. It is not sentimentality which has made Hanna's aureole the brightest. In a period dominated by the vision of the endless march to the extermination center, every figure who rose out of the nightmare to the level of action was cherished in proportion to the will that he displayed. The sensitive poetic girl became the symbol of awakening.

Every Jew in Palestine can recite the four simple lines of the poem Hanna wrote shortly before she was executed.

Blessed is the match that is consumed in kindling
flame.
Blessed is the flame that burns in the secret fastness of the heart.
Blessed is the heart with strength to stop its beating for honor's sake.
Blessed is the match that is consumed in kindling
flame.

The Hebrew original has a beauty which is lost in a
literal translation, but the concept is clear. The poem
celebrates the self-immolation of the hero. There is no
assurance that the ultimate issue will be life. There is
only insistence on the sacrifice. That such a sentiment
can be described as the national slogan of Palestine
Jewry indicates the bitter lesson learned from the Nazi
decade. The attempt to cling to life will surely result
in death. The only hope lies in the readiness to die.
Ashrei ha-gafrur —"Blessed is the match"— I heard
these lines many times in Palestine. The application
was always immediate. The youth I encountered was
prepared to be consumed, as Hanna had been, in the
hope that their people might live. This ardor is to be
found in no other Jewish community; and when one
senses this prevailing mood, Hanna and her fellows
become more comprehensible.

I have no intention of writing Hanna's biography.
One cannot, however, disassociate her career as a parachutist from her past. Her evolution helps one to understand the paradoxical Jewish hero who emerged in the
Hitler era — this being, hyper-intellectual, ultra-sensi-
tive, who became under the pressure of events a parachutist, a partisan leader, or a ghetto fighter. The
heroes of other peoples have, for the most part, back-
grounds which explain their subsequent careers, but

24

the Jewish heroes did not come from the playing-fields of Eton. Most of them had not been athletes delighting in swiftness of limb and strength of muscle.

The Shield of David was forged in the ivory tower, in the synagogue, in the meeting-halls of sects arguing fiercely how Utopia should be shaped. The visionaries and artists became the chief doers. The Jewish hero became such, not because of temperamental or physical aptitude, but because of faith. Perhaps the paradox is not as strange as it first seems. Where the odds were so great, only the exaltation of the believer could provide the necessary impulse. This type is to be seen at its purest in Hanna Senesch.

Under ordinary circumstances she would probably have devoted herself to one of the arts, but the Nazi triumph ended all chance of anything approaching a normal existence. The span of her life — July 7, 1921 to November 7, 1944 — coincided with the development of the Nazi party, its seizure of power, and World War II. And whereas another girl similarly situated might have sought to escape from the cataclysm, it was inevitable that she should be drawn into its center.

She was born in Budapest into a wealthy, distinguished, assimilated Hungarian Jewish family. Perhaps, without Hitler, Hanna would have become a Hungarian minor poet instead of a major Jewish heroine. She was too self-conscious, and too conscientious, to have been without awareness of herself as a Jewess even in the best of circumstances; but in another period there is no telling what form this awareness might have taken. Once, however, the Jewish issue had been posed on any part of the European continent, Hanna, though living in the material comfort and apparent safety of a well-to-do

Hungarian home, could not fail to react. Her solution was Palestine.

She was caught early by the Zionist fever.

Before she is eighteen, she is already proclaiming in her diary: "I want to read the Bible in Hebrew," and on the same day she quotes a letter from her brother in which he writes, "It is good to die for one's country." The seventeen-year-old girl remarks: "This last is very actual in Palestine, for the British have just concocted a White Paper with dreadful contents." This is 1939 and her reference is to the Chamberlain White Paper.

On her eighteenth birthday she writes: "To-day is my birthday . . . I am eighteen. It is hard to believe that I am so old already." But this typical adolescent melancholy is accompanied by another note: life is beautiful because "my idea fulfills all my life." Friends warn her of disappointment, but she is sure! "I know I will not be disappointed. I want to do everything to bring this dream nearer to reality, or the reality nearer to the dream."

A few days after the birthday which made her feel old, she writes exuberantly: "I've got it. I've got it — the certificate to go to Palestine. I read the good news again and again." There is only one drawback to this joy. Her widowed mother dreads the young daughter's departure. Hanna, who is passionately attached to her mother and brother — these are to remain her chief loves — is aware of the suffering she is inflicting on her family, but she is as one possessed. She describes her mother "as a great heroine. This is a great sacrifice for her," but her own course is set.

A few months later she is already in the agricultural school of Nahalal in Palestine, training herself for a life on the soil. It is a very different world from that of Budapest and begins a crucial period of adjustment. More than one enthusiast, who came to Palestine full of a poetic fervor for "pioneering", found his resolution unequal to the actual business of draining swamps and "making the desert bloom."

Even Hanna has her moments of faltering, which can be sensed in the diary. She has received a letter from a friend in Hungary describing a gay party. Hanna, remembering the frills and furbelows of the past, writes: "My eyes surveyed my hands, sore from work . . . . I wondered if it was not simply romanticism which had driven me from a comfortable home to a life of physical work . . . . but, no, I am right."

She is too complex, too full of eagerness for intellectual and artistic experiences, not to be aware of what she has relinquished by her choice. In Nahalal, in addition to the practical branches of farming, the students learn something of the science of agriculture. After a botany class, she writes: "To-day we learned about certain cells which penetrate the soil first, which prepare the way but are themselves destroyed in the process. The teacher called them 'the pioneers of the plant'." And Hanna, thinking of the girls with whom she is training in Nahalal and of their future, adds: "These cells are cleopadra. And we, shall we all be such cells? Is this our fate? These questions interest me more than a lecture on botany."

The sense that she is dedicated, or, rather, that she must dedicate herself, pursues her everywhere — in a botany class, in her room, on a hike. She visits Kfar Gileadi, in northern Galilee, where Trumpeldor and those who fell with him in defense of the settlement lie buried. The wild beauty of the Galilean hills, the purple mountains of Moab towards Transjordan, can move even the most apathetic. The memories associated with this place, both ancient and recent, stir the young girl deeply. She observes in her diary: "In the freshness of the dawn, I understand why Moses received God's command in the morning. In the mountains, the question arises of itself: 'Whom shall I send?'"

She answers the immense question that she senses everywhere. "'Whom shall I send?' Send *me* to serve the good and beautiful." And though she adds, as any young girl might, "Will I be able?", the fundamental assurance that *she* must be sent, although she is as yet uncertain as to what form this sending must take, is hers already.

Her diary reflects the history of the period as well as the *Sturm und Drang* of her spirit. The day when Jewish refugees are sent from Palestine to Mauritius is specially black. But on the same page she writes: "I feel that I can't live without writing . . . I have much to write . . . I would like to write about my mother. The theme involves not only my mother, but all Jewish mothers . . . however, not all have her modesty and her heroism."

The longing to be a writer in no way weakens her determination to become a member of an agricultural collective where the day's labor leaves little room for the cultivation of the spirit. She faces the problem squarely. A play composed by her indicates the nature of the conflict. The heroine, a gifted violinist, must choose between developing herself as an artist, or living in a collective settlement. She decides that service to her people through the collective is more significant than the development of an individual, no matter how en-

28

dowed. The plot of the play is transparent. It is Hanna's problem and choice. "I have chosen to work on the soil. I want to be a part of the working class in Palestine. This is not theoretical, because it permeates all my actions."

This is not theoretical! These words explain Hanna's peculiar strength, for she is never lost in a daydream. At the same time that she is consumed by the vision of a heroic future, she becomes an expert and competent worker in the various branches of farming. She even tries to devise all kinds of little innovations to improve poultry raising. "I am thinking of a device to mark the color of each egg . . . but I suppose the poultry will be organized without me."

She does not spare herself in her diary. In a mood of scepticism, she exclaims: "Sometimes I think I am deceiving myself — playing a game — and that the only thing I really care about is whether my blue blouse and shorts are becoming." She has a normal girl's liking of a pretty dress, a normal girl's interest in boys, but the boys she meets do not content her. She is looking for an "impossible he." And whether the blue blouse is becoming is essentially a minor concern among the passions which possess her.

She has intensity, but not simplicity of purpose. Joan of Arc left no diary, but from what we know of the young shepherdess all her emotional capacity could probably have been concentrated within the range of the religious exaltation and conviction which ruled her. The call of the archangel was unmistakable. Hanna Senesch belongs to another category. She is the complex child of a more complex time. Conflicting impulses agitate her: the need for artistic expression, the quest for personal happiness, the desire to play a part in the political life around her (she admits that), the stern creed which bids that all this must be subordinated to "poultry-raising," and, above all, the mysterious assurance that she has been chosen for some great purpose. "Sometimes I feel I have a mission; what it is, is not clear to me. Sometimes I think this is all nonsense. Why all these efforts of the individual?"

In the midst of her work in the settlement of Caesarea, which she enters after completing the course at the training school in Nahalal, she is active and gay. She mentions the unexpected satisfaction one can have even from working in the laundry of the settlement. She is as good a comrade in the actual life of the communal settlement as she had been in the school. Her comrades testify to that, and the witnesses are significant. They would be quick to spot a shirker and mercilessly critical of one who proved unequal to the exigencies of hard, unglamorous work. Hanna is never paralyzed into inactivity by the dream, nor does she substitute a grandiose fantasy for scrubbing clothes or cleaning the chicken coop. The processes are simultaneous.

The climax is approaching. On January 8, 1944, she writes: "This week has been an agitating one. Suddenly an idea occured to me: I must go to Hungary, be there at the present time, help to organize youth-*aliyah*, and bring out my mother. I realize the absurdity of this notion, and yet somehow I think it possible, and I keep figuring how it could be done."

But the "absurdity" becomes real. Within two weeks she is approached by the organizers of the parachutist group. She cannot write the details in her diary, but the answer is clear:

30

How strangely things develop! On January 8, I wrote of the idea which suddenly stirred me ... a few days ago a comrade came and told me of the mission being planned ... just what I had dreamt of .... I feel a fatality in this, just as at the time before I went to Palestine. Then too I was not my own master. I was caught by an idea that did not let me rest. I knew that I would enter Palestine, no matter what difficulties were in my way. Now I again feel this tension towards an important and necessary task — as well as the inevitability of the task. Possibly nothing will come of all this. I may receive a brief notice telling me the plan has been abandoned, or that I will not be accepted. But I think that I have the maximal capacities for this task — and I shall fight with all my strength for it.

At night, I find it hard to fall asleep because of what I picture. How will I act in this situation — how in another? How will I inform my mother of my arrival? How will I organize the youth? All is unclear. We will see what the future brings.

She is accepted for training as a parachutist. Any day she may be called to Cairo. The fantasy has come true. She will go to Hungary, descending from the skies in a parachutist's dress. One of the last entries in the diary reads:

May 27, Caesarea, I am wholly taken up with one thing — my departure. It has become actual and close at hand. I may be called in the next few days.

I place myself in various situations and sometimes I think: "To leave this land, and freedom?" I would like to fill my lungs with fresh air with which I will be able to breathe in the choking atmosphere of the *Galut* and to dispense it to those who have been so long denied the taste of freedom. But these are merely thoughts around the undisputable fact and the necessity for my departure. I am aware of the difficulty and the danger, but I have the feeling that I will be able to fulfill my task. I see everything that happened before as a behest and preparation for this mission.

The final entry of the diary is made on June 14, 1944:

This week I go to Egypt. I am mobilized; I am a soldier. I want to believe that what I do and will do is right. The rest time will tell.

One cannot help comparing these sober, restrained words with the exuberant "I have it, I have it, the certificate to Palestine" written in Budapest, in 1939, just five years earlier. The vague ecstasy of the eighteen-year-old girl is approaching fulfillment; the young woman of twenty-three makes this last restrained entry, gives her diary and her poems to her *kibbutz* (collective), and leaves for Egypt. The five years in Palestine are over.

3

Behind the Lines with Tito

❂

F ROM this point on the story of Hanna becomes involved in that of her fellow parachutists. The accounts
of her activities in Yugoslavia with Tito's partisans and
of her capture and imprisonment in Budapest come from
the companions who shared her mission. Actually, it is
the accomplishments of those who returned which make
it possible to reconstruct the picture of what happened
behind the enemy lines after the leap had been made.
Each of the parachutists to whom I spoke began his
story with the declaration that he had felt himself personally called to answer the cry of the Jews of Europe.
The statement would be made simply, with a minimum
of melodrama, but it was the inevitable introduction.

Reuben Dafni and Joel Nussbacker, the two parachutists who were with Hanna at different stages of the
mission, have an impressive series of exploits to their
credit. So has each of the other parachutists whose histories have become known since the conclusion of the
war. I dwell on the trio of Hanna, Joel and Reuben because between them the various aspects of one mission,
its failures as well as triumphs, were covered.

The plan of the group of which Hanna was a member was, of necessity, broad in outline. The parachutists, four men and one woman, were to be dropped in Yugoslavia — in territory controlled by Tito's partisans. From there the task was subdivided. According to the plan, some were to remain in Yugoslavia, whereas Hanna was to try to cross into Hungary, the land of her birth. The parachutists, particularly Hanna, were eager to be dropped directly in Hungary but the military authorities refused, on the grounds that this would be too risky.

In each operation involving the parachutists, it was possible to use one of two methods. Either they could be dropped blindly in the country selected and left to their own devices to discover a way of establishing contact with friendly elements and of conveying information back to headquarters, or they could be dropped in the liberated country closest to the target. From there, they could smuggle themselves across the border into the occupied country. Both methods were used. Hanna's group was dropped in Yugoslavia. Its experience was to serve as a guide for future operations. If successful, a second group was to be dropped shortly in Yugoslavia.

It must be remembered that the parachutists wore British uniforms, and if captured were to represent themselves as Palestinian members of the British air-force who had met with an accident over enemy territory. Their special function involved a dangerous military secret, which had to be closely guarded for the sake of future plans as well as the safety of the individuals involved. If captured, they had to make every effort to establish their right to be treated as prisoners of war. Otherwise, they would be shot as spies.

The first lap of the journey was from the training center in Egypt to Italy. They landed in Bari. The jump into Yugoslavia was to be made from Brindisi. The crew of the plane consisted of Poles, who were stunned at the discovery that the parachutists were Hebrew-speaking Palestinians, with a girl among them. This was a new type of Jew.

At 1 A.M. on March 13, 1944, which Reuben remembers as a beautiful, moonlit night, the parachutists jumped. Reuben had an incendiary bomb with a complete set of false documents for the whole party strapped to his leg. If the parachutists fell into enemy hands, he merely had to strike the bomb. It would at once go up in flames destroying the incriminating documents.

On this occasion even the neophytes had little inclination to worry as to whether the parachute would open. They had too much else to trouble them. Some of Tito's partisans had been contacted previously and been informed of the proposed drop of the parachutists. Now the problem was whether they would succeed in landing in the designated territory.

The pilot misjudged the distance and dropped them eight miles from the target. However, the four men found each other immediately. But Hanna, who was lighter and weaker, could not fight against a wind carrying her away, and drifted off in a different direction. In the meantime, two figures approached who challenged them in Slovenian. Reuben answered in English, not being sure whether they were partisans or quislings. He stood ready to strike the incendiary bomb. Then in the clear moonlight, he saw the red star on his questioners' caps. They were Tito's men — poorly dressed, without boots, though snow was still on the ground.

A signal that friends had arrived was given to other

partisans in the hills. They came down and welcomed the Palestinians with their greeting: "Death to fascism; freedom to the people."

Together they started to search for Hanna. After about an hour she was found. The partisans were extremely cordial, though they were Slovenians, among whom anti-Semitic feeling had been rife. At a banquet which they gave the parachutists later, one of the welcomers announced that they were glad to have in their midst representatives of a people who had suffered from fascism even more than the Slovenians. Everything about the parachutists was remarkable. They were Jews; they were Palestinians; and they were members of a collective settlement. Tito's men listened with respectful interest to the descriptions of the "Jewish *Kolhoz*" * which they received ... The presence of a pretty young girl among the parachutists was, as might be expected, an additional source for marvel.

Military headquarters in the woods were contacted, as well as the British and American missions with Tito. The work was in the process of organization, but a catastrophic turn in events compelled a complete revision of the plans. On March 18, Germany invaded Hungary. According to the original plan, Hanna was to have entered Hungary as a Jewish refugee. Now this scheme was no longer feasible. The disappointment was acute. Reuben relates that this was the first occasion on which he saw Hanna cry. Nevertheless, she at once began to make other plans for smuggling herself across the border, though obviously, with all Hungary occupied, the controls would be much stricter.

A few days later another blow fell. The parachutists

* Collective colony.

had jumped into Slovenia because there was a stretch of liberated territory near the Hungarian border. The Germans started a big offensive and succeeded in dislodging the partisans from this section. Here was a new complication. Information, however, reached the parachutists that, in Croatia, the 10th corps of the partisans controlled territory along another part of the Hungarian border.

They decided to make their way to Croatia. To do so they had to go through two hundred miles of enemy territory, along the path of the main railroad which runs from Vienna to Belgrade. It was a dangerous task because the route of the railroad was under specially careful guard. The line bristled with pillboxes. They trudged for ten nights — the only possible time for moving — carrying their radio equipment as well as their weapons. They went as part of a partisan battalion of 110 men who were headed for the same destination. On the way they had clashes with enemy patrols, but they finally reached the little town in Croatia which was the partisan headquarters of the region. The Palestinians were the first British officers to appear in this part of Yugoslavia.

The partisan general in Croatia made a painful request, to which the Palestinians had to accede. He explained that his troops were operating in territory which had been strongly infected by Nazi indoctrination. This was the first British mission that his men had seen. If the partisans should learn that it consisted of Palestinian Jews, the troops might be inclined to accept this as proof of the Nazi propaganda slogan that "the Jews rule Britain and the world." The partisan commander promised that the leaders would know the true identity of the parachutists, but he insisted that it would be more politic not to take the troops into their confidence. This demand presented a difficult problem. The Palestinians had started on their mission originally because they felt impelled to assert Jewish independence and dignity. Now they themselves were being asked to soft-pedal the fact that they were Jews. Military considerations, however, were paramount, and other aspects of the enterprise had to be subordinated to the primary purpose of doing as much harm to the enemy as possible. The commander's recommendation was accepted. There was only one hitch — the language. As only Reuben could speak English, and the parachutists did not wish to disclose their antecedents by speaking the Balkan languages with which they were familiar, they spoke Hebrew among themselves. This, they explained to their hearers, was Welsh. Hebrew and Welsh were all one to the Croatians, consequently the Palestinians had little difficulty in posing as Welshmen before the soldiers.

Bad luck continued to disrupt their plans. Just before their arrival in Croatia, the Germans had started an offensive against the particular sector which they had managed to reach. Again the problem of crossing the border became more complex.

Nevertheless, Reuben began to work on his military mission, which was to assist in the escape of American prisoners and of airmen. Great American air attacks were being carried out over Hungary and Ploesti at the time. Airplanes with American aviators were being downed throughout this period. It was essential to aid the fallen aviators to reach partisan territory from where they could be sent on further to the Adriatic coast. Reuben plotted maps which indicated exactly where liberated territory was to be found, and what sections were in no man's land. These maps, supplemented by radio information, served as guides. Leaflets were composed asking the cooperation of civilians. Searching parties for stranded aviators were organized, and many an American aviator who has returned safely home has cause to be grateful to the Palestinian parachutist. The Germans showed their appreciation of Reuben's efforts by putting a price on his head. The British and Tito decorated him for exceptional gallantry.

In the meantime, the second group of Palestinian parachutists arrived from Cairo, among them Joel. It was decided that Reuben should remain in Yugoslavia to continue his work in conjunction with the partisans, while Joel and Hanna should attempt to cross into Hungary despite the fact of complete Nazi occupation. In order to increase the chances of success, the attempt was to be made at two different places. Hanna went with one group, Joel with another.

Crossing the border involved an elaborate technique and the connivance of smugglers who knew the points at which such attempts could be made. The first attempts were unsuccessful. On one occasion, when the parachutists were in a peasant's home, they were involved in a shooting foray which almost ended fatally. After several more attempts, however, Hanna finally succeeded in getting into Hungary, on June 9, 1944.

Of Hanna's further fate we learn from Joel, the parachutist who also crossed into Hungary and eventually found himself in the same prison with her. Joel was to play a vital part in organizing the Jewish underground in Budapest, so that it is essential to know something of his history before the last act of Hanna's tragedy unfolds.

Like Reuben, Joel had served in the British Army before he volunteered for the parachutist corps. Having come originally from Hungary, just as Reuben had from Yugoslavia, he possessed not only the military training but the particular linguistic and personal qualifications necessary for behind-the-lines service in the Balkans.

Since it had been decided that Joel should cross into Hungary from the east while Hanna and her companions were to make the attempt further north, Joel had the opportunity of working with a different group of guerrillas. The partisan corps with which Joel established contact was also one of Tito's detachments, but Joel's experiences were less fortunate than those of Reuben, nor do his impressions tally with those of his friend.

Joel missed the warm welcome given to Reuben and Hanna. The partisans he met refused to trust the Palestinians unreservedly, viewing them as possible British agents. Because of these suspicions, various snags arose. Joel discovered that one partisan commander had warned his men to be careful in regard to the information they gave. The Palestinians were to be given free access to data about the enemy, but strict limits were to be placed upon any knowledge of partisan movements and operations. Permission was given to cross the border, but only with the help of professional smugglers, not through the contacts available to the partisans themselves. This made the crossing more hazardous. Since professional smugglers had no scruples about working for the Germans as well as for the partisans, there was constant danger of betrayal.

Nor was there smooth sailing in other respects. The

commanders were anxious to start a partisan movement in Hungary to cooperate with the Yugoslavs. They suggested that Joel recruit Hungarian Jews for this purpose. Joel, however, knew that such a scheme had little likelihood of success. A partisan movement must base itself on a friendly local population. In view of the virulent anti-Semitism in Hungary, the presence of a large number of Jews among the first partisan units to be formed might have antagonized the people and alienated mass support. He therefore proposed a more feasible alternative: that he be enabled to recruit Jews in Hungary and bring them into Yugoslavia to join Tito. The proposal had such obvious merits that it aroused a sympathetic response. The partisan commanders were prepared to weigh the considerations which prompted Joel's plan. But a new series of suspicions arose to block the scheme. One of the chieftains was afraid that such a plan would provide a pretext for the escape of Jewish families. The men might take their wives and children with them, thus adding to the number of mouths that the partisans would have to feed. To discourage the flight of Jews into partisan-held territory, the commander was prepared to libel his own men; he spread the canard that partisans kill Jews who fall into their hands.

This incident illustrates how unpredictable was the attitude of even supposedly friendly groups whenever active help for Jewish sufferers was required. The partisan movements reflected the temper of their environment fairly accurately. In Poland, Jews had almost as much to fear from the native bands fighting the Nazis as from the Nazis themselves. In Yugoslavia, particularly in those regions where no violent anti-Jewish feeling existed among the people, the attitude of the partisans was kindlier. But even in Yugoslavia, one of the most enlightened countries in the Balkans as far as the Jews were concerned, there was enough anti-Semitic contamination to make all efforts at collaboration in the rescue of Jews uncertain and hazardous.

The partisans, however, were sufficiently convinced of the importance of other aspects of Joel's mission to enable him to cross the border into Hungary. With his young friend Perez, a fellow parachutist from Palestine who was only nineteen years old at the time, Joel finally made his way into Budapest.

4

In a Hungarian Prison

◎

THE goal had been reached; the Palestinians were in the heart of Europe. Unfortunately, among the guides provided by the partisans were members of the Hungarian counter-espionage force. The Palestinians were permitted to reach the Hungarian capital because the police were anxious to discover their true purpose and to learn the nature of their contacts. Joel and Perez soon realized that they were being shadowed and attempted to find safe hiding-places. For several days they thought that they had shaken off the trail of the Hungarian sleuths, and they attempted to utilize the time to establish contacts with the underground movements, particularly the Jewish underground. Once this had been done, the first link in the chain of communication would have been forged. Even if arrest should follow, the local underground would know of the presence of the parachutists and further links could be created. But despite all precautions, the feared arrest followed soon after Joel's arrival in Budapest. He was taken into custody.

In the prison Joel learned from the guards that a young Palestinian girl had been captured two weeks earlier. As a final blow he was shown the uniform and weapons he had left in Yugoslavia, presumably in a trustworthy hiding-place. The Palestinians had been betrayed at every point. Joel was questioned about the whereabouts of his friend, Perez. Following the usual underground technique, they had lived in separate quarters and been careful not to know each other's address for fear of weakening under the third degree. He soon discovered, however, that Perez had also been arrested. The whole group was in prison.

Convinced that the cause was lost, and anxious to forestall torture by the Gestapo, Joel attempted to commit suicide by cutting his wrists with an American aviator's aluminum identity disk left behind in his cell. A guard found him after he lost consciousness. The Hungarian prison officials did not allow him to be taken to a hospital; he was revived and kept for questioning.

The grilling began. It was essential that Joel's antecedents and the nature of his military mission remain undisclosed. He kept assuring his interrogators that he was a Palestinian who had enlisted in the British army, and who therefore was entitled to the rights of any captured British airman, since he had been arrested in uniform. The Hungarians, on the other hand, were convinced that he was not a simple prisoner of war, but a dangerous character with a special espionage and sabotage mission whose sponsors and scope it was imperative for them to discover.

Joel insisted that he had no military mission. He admitted only that he was a Palestinian — not a Hungarian or a Rumanian — whose purpose was to help

44

save the Jews of Hungary of whom hundreds of thousands still remained alive.

The interrogations revealed the fears and confusions of the Hungarians. On the one hand, they behaved like victorious captors determined to break their prisoner down by any means. On the other hand, they were anxious to discover what their own chances might be in the case of a German defeat. This was already the end of June, 1944, and even the most enthusiastic of Germany's cohorts were growing nervous. The Hungarians were particularly eager to know if the long-hoped-for Anglo-American attack on Russia was likely to take place. The desire to get information on these troublesome questions made Joel's cross-examination a combination of third degree and discussion. There would be periods of torture alternating with hours of political debate which Joel would use to score his own points, and, though he did not succeeed in convincing his examiners, some of his arguments made a visible impression.

Joel assured the Hungarians that an understanding between Nazi quislings and the Allies was out of the question — particularly because of the Hungarian adoption of the Hitler anti-Jewish program. Paradoxically enough, both the Nazis and their henchmen in Nazi-occupied countries seriously believed that the democratic powers would make an issue of the Jewish massacres, and that the Jews were, consequently, a hostage in Axis hands. The Goebbels propaganda in regard to the extent of Jewish influence had convinced not only the ignorant masses, but even the supposedly hard-headed leaders. Naturally, this was a belief which Joel attempted to exploit to the utmost. He urged the Hungarian police to enable him to meet the Secretary of State, so that he could lay his plans for the rescue of Hungarian Jewry before him; such cooperation would later aid the Hungarians in their hour of defeat. Though Joel's arguments were listened to, not only for the purpose of discovering his aims, but on their apparent merits, the Hungarians decided to hand him over to the Gestapo. They were still not sufficiently sure that the Nazi cause was doomed.

The German officers treated both Hanna and himself in a "gentlemanly" fashion. They never failed to address him in accordance with his rank, *Herr Lieutenant*, and never called him *Jude*, as they did the other Jewish prisoners. Towards Hanna they were especially respectful. This Joel explains on the basis of an unwilling admiration elicited by the Palestinians' courage and refusal to cringe. But the "gentlemanly" behavior of the Nazi officers in no way interfered with the brutality of their orders. The "gentlemanly" Germans dispatched prisoners to death as unblinkingly as the ruffianly S. S. men.

Life in a Hungarian prison was apparently less rigidly controlled than in a purely Nazi establishment. The sense that the war was running to an unsuccessful close affected the guards and made them willing to curry favor with the prisoners, particularly the British and the Americans. The cells faced the courtyard, and it was possible to shout to friends from the windows. By means of strings they could throw messages across the yard. Some guards could be bribed to open the cells at night. This made meetings between the prisoners possible.

Finally, after two months, through bribery, Joel and Hanna had an opportunity of meeting. They had a

ans, more pedantic than the Hungarians, began
xhaustive interrogation, which lasted for several
in the attempt to discover whether the mother
anything of her daughter's acts. At this time,
Senesch still had no idea as to how Hanna had
d Hungary from Palestine. The Germans were
satisfied that the mother had no share in the mis-
ut she was not released. She was kept in prison
eral months. This, however, had its compensa-
Vithin a few days Hanna was brought to the same

y of the prison attendants were apparently im-
by Hanna's valor and charm and by the pathos
mother's presence in the same prison. At any
veral of them cooperated in making an occa-
limpse of Hanna possible. Once, the mother
d when Hanna was in the toilet, and they had
nutes together. Hanna looked better. Her hair
ing were neat. The bruise was gone. But the
ad to find out about the broken tooth. "I got
g down in the parachute," Hanna explained
d laughing: "Mother, if I only lose a tooth in
ll be well."

their brief, stolen meetings — sometimes while
e in the courtyard, sometimes through the
e of a sympathetic attendant — the mother
: "What did you undertake?" But on this
na was silent. Finally, the mother asked:
omething of Jewish interest?" And Hanna
are on the right track." And when the
nted to know: "Is it worth risking your life
alistic impulse?" Hanna answered simply:
is worth while."

long talk in the course of which Hanna was able to tell
Joel of the series of events which had led to her capture.
She had been caught as soon as she had crossed the
border, because the smugglers who had been engaged
to assist her lost their nerve. Two of her three escorts
had gone into a village on the Hungarian side of the
frontier to look for smugglers who would help her board
a train to Budapest. They were caught. One committed
suicide. This frightened the local peasants who knew
that Hanna and a partisan were hiding in the vicinity.
To protect themselves from charges of complicity, they
disclosed her whereabouts.

The Hungarian police found her radio code and her
radio apparatus. By means of the third degree, they
tried to force her to reveal its purpose. When physical
torture failed, they hit upon something even more per-
suasive. They located her mother who was still in
Hungary.

Those who have read Hanna's diary and poems know
how passionate was her attachment to her mother and
how bitter were her self-reproaches in regard to what
she conceived to be her "unfilial" conduct. It had not
been easy to leave her widowed mother alone. The
five years in Palestine had been lived under the cloud
of this separation and of the sense of guilt from which
the daughter suffered, particularly because the mother
had been unfailingly tender and understanding.

At last, the long-awaited meeting took place, in a
Hungarian prison, under the eyes of police who threatened Hanna that the mother would be killed unless she
revealed the nature of her mission.

Hanna did not tell. Somewhere the sensitive girl
found the will to face her mother and her torturers and

permit the adored and adoring mother to be led away without knowing what her fate would be.

The most intimate picture of Hanna's last days is that provided by her mother. The story of Mrs. Senesch is in its way as dramatic as that of her daughter, and as organic a part of the tragedy of the Jews of Europe. The tall, slender, gracious woman — originally remote from Zionism and with few specific Jewish interests — came to Palestine in the fall of 1945, a year after her daughter's execution. I saw her for the first time at a memorial service for another parachutist, Enzo Sereni, who had been executed in Dachau. In the quiet, grave face of the woman I watched from a distance one could sense the stoicism which had flamed into a more spectacular heroism in the daughter. But this was a year after the girl's death. Since that summer day in 1944, when she first saw her daughter again after five years of separation, there had been time not only for Hanna's execution but for the apotheosis of the girl into a national heroine. A year before, in the prison, the comfort of the legend had been absent.

Sitting in a small hotel room in Tel Aviv, Mrs. Senesch told me of her reunion with Hanna in a Budapest prison. The cultivated Hungarian lady symbolized a phase of modern Jewish experience as vividly as Hanna herself. She had been thrust fiercely into the very vortex of the Jewish tragedy; her daughter had leapt into it of her own volition. The path which led Mrs. Senesch to a new life, in the collective farm of which her daughter had been an eager comrade, has its place in any account of contemporary Jewish history.

When Mrs. Senesch was summoned by the Hungarian police she went secure in the conviction that, whatever

happened, her children were safe in
son had reached Palestine the day
out on her mission.) To her surprise sh
about Hanna. Why had the girl le
had she studied? The mother coul
official to the girl's brilliant school
mother added that despite the pai
she was glad that her daughter was
questioner smiled mockingly. Fina
"Where is your daughter now?" Ar
again, "In Haifa," he seemed conv
was truly ignorant of her daug
announced: "She is in the next
her in. Persuade her to speak,
your last meeting."

Hanna was brought in. She
embraced her and began to v
forgive me."

She was not in uniform. Her
her hair dishevelled. She had
and one of her teeth was brol
spoke to me, a year after the
that she was still troubled by
tooth.

Mother and daughter were
Stunned and bewildered, the
are you not in Palestine? Ho
To which Hanna did not ar
ing: "Are you hurt?" to wh

The mother was sent h
not to talk of her experien
ever, she was arrested, th

Gerr
an e
days,
knew
Mrs.
reach
finally
sion,
for sev
tion.
prison.

Man
pressed
of the
rate, se
sional g
was call
a few m
and clot
mother
it comin
and add
this, it w

During
at exerci
connivan
would asl
point Har
"Was it s
said: "Yo
mother wa
for an ide
"For me it

Hanna told her mother that she viewed her stay in the prison as not wholly unprofitable, because she had converted many of her fellow-prisoners to Zionism. She had an unerring sense for the grand gesture. Her fellow-prisoners, being Hungarian Jews, all wore the Star of David. As a British subject she was free from the requirement. So, to demonstrate her solidarity with Israel, she traced a Star of David in the dust of her windowpane and maintained it there for all to see.

In September, after nearly four months, the mother was freed. The parachutists also hoped for release. By the beginning of October, every one knew that Hunary's collapse was certain. In the desire to forestall vengeance, the prison guards would come in and introduce themselves with the communist greeting and offer the prisoners cigarettes.

When Hungary capitulated in October, the mood of the political prisoners was jubilant. Each one had a daydream to fulfill. The Palestinians had their program. They would meet Hanna. Then they would go to a hotel where they could get a big dinner, a hot bath — all the things which had been impossible in the months of imprisonment. It would have been easy to make a jailbreak. Discipline was at its lowest, and there was no real attempt to enforce it. But the guards begged the political prisoners to wait a few hours more for their formal liberation. Otherwise the common criminals who were in the jail would take part in the escape. Since the prisoners had no knowledge of actual conditions in the country, and believed that if Hungary laid down her arms there could be no fear of a fascist counter-attack, they agreed to wait.

But the fascist coup came at once. That night, shots

were heard in the city. In the morning the guards did not come near the charges they had so recently wooed. No breakfast was served. The brief interlude of hope was over.

Within a few days, new interrogations began. The men were summoned to a court-martial. Hanna was sent to a civil court. This increased the belief that Hanna would be the one to survive. Joel and Perez were certain that they would be shot, but confident that the story of their venture would at least be told by Hanna.

Hanna was the first to be tried. The accounts of the trial are pieced together from the reports of eyewitnesses and of Joel's information received through the usual prison channels. Hanna was brave, and she made the kind of addresses to her judges that might have been expected. Perhaps they were impressed by the girl's valor and touched by her youth and charm; but the prosecutor nevertheless demanded the death penalty. The judges did not pass sentence at once. Hanna was remanded to her prison. On November 6, 1944, an officer came to her cell and told her that she had been condemned to death. Did she wish to plead for mercy? Hanna answered that she had been condemned by a lower court, and demanded the right to appeal to a higher court. Again she was asked whether she wanted mercy. And she answered: "I ask for no mercy from hangmen."

The execution took place on a cold, foggy autumn day. Joel remembers it because he heard the shots of the execution. Hanna was brought into the courtyard. Witnesses tell that she refused to have her eyes bound, but stood straight and unmoving as the order to fire was given.

In the meantime, the mother had no knowledge of her daughter's fate. Mrs. Senesch kept trying to arrange for a visit to the prison but was prevented by a series of obstacles. One day there was an air-raid. Another time the officer who could grant permission for visits was out of town. Besides, Jews had the right to leave their homes only between the hours of 10 and 12 in the morning. As the prison was some distance from the mother's home, it was impossible for her to complete the trip in the alloted period. Finally, on the fatal November 6, completely ignorant of what was to take place that day, she covered the yellow star on her coat lapel with her handbag and ventured out an hour before the permitted time.

When she gave her name to the guard at the prison, he seemed startled and embarrassed. "Hurry," he said and directed her upstairs to the officer in charge. The officer bade her sit down; he glanced toward the window which gave on the courtyard; a shot was heard. Then he turned to the mother. He recounted all the acts of which the daughter had been guilty. He concluded his indictment with the sentence: "Those acts merit the extreme penalty which has just been executed."

That was the end of the story. There was nothing more to tell beyond the shot in the courtyard whose significance she had not known at the time. The girl, vibrant, gay, affectionate, who had been so vividly evoked by the mother's words that there were moments when we both forgot that she was dead, vanished with the shot. In her stead came the national heroine who had chosen to dash herself against Hitler Europe.

Several years before, Hanna had written:

> To die, to die in youth,
> No, no, I did not want it;
> I loved the warmth of sun, the lovely light.
> I loved song, shining eyes, and not destruction.
> I did not want the dark of war, the night.
> No, no, I did not want it.

The poem went on to declare that since fate willed that she live in the midst of bloodshed and ruin, she was grateful that she could live — and die if need be — on the earth of her homeland.

She did not die upon the earth she loved. Her body lies in the Jewish cemetery of Budapest, in the "lot of the martyrs." But her wish was fulfilled in even richer measure than she dared imagine. There is a special memorial room for her in Caesarea, the settlement in which she worked. And her young, smiling figure, in military uniform, may be seen in every village and town of Palestine.

Hanna Senesch's poems and diary have become part of the national literature of Palestine and quotations from her writings have become daily slogans: "Whom shall I send? Send *me* . . ." In her life, as in her words, she had been the ideal *shaliach*, one of the "messengers" who appeared in various guises in every ghetto of Europe. And be it remembered, when one strives to measure the achievements of those who answered the call, that, etymologically, even an angel is only a messenger.

5

Resistance in Budapest

❀

DESPITE the crushing blow of Hanna's execution, Joel did not lose the will to complete the mission which so far had ended in failure. Prison supervision had become much stricter again and the possibilities of escape correspondingly slimmer. In view of the Red Army's advance, political prisoners were being sent to Germany. When the Russians reached the outskirts of Budapest, the evacuation of Joel's prison started. Three hundred prisoners, including British officers, Russian parachutists, Yugoslav partisans and Hungarian communists, were herded into five cars. Joel knew what awaited him in Germany. There was little to lose, and with several others an attempt to escape was made. The train was of wood, and by scraping carefully at night with a knife which one of the officers had secreted, a hole large enough to squeeze through was cut. Joel and a few others jumped from the moving train; they found themselves still in Hungarian territory.

After a series of adventures which would form a chapter in themselves, Joel managed to get back to Budapest, the original object of his mission when he was first parachuted into Europe some seven months earlier. In Budapest he at first found shelter with a de Gaullist at the French Legation. It was, however, impossible to remain at the Legation indefinitely. Joel lived in bombed-out houses till he found a British lieutenant who offered to take him to Russia. But there was still the long-delayed job to be done. The British lieutenant shared Joel's sense of the primary importance of helping the Jews of Europe. He had contacts with the Jewish underground in Hungary and, through him, Joel was able to resume his work.

Till October 15, 1944, the date of the fascist coup, the 250,000 Jews still remaining in Budapest had been able to exist after a fashion. They were confined to special quarters; they had to wear the badge with the Star of David; and they suffered acutely from discrimination and persecution; but they were not being murdered. In comparison with the Jews of Poland, whose slaughter had begun two years earlier, they were fortunate. After the fascist coup, the situation changed. Jews began to be hunted down for the dreaded shipments to the death-camps. The ostensible reason given was that Jews had taken an active part in street battles during the revolution and that Jewish houses had been used as pillboxes for partisan activity. Therefore, German tanks destroyed whole blocks of houses where the Jewish underground had been active. The members of the Jewish underground, armed only with small weapons, were no match for tanks; their losses were enormous. In addition, the local population had no compunction about abetting their German overlords.

Hungarian fascists joined the sport of murdering Jews.

Every Jew caught on the street was brought to a big square, tortured and shot. The annihilation of Hungarian Jewry was well under way.

An organized attempt to save Jewish lives had to be launched. A last desperate stand such as that of the Warsaw ghetto was still premature. It would be made when all hope of saving considerable numbers of lives was gone. As long as it was possible to rescue Jews by acts of individual valor or strategy, all the ingenuity of the Jewish underground had to be brought into play. In addition, it was essential to instill courage into a terrorized population. If the calamity of Poland was not to be repeated, initiative had to be taken and direction given. Whatever the outcome, the spectacle of helpless masses permitting themselves to be herded for the slaughter had to be avoided. The special function of the Jewish underground, in which the Zionist youth groups played a leading part, was to prevent the passive extermination which had so bewilderingly taken place in other parts of the European continent. Joel's role in the organization of resistance in Budapest in this final critical period was a historic one.

One of the devices which resulted in the saving of thousands of Jewish lives sounds suspiciously like motion-picture melodrama of a not too inventive sort. But in a period in which the primitive fantasies of a Julius Streicher or a Hitler determined the plot, it is not surprising that the resistance movement had its movie-thriller episodes as well as its epic grandeur.

The Jewish underground managed to secure Hungarian uniforms. Dressed up in these, young Jews would approach bands engaged in seizing Jews on the streets and would offer to take charge. The Hungarian mobs would willingly hand over their victims to what appeared to be the proper authorities. When a sufficient number of Jews had been gathered together, they would be taken away by the Jewish underground, presumably for immediate execution.

The masquerade worked on other occasions also. Pretending to be an execution squad, members of the Jewish underground in Hungarian uniforms presented themselves at the Budapest prison with faked orders. They succeeded in liberating forty-eight non-Jewish political prisoners. (A number of the resistance leaders saved by Jewish youth groups assumed high posts in the Hungarian government after the country was liberated.)

But the Jewish position continued to deteriorate. Jews were no longer allowed to leave their homes. It then became essential to evacuate the houses if the residents were not to be murdered wholesale. Again squadrons of the Jewish underground, in fascist dress, would enter the houses and examine the inhabitants. Those of Aryan appearance were provided with forged documents. Those with unmistakably Semitic features were hidden in secret cellars or "bunkers."

These seizures by the Jewish resistance groups were no simple matter. The Jews whose houses were invaded had no idea that the young men in fascist uniforms were actually their saviors. Fascist methods had to be mimicked faithfully, otherwise there was the danger that the nature of the trick would be bruited about and it would be impossible to repeat such manoeuvers. It was particularly important to hide children, as the very young, the sick, and the very old were those in the most immediate danger of extermination. Consequently, children would be torn from protesting mothers who would have to be forcibly thrust aside with no word of comfort. Parents did not learn of the survival of their children till after the liberation of Budapest. Then the revelations were made. Had parents been informed of the truth, it would have been humanly impossible to keep the secret. Furthermore, they would not have been able to simulate convincingly the natural agony felt. The procedure was harsh, but several thousand people were saved this way.

This was only one way of helping. All Hungarian Jewry was in the process of being massacred. If the butchers were to be foiled — in some measure at any rate — more extensive methods of salvation had to be devised. One way to protect Jews from deportation to the death-camps was to provide them with passports of neutral countries. Such passports were forged in large numbers and kept in circulation. After a number of weeks, the Hungarian government became suspicious of the authenticity of these passports and demanded that the consulates check on the identity of those claiming the protection of their citizenship. In the meantime, however, several valuable weeks had elapsed in the course of which it had been possible to make other arrangements for Jews threatened with deportation.

Sometimes a neutral passport would be given for only a few days, in order to develop a sense of confidence in the possessor. Then he would be given Aryan documents and concealed. The reason for this was psychological. One of the chief causes why possessors of Aryan documents betrayed themselves was fear. This factor has been stressed so often by leaders of Jewish underground movements from every Nazi-occupied country that it must be given full weight. If a man questioned by police, in the customary check-up on streets and trains, took out his documents with the assurance born of the knowledge that all was in order, he might be examined casually. A nervous manner was fatal. Many Jews, shattered psychically by years of hounding, were unable to simulate the easy manner essential to prevent suspicion, even when they were of so-called "Aryan" appearance. Sometimes marked Semitic features with a confident air were a better guarantee of safety in a routine examination than Nordic blue eyes and blond hair plus a hesitant demeanor. The neutral passport enabled the owner to appear on the street as a Jew of a neutral nationality. After he had gained the necessary assurance to appear in public, he could be placed in concealment and furnished with Aryan papers.

I deliberately refrain from naming those neutral consulates and those international agencies of mercy who assisted, either actively or passively, in these schemes, because their help might be construed as "illegal." There is apparently some diplomatic hocus-pocus which respects the right of the murderer to murder and sharply limits the forms in which some sanctuary may be offered to the victim. Even after the Nazi defeat, it is not possible to give due honor where honor should be given because some convention of international usage may have been violated by those who dared to save the innocent from butchery.

When a ghetto was decreed in Budapest, a plan for a general uprising was worked out. It was decided to defend each individual house to the last possible moment. This necessitated the construction of large numbers of bunkers and the organization of flying squads who would be prepared to maintain contact between those hiding in the bunkers and the militant underground. Nobody knew when the hour for the final stand would come and preparations were being feverishly made for all eventualities. A heavy blow fell when sixty of the best trained men of the underground were arrested through betrayal. A member, who was caught, weakened under cross-examination and informed the police of a meeting of leaders. The loss was so great that the motion-picture masquerade was again resorted to. A daring member of the underground, dressed in the uniform of a Hungarian officer and accompanied by a group of supposed Hungarian soldiers, appeared at the prison with a faked list containing the names of the prisoners and demanded that the men be given to him for immediate execution. They were handed over.

On December 24, 1944, the Russian Army surrounded Budapest. At that time there were still about 80,000 Jews in the ghetto and many thousands hiding with "Aryan" documents. Because of the Russian siege the food problem became extremely acute, as supplies from the country and other towns were cut off. Death by starvation seemed imminent.

On December 25, when Russian artillery began to shell Budapest, the fascists commenced a wholesale massacre of the Jews — those in the ghetto, the Swiss International House, and wherever else they could be found. There was no methodical German murder-camp available in Budapest, so the Hungarians had to use the less scientific methods of simply taking groups of Jewish men, women and children and shooting them near the river. Again the Jewish underground, dressed in the uniforms of Hungarian military patrols, tried to liberate the victims. Sometimes the device still worked. No doubt the general disorganization and demoralization of a besieged and doomed city helped to make any assertion of apparently legitimate authority respected. Nevertheless, despite the efforts of the underground, in the course of the nineteen days of the siege, till the Russian liberation of the ghetto, 18,000 Jews were murdered by the fascists on the streets of Budapest.

On January 6, 1945, information was received that German and Hungarian engineer troops planned to demolish the ghetto as a last act before capitulation. It was obvious that at this stage an armed uprising would be able to accomplish nothing except to precipitate the end; there was a chance that the remaining Jews could be saved through other channels. In this the situation differed from that of the Warsaw ghetto. In Budapest were officials of the Gestapo with whom negotations for the rescue of Jews had been under way, notably Becker of the S. S. The Jewish underground determined on a bold stroke. They sent a delegation, including Joel, to Becker with the demand that the ghetto be not razed. They followed a line of argument that had been used in all other efforts to negotiate with the Germans. The head of the delegation suggested: "You have lost the war; you will certainly be tried and punished for your deeds. If you destroy the ghetto with the thousands of Jews still alive, you will add to the roster of your crimes. But if you will not carry out this plan, we promise you a visa for Switzerland together with enough funds for subsistence." Becker accepted the proposal, but warned that if the agreement were not carried out, he still had half a million Jews left in his lands whom he could slaughter.

Naturally, the whole negotiation was a play for time.

The entrance of the Russians could not be long delayed. Every day gained increased the possibility of saving the lives of thousands of Jews. There may be some delicate souls who feel that promises given to the Gestapo assassins should have been honored and that, consequently, Becker should either not have been approached or should have been provided with the means for a quiet life in Switzerland, since he forbore to raze the ghetto. Fortunately, the young men struggling to prevent the murder of the remnant of Hungarian Jewry were not troubled by such scruples. Any ruse that could outwit the criminals with whom they dealt was eagerly employed.

On January 18, the Russian army reached the east bank of the Danube and the illegal phase of the work was over.

In all the work of rescue which has been described, Joel took a prominent part. Of course he was not alone. There was an active rescue committee in Hungary whose role will be described later, but it must be borne in mind that the appearance of the Palestinian parachutists and *shlichim* in Nazi Europe had a value far beyond the actual numbers involved. The psychological effect on the Jewish communities to whom they came was enormous. One must remember that they appeared in the midst of human beings reduced to either terror or apathy by a long period of suffering and persecution. The sense of having been forgotten by the world, of having been handed over to carnage without any apparent attempt at help or interference, was in itself paralyzing. Each Palestinian who appeared among them stimulated hopes and energies fast becoming extinct. Even when the mission failed, as in the case of Hanna who was executed before she could achieve any of the tasks which she had set herself, the mere story of her attempt quickened courage and indicated new possibilities of struggle.

Reuben in Yugoslavia working with the partisans, Joel and Hanna in Hungary — these are a few of the names of those that went. But they were only part of a gallant company whose existence they never let me forget.

6

A Shepherd in Rumania

◉

ALL OF the Balkans had to be breached. Rumania, too, had its parachutists from Palestine. I spoke to Avi while he was still nursing the broken leg he got when he landed on a rooftop in Rumania.

Avi was a shepherd. A mild, blue-eyed chap who originally came from Rumania, he had spent his years in Palestine in an agricultural settlement where he had tended sheep. When I came to see him, he could already hobble about; but for months previously he had lain in a cast trying to set the fractured bones straight.

Like the other Palestinians, he had been obsessed by the desire to reach the Jews in Europe. From 1941 on, he had been meditating on how this could be achieved. In the winter of 1943, when he would get up at dawn to milk his sheep, he would be haunted by the thought of European Jewry and its fate. His comrades knew of his preoccupation; when plans for a parachutist group began to crystallize, he was among those considered. In view of his knowledge of Rumania, the place for his mission was obvious.

Before he could begin training, he had to receive the permission of his settlement, as was the case with the other parachutists, all of whom came from collective farms. He was the only trained shepherd in his settlement — which complicated the problem of finding a substitute. The question was threshed out at a meeting of the collective. Avi could reveal nothing more than that the undertaking was in the interests of the war and of the Jews of Europe. It so happened that the sheep were lambing — a particularly bad time for a shepherd to leave his flock. The secretary of the settlement warned that, if Avi left, the sheep would have to be sold. Could the settlement afford such a sacrifice? Finally, one of the comrades who worked in the apple orchard volunteered to leave his apple trees and take charge of the sheep. Years before, he had had some experience as a shepherd and might succeed. After an agitated session, the settlement gave its consent: Avi could go to his unknown task.

He started training as a parachutist with considerable misgivings. He had been anything but a sportsman. The leisurely pace of tending sheep was hardly preparation for a life of strenuous physical activity. Unlike Reuben and Joel, he had not been a soldier. His wife, his child, his sheep, had filled his life. But the cry of the Jews of Europe kept reaching him in the fields of the Emek. Many shepherds were needed for the flock beset by wild beasts. Avi told me that he found strength in remembering the favorite characters of Jewish folk-lore — simple men who performed miracles for the nation, shoemakers or tailors who became capable of fantastic acrobatic feats in a moment of exaltation! "You see," he said to me, "it is not the wonder-rabbis who became our saviors. In the legends, it is the plain, humble man, the shoemaker who is able to perform *kefitsat ha-derech* (leap over the road, that is, annihilate distance); he is the original parachutist!"

In the fall of 1943, after a brief training period, Avi and Aryee, another Palestinian, were dropped in Rumania. According to the original plan they were to jump in the vicinity of Timisoara, where members of the Jewish underground were supposed to receive them. Documents and facilities for the later transfer of the parachutists to Bucharest had been prepared; owing to bad visibility, however, they were dropped not on the designated point but amidst anti-aircraft fire in a small Rumanian town. Aryee fell in the courtyard of a police station where he was promptly seized. Avi landed on a rooftop, breaking his leg in the fall. In the morning, he too was arrested.

This seemed like a hopeless end to the mission. What could be accomplished by a prisoner of war lying with his leg in a cast in a Rumanian prison hospital? The first problem, naturally, was to prevent the Rumanians from discovering his identity or the nature of his mission. Since he was captured in uniform — that of a British lieutenant — Avi was in a position to insist on his rights as a prisoner of war. He claimed that he and his companion had been obliged to bail out because of engine trouble. As a Palestinian, he could be a British airman without knowing English. The Rumanians, however, were suspicious. They accused him at once of being a Rumanian native, who knew the language and who had been deliberately dropped for some Allied task. Avi's great concern was to keep them from discovering that he knew Rumanian. He spoke only German to his interrogators.

The Rumanians kept trying to trap him by wearing him down physically and nervously. His leg was in a bad state — infected and badly fractured — and he was in great pain. Nothing was done to alleviate his suffering, on the pretext that the Rumanian nurses did not understand what he wanted. He would not be given the flask for urine and other necessities when he made the request, on the theory that in a moment of distress and impatience he would betray his knowledge of Rumanian. When the cast on his leg bothered him, the nurse would manipulate the leg in some particularly painful manner and ask in Rumanian: "Does this hurt?"

When these devices failed to elicit the desired response, the Rumanians decided on a more drastic course. He was told that his leg would be X-rayed. In the elevator the nurse said to the porter in Rumanian: "If I could throw this ugly Jew down the shaft, I would do so." Avi had to pretend not to understand.

In the X-ray room, while the apparatus was being made ready, the physicians began a discussion in Rumanian as to whether they should arrange the machine in such a fashion that there would be an explosion. Apparently they had read Jules Verne. Finally they announced that they would remove the usual safeguards. During this discussion, they kept watching Avi, and he, though uncertain whether this was a trick or whether the doctors were in earnest, had to look calm and uncomprehending.

After the photograph had been made, the physicians told Avi that his leg would have to be stretched, and that he would be given an opiate. This was a real danger. Avi knew that under the influence of an opiate, he might readily answer a question in Rumanian. Only an enormous effort of the will could save him. He determined that, if possible, he would repeat only one German phrase: *Was wollen Sie?* (What do you want?). When they began giving him ether the doctors started counting in German and then switched to Rumanian, requesting him to repeat the numbers. He forced himself to say nothing. Then as he began to lose consciousness, they squeezed his body painfully, while asking in Rumanian: "Shall I stop?"

Somehow, Avi managed to get through this trial without betraying himself. Even when he regained consciousness he heard himself repeating mechanically: *Was wollen Sie?*

The net result of this episode was that the Rumanians began to fear that he was a German, involved in some Nazi double-cross of the Rumanians. This suspicion made his stock rise, and his life became more endurable.

His fellow-prisoners, however, who were for the most part American and British aviators, also got wind of his conduct under ether and began to suspect that he was a German spy. Fortunately, he had means of persuading them of his true identity.

Though bed-ridden, Avi managed to establish contact with the Jewish underground in Bucharest, and by that means to fulfill some of the purposes of his flight. First of all he had to discover a friendly soul among the guards and attendants. After tactful probing, he established good relations with a soldier and a nurse, both of whom began to assist him. The initial step was to get messages out of the hospital. A regular correspondence developed between Avi and centers in Bucharest, Istanbul and Cairo by means of those go-betweens, whose cooperation was absolutely trustworthy and who were inspired by a genuine desire to help rather than by the usual motive of a fat bribe.

Once Avi knew that his contacts with the outside world had been established and could be brought into play, he began to carry out a principal point in his program: to help in the escape of American and British prisoners of war. He made his presence and purpose known to an American major in the prison and began to work out plans for escape. At that time the prison camp had in it one hundred and twenty American prisoners of war, all of them aviators who had been downed in the costly bombardments of the Ploesti oil fields.

Shortly after that, a directive in code was received from American headquarters indicating to the Americans that Avi (this was not the name by which he was known in the camp) was to be obeyed by all United Kingdom and United States prisoners in matters of escape. This settled the question of his authority.

It is irrelevant to the purpose of this narrative to recount the various methods of escape attempted, some of which were successful and some of which failed. The stories of the tunnels dug, the flights at night, can be duplicated by any account of a prisoner-of-war camp. What is significant, however, is how Avi, from his sick-bed, managed to spin the threads which made the schemes practicable. In order to escape, the prisoners had to be provided with maps of the surrounding country, with money, with flashlights. A wire-cutter to cut the wires around the camp was required. All these essentials were received by Avi, once he had made his contacts with the Jewish underground. The chain went from Avi to a doctor who came daily to the hospital, to a center of comrades in Bucharest, and from there radiated out to

Istanbul and Cairo. It became possible to make requests known to British and American headquarters and,
when these requests were fulfilled, to bring the articles
to the prison camp. All this involved daily danger, but
the Rumanians never discovered that Avi was the central figure in many of the escapes that took place.

When the Rumanian armistice was signed in August,
1944, there were a thousand American aviators in Bucharest. In the chaotic period, before new authorities took
over, it was essential that these aviators be concealed
and enabled to escape, since it was feared that the
Germans might march in at any time. The Germans
immediately began an intensive bombardment of Bucharest which lasted for several days. During this period,
under the direction of Avi and with the help of the
Jewish underground, the aviators were provided with
civilian clothes, places for hiding, money and medication. Radio communication was established with Cairo.
Thanks to these measures the aviators were kept safe till
the Americans could take them out of Rumania. It is
therefore no exaggeration to say that, due to the immediate assistance given by the facilities of the Jewish underground, a thousand American airmen were free and
alive who might otherwise have been lost. This phase of
Avi's mission was successful, despite the unfortunate accident with which it began.

As far as the second phase — the rescue of Jews — is
concerned, it is harder to speak in round figures. Even
from the hospital, the Palestinian parachutist helped in
the organization of defense units. And, of course, he
formed a living link with Palestine. He brought the
authority of a reborn people to the dying remnant. A
concrete example of how his influence made itself felt

THE PARACHUTISTS FROM PALESTINE

may be seen in the following incident. After negotiations with Antonescu, involving handsome sums of money, an agreement was reached between the Rumanian authorities and the Jewish Rescue Committee, directed from Istanbul, permitting three hundred Jews to leave from Constantza for Turkey. From there refugees, who had certificates for Palestine, would proceed by train. The ship was the *Maritza*, the first refugee ship to leave Constantza since the outbreak of the war.

The crossing was known to be perilous. The ship was small, the conditions of the sailing dangerous and uncertain. Consequently there was a good deal of hesitation among the Jews selected for the journey. They had heard, however, of the Palestinian in Bucharest; word was sent to him. They asked simply: "Shall we go? We are afraid the boat will sink." Avi sent back the message: "Members of he-Halutz (Zionist Pioneers) will go first. Then you must embark. Every Jew given a chance must leave Rumania."

The order was obeyed. The *Maritza* left Constantza in February, 1944. The fact that Avi could persuade a terrorized group to take a bold step is no tribute to his personal power. The people involved did not know him. It was a tribute to the inspiring power of Palestine. Avi was a symbol of strength, of independent action. When the parachutist from Palestine said "Go," even the frightened and feeble went.

7

What Did They Achieve?

❀

I ASKED each of the parachutists: "What did you
accomplish?" Each, after he had recounted the details
of exploits which, no matter how brave, were in themselves confessedly not unique — each said to me: "The
mere fact of our presence was important."

The actual accomplishments of the parachutists were
by no means negligible even when compared with similar attempts by greater powers than Jewish Palestine.
The numbers seem small: two hundred and forty men
were trained; of these, thirty-two reached their destination, of whom seven were lost. In considering these
figures, one should bear in mind that the entire British
Empire at no time had more than about two hundred
and fifty parachutists working behind enemy lines. Compared with this number, the thirty-two Palestinians do
not appear so few. Furthermore, in Rumania, in parts
of Yugoslavia and in Austria, the Palestinians were the
first behind-the-lines parachutists on the scene.

Reuben working with the partisans in Yugoslavia, Joel
and Perez in Hungary, Avi and Joshua Trachtenberg in

Rumania, Haym Hermesch in Slovakia, Enzo Sereni in Italy, and others whom I have not mentioned, fought bravely and well for the Allied cause.

Joshua Trachtenberg was particularly successful in organizing a Jewish underground railway. Over three thousand people were gotten out of Rumania and sent to Palestine.

When Bucharest was in danger of being recaptured by the Germans, the Palestinians helped to organize resistance in the Jewish quarter. These groups formed part of the general resistance movement of the workers of Bucharest who rose to defend their city against the Nazis till the Red Army entered.

In Yugoslavia, they worked as liaison officers with the partisans and tried to maintain the links with Hungary and Rumania. The activities in Hungary and Yugoslavia have already been described. One of the groups dropped in Yugoslavia reached Austria, the first Allied airman to do so.

Slovakia also had its Palestinian parachutists. In September, 1944, during the Slovak partisan uprising, a mission of five left Italy by plane for Yugoslavia. One of these was a young woman (Haviva) who, like Hanna Senesch, lost her life in the course of the mission. They set up a wireless station and established contact with the Jewish underground in German-occupied Slovakia. They assisted hundreds of refugees from forced labor camps.

With the help of local Jewish resistance groups, they formed a Jewish partisan unit which went into the mountains two days before the town in which they operated was recaptured by Germans. Three of the five, including Haviva, lost their lives in a German raid on their camp.

74

In May, 1944, Enzo Sereni was parachuted into northern Italy, the part still occupied by the Germans. His task, too, was to organize the escape of allied war prisoners and to aid in Italian resistance. Enzo Sereni is as much a legend in Palestine as Hanna Senesch. A son of the personal physician to the king of Italy, a scholar and adventurer with a touch of the Italian *condottiere*, Sereni's exploits had for years been a part of the verve and valor of Palestine. A *halutz* long before Hitler's advent, he had entered Germany after 1933 to organize Jewish youth. When the mission of the parachutists was undertaken, he was 39 years old, but he insisted on being accepted. His fellow-parachutists idolized him as teacher and leader. It was Enzo who, with characteristic assurance, told his young comrades when they parted in Bari: "Remember, only he dies who wants to die." He was captured and executed in Dachau.

Indisputably, there were men and women working in the Jewish underground in every European country who were of heroic stature, and who were equal to any act in which valor and intelligence could avail. They too have become legends, but as far as the Jews of Europe were concerned, the parachutists' appearance was the sign that the tomb in which they were perishing was not sealed.

Word of the parachutists reached every Jewish community. In Yugoslavia, Jewish partisans marched for miles to see Reuben. The story of Avi spread throughout Rumania. Of course, all kinds of legends sprang up around the parachutists. Their numbers grew in the popular mind; the nature of their deeds assumed a more spectacular character. This idealization was inevitable.

75

The combination of desperate need and poetic answer — the parachutist from Palestine — was bound to create the myth. The folklore of every people has the figure of the savior who comes to help in a black hour. France has the vision of the Maid of Orleans who always returns to defeat the enemy; the Germans wait for Barbarossa to rouse himself from his long slumber. For the Jews of Europe, as every rational expectation of help proved illusory, as no great power intervened, no "conscience of mankind" revolted, hope began to center on the resurgent "homeland" — the only place which offered welcome, if it could be reached. When the miracle took place, and the homeland voluntarily sent its sons and daughters into the abyss, it is readily understandable what emotions were aroused.

One of the songs chanted in the ghettos of Poland and in the extermination camps consists of a single statement reiterated over and over: "I believe the Messiah will come. Though his coming be delayed, I believe that he will come." Even on the way to the slaughterhouse the need to believe could not be crushed. And for many the young parachutists from Palestine were an affirmation of their faith.

"Blessed is the match that is consumed in kindling flame."

III. The Underground Network

1

The Office in Istanbul

❀

T HE parachutists leapt from the sky in the last year of the war into Nazi-held Europe to discover what could be done to bring aid to the Jews who were being systematically murdered at an ever increasing tempo. Other attempts, however, to penetrate the fortress had been in progress for several years. These were less obviously spectacular, but they too had their full share of drama and heroism. The Jewish underground which the parachutists found when they arrived was part of a network which extended over Europe. Independent cells of Jewish resistance, led by the Zionist youth groups, came into being in each country under Nazi rule, but the contacts and coordination between these cells had to be created by central bodies who could survey the whole grim prospect.

The opportunity to parachute into the Nazi slaughterhouse had been granted very late. Before that, a constant effort had been going on to burrow into the core, to dig a way from the frontiers toward the center. Inside Western and Eastern Europe, inside the Balkans, the Jewries of France, of Holland, of Poland, of Hungary, of Rumania, of Slovakia, were trying to dig their way out of the tomb. With infinite courage and patience they constructed the corridors through which a few might escape. From the other side the digging went on also. At some points the tunnels met; salvation became possible. It was often a tedious process, always a dangerous one, and never a pretty one. Each human being wrested from the German murderers involved an enormous expenditure of money, ingenuity and daring.

At the outset the entire rescue action was a Jewish one. The Great Powers displayed no active concern in the macabre drama enacted behind the Nazi curtain — the deliberate, scientific massacre of six million men, women and children. It is important to stress this point not for the purpose of framing an accusation against the world's incomprehensible indifference in regard to history's great crime — no accusation can be bitter or grave enough — but so that one can appreciate with what limited strength and by what few hands the work was done.

Boring from without could only be done through a neutral country. As soon as the war broke out in 1939, a rescue center was established in Geneva which directed activities in Western Europe. After the entry of Italy into the war, however, Switzerland became encircled by the Axis powers. As a result, the effectiveness of Geneva as a center of rescue was sharply curtailed. It continued to function throughout the war; the role of Switzerland in relationship to rescue from France, Holland and Belgium remained important, but it became essential to find other ways of entering Central and Eastern Europe.

After the liberation of Syria in 1941, the way to Turkey became open. Here was a neutral country from which access could be had to the Balkans, and from the Balkans to Poland. Therefore, in the fall of 1941, a group of Palestinian Jews, representatives of the Jewish Agency and of the Histadruth, the workers' organization of Palestine, came to Istanbul and set up a secret rescue and resistance center which functioned actively till the close of the war.

Three years later, in February, 1944, Ira A. Hirschmann arrived in Turkey as the special representative of the United States Department of State. His instructions were to carry out the orders of the War Refugee Board created by President Roosevelt in January, 1943. The purpose of the War Refugee Board was "to take action for the immediate rescue from the Nazis of as many as possible of the persecuted minorities of Europe, racial, religious or political, and all civilian victims of enemy savagery." America's action, though long delayed, was instrumental in saving many lives, and Ira Hirschmann's work was of historic importance. As a government representative, his activities are a matter of public record and officially had to be confined to legal channels. However (as he relates in *Life Line to a Promised Land*), he soon met the young Palestinians whom he calls "the boys." He pays tribute to their boldness and energy. "It was 'the boys' who had begun the organization of the traffic of small, illegal ships to carry men, women, and children by underground and underworld routes into safety." Though Ira Hirschmann could not openly associate himself with the Palestinians, he gave them his blessing and cooperation: "As a government official I cannot approve your illegal work, but go ahead by all means."

I spoke to the men who worked in "Kusta," Istanbul. I asked them questions which perhaps impressed them as superficial or naive, but these were the usual layman's questions. The answers they gave me will no doubt provide the explanation for much that must puzzle the average person with no knowledge or experience of the ways of the conspirator.

The young men whom I interviewed were secret agents. Daily they plotted and contrived to snare the victim out of the hangman's noose. Yet no less than the parachutists they were dedicated. Despite the difference in tactics and methods, they operated on the same plane. They, too, were zealots and visionaries consumed with the passion to reach the Jews of Europe. As I sat with them, I could not help asking myself for the hundredth time: why was there no such inner compulsion among the Jews of America? Why were they content merely to contribute funds and attend meetings? To how many of them would it have occurred that it was their appointed task to breach Nazi Europe? The Jewish American relief organizations did their work faithfully and well in accordance with permitted and prescribed methods. I exempt these from the question. Nevertheless, the fact remains that as with the venture of the parachutists so with almost all other instances of bold and imaginative action, it was Palestine that accepted the responsibility and took the initiative. That was why I had to go to Jerusalem to examine the records and meet the people who could tell me how the web was spun, how the tunnels were dug.

The rescue center in Istanbul had to be set up under

the guise of a commercial bureau. Though Turkey was neutral, there were strong pro-German leanings in the country; nor was the Turkish dictatorship inclined to countenance activities which might incur the displeasure of the possibly victorious Nazi war lords. Various devices were used to conceal the true character of the "businessmen" who had arrived from Palestine — devices which it would be inadvisable to reveal at the present time. But one point should be stressed. The Palestinians in Istanbul worked in cooperation with the British and American intelligence services. Though the British consulates and embassy in Turkey were no more sympathetic than the London government officials had been to the proposal that Palestinians be used as parachutists, the military authorities appreciated the potential value to the war effort of the Istanbul office. They knew that whatever information would be secured by the Jewish agents, in the course of their attempts to establish contacts with the Jews of the occupied countries, would be relayed to the Allied Intelligence. Much valuable information was, in fact, transmitted by the Jewish Agency "messengers" who finally penetrated into the lands of the Nazi.

Despite the hazards of the operation, a chain of contacts was eventually created which established the links between the severed Jewish communities of Europe. The chain went first from Palestine to Istanbul. From Istanbul there were links to Budapest, Bucharest and Sofia. Sometimes the chain stretched directly from Istanbul to Poland. More commonly, however, the links, reaching farther into the heart of Central Europe, came from Budapest where an effective organization of couriers was built up under the supervision and with the financial assistance of Istanbul. Budapest served as a relay-station which sent out further lines to Poland, to Theresienstadt, to Germany, Austria and Italy. To complete the picture, Istanbul had a direct contact with the Geneva office which carried on rescue work in Western Europe. All Europe was finally embraced.

How was this accomplished? The initial problem was to let Jews in Hungary, Rumania, Poland and Slovakia know that an attempt to reach them was being made. At the same time, it was essential to discover what, if anything, could be done by these Jewries immured in ghettos or in the process of being shipped to extermination camps. One had to tap inch by inch along the ground of the graveyard to discover if a living response could still be heard.

The first attempt made was to try to establish a contact by mail. The Istanbul office had in its possession the names and addresses of Jewish leaders in every Jewish community in Europe. Nobody knew whether these people were dead or alive, but, if they were alive and able to act, the chances were good that they were active in any Jewish underground cells that might have managed to come into existence. Therefore hundreds of letters were sent to the old addresses. The letters were signed by a Turkish girl, and were mailed from all parts of Turkey so as not to attract attention in any one post office. They were in code — a very simple code. A sample might be: "Uncle Ezra has sent me to find out how you are." *Ezra* is the Hebrew word for "help." It might be signed "Artzi." Every Zionist would know that that meant "one from the *Eretz*," or a Palestinian, just as he would know that a signature like "A. Moledetski" was derived from the word *Moledeth*, homeland.

Most of the letters, as was inevitable, were never received. The addressees were already dead, or had long since been driven out of their homes. But a few did reach their destination. At first the recipients did not understand the missives they were getting. Then they became suspicious. But the letters continued to come, with their innocent text interspersed with camouflaged Hebrew words which stressed "rescue" and "Palestine." At last, equally veiled answers began to arrive in Istanbul. Within four months, contacts had been made with the Balkans. Poland came last. Finally there came a day when a postal card arrived signed "Zivia," the name of the heroine of the Warsaw ghetto. One has to appreciate the aura around her person to realize what this postal card meant to the workers in Istanbul.

A telegram came from Slovakia in German: "Please inquire as to address," but the signature was *Rachmim Maher* — Hebrew words meaning: "Mercy, Quick." The device of using Hebrew words appears to be so childishly simple that it is impossible to understand how it escaped the Nazi censorship. Perhaps the German and Balkan experts were so busy looking for intricate codes that they were baffled by the very simplicity of the method. At any rate, this primitive code became the means for disseminating information about every Jewish community in Europe. When Istanbul wanted to know the fate of Czerniakow, the head of the Warsaw ghetto, they received the reply: "Czerniakow has gone to visit Dr. Ruppin." Since Ruppin was a well-known Palestinian economist who had died some time before, the inference was clear. That was how the world first learned of Czerniakow's death. The details of his suicide came later, as survivors of the Warsaw ghetto began to appear outside the confines of Nazi Europe. It is obvious that the code depended on a body of common knowledge and common interests. The Gestapo censor had never heard of Dr. Ruppin, but every active figure in this chain which stretched across the European continent to Palestine was able to interpret the answer.

Once contacts by means of letters had been established, it was necessary to proceed to the next stages. Money had to be sent. Rescue plans had to be contrived. And, not least important, each country had to be informed as to what was happening to its neighbor. Bucharest in Rumania did not know what was taking place in Budapest, Hungary. Neither knew of the events in Poland. Each country was a sealed ghetto in which the Jewish communities were steadily being destroyed without knowledge of what was taking place in other parts of Europe. It was essential for the success of the German extermination plan that this ignorance be maintained. Of course, rumors circulated; an occasional survivor from Poland found his way outside the border to give the alarm. But the information was scanty and uncertain. No real picture of the truth could be had till a reciprocal process of sending in reports to a central clearing house, which in turn gave word to its branches, had come into being. Istanbul served as this clearing house.

After the existence and location of many individuals had been ascertained through answers to some of the letters which had been sent throughout Eastern Europe, a courier service was developed. Money and instructions could not be sent by mail, which had to be restricted to a few innocuous sentences. Anything more complicated required delivery by a personal messenger.

The people who were used as messengers varied. Some were paid agents and some were *shlichim*. It was most feasible to use individuals belonging to the nationalities of the countries to which access was sought. For instance, one of the workers in the Istanbul office saw a notice that a Turkish-Rumanian football match was going to be held in Istanbul. He went to the game, struck up an acquaintance with a member of the Rumanian team, and inquired whether the latter had any Jewish acquaintances in Rumania. After some negotiations, the man agreed to take a letter back with him. This is an example of a casual, and not necessarily reliable, attempt to establish direct contact. As the months passed, an elaborate system of paid agents was set up. These were non-Jews of German, Hungarian, or Rumanian nationality, who had adequate reason for travelling and were therefore permitted to move about. Railway conductors were a particularly desirable class. An even more useful group were minor employees attached to various consular offices. These enjoyed a limited diplomatic immunity as far as travel restrictions were concerned. In most cases for bribes, in some cases out of a genuine impulse of human sympathy, these individuals became regular agents who carried messages and funds to the places designated. It is impossible, even at this stage, to reveal all the details which made the operation of the messenger service possible. The broad categories of collaborators included couriers of neutral countries, merchants, and such enemy functionaries or agents as could be reached through bribery. In addition, but in a class apart, was the large body of young Jews of "Aryan" appearance who, with forged papers, engaged in the life-and-death task of serving as bonds between one ghetto and another.

The first communication sent by messenger reached Budapest in Feburary, 1943. By the spring of 1943 messengers from Istanbul were bringing money and directives into all the Balkan lands. The immense, heart-rending problem, however, was to reach Poland. There the major horror was being enacted, there the sealed trains from all Europe went, and there the slaughter was raging day in, day out. Istanbul knew this from the letters stating laconically: "Uncle Mavetski is with us now" (Uncle Death), or else that: "Gerushunski is getting stronger daily" (deportations are increasing).

To reach Poland by messenger was a real feat. From the overwhelming moment that the postal card from Zivia was received, Istanbul had been engaged in a more or less regular correspondence with leaders of the Jewish underground in Poland. But no direct personal contact had as yet been made. A paid German agent undertook to reach the ghetto of Bendin to deliver a letter to Frumka. (We shall hear of Frumka later, just as we shall hear of Zivia, for Frumka, too, was a heroine of the Warsaw uprising.)

The German succeeded in reaching Bendin in the heart of Poland. He managed to bribe the S. S. guards in order to gain access to the ghetto. It was not easy to find Frumka. As an active leader of the underground, she was watchful and suspicious. He finally located her, but she was unwilling to speak to him. Fearing a trick, she at first refused to take the letter he brought her. By references to mutually familiar individuals, he persuaded her to accept the message. Its code contents were unmistakably authentic. When Frumka realized that she was at last in direct contact with comrades in Palestine, she broke down and wept.

The German had orders to try, if possible, to bring Frumka back with him. False papers had been prepared for her, and her chances for escape were good. The agent offered to take her to Hungary where Jews were as yet not threatened with immediate extermination. From there a road to Palestine might be found. But Frumka refused to accompany the German to safety. She took the money he brought; sent a message back with him to Istanbul — the message is in the archives of the Jewish Agency in Jerusalem — and, instead, made her way to Warsaw where the ghetto was in its death-throes. There she was killed. Even the German was affected by Frumka's courage and self-sacrifice. Though a hard-boiled agent, who had engaged in the business of being a courier out of a mixture of motives in which greed and a sense of adventure had predominated, he came back to Istanbul profoundly, shaken by the heroism of the young Jewess.

They make extraordinary reading, these letters in the files of the Jewish Agency at Jerusalem. From Bratislava in Slovakia, from Jassy and Bucharest in Rumania, from Budapest in Hungary, from Rasgrad in Bulgaria, from Prague, from Geneva, from Versoix, from as far north as Stockholm, the coded letters came. The names of the signatories have — many of them — entered into history. Some of the workers have remained alive, some are dead, but they are all a part of the record of our time — Zivia, Frumka, Gisi Fleischman, Joel Brandt, Zukerman and many others. These names are not written down because I feel that honorable mentions are in order; nor am I attempting to allot credit and make certain that each individual who pitted himself against the implacable German murder machine get his due meed of praise. Nothing so mechanical or presumptuous is at issue. Each of these human beings became involved in so vast a struggle, each planned his campaign from so different an angle, that, no matter what his individual qualities might have been, he became transfigured by the events in which he took a part. One cannot describe the events without reference to some of these figures even though other names might be added.

There may have been no Titans among them, but their effort was titanic. The mortal men and women who moved in this abyss, and stumbled over a thousand corpses to save one living child, reached a stature amplified by the size of the forces they challenged. Each one, in his way, illumines a strand in the web, a cell in the corridor, and as such stands for the host of his comrades who were engaged in the same task.

2

Eichmann Makes an Offer

❁

H AND in hand with the daily effort to rescue a life here and there, there periodically arose the dream of wholesale salvation. Perhaps it would be possible to come to terms with the Germans, to persuade them not to carry out their program of annihilation. Representatives of the Jewish Agency began discussions with the Gestapo as early as 1939. It is time that the story of these negotiations be revealed, for it throws light, as clearly as any other factor, on the reasons why European Jewry perished. The web of the negotiations was spun at different points by different people, but the central impulse came from one source — the Zionist cells inside Europe, that is, ultimately, the Jewish Agency in Palestine.

Shortly after the war broke out, Storm Troop *Fuehrer* Eichmann, head of the Jewish Section in Germany and later in German-occupied countries, summoned the representatives of the Jewish communities in Berlin, Prague and Vienna, and announced that Germany proposed to found an autonomous Jewish State near

Lublin, Poland. He ordered the Jewish representatives to prepare lists of Jews for voluntary deportation to Lublin. The heads of the Prague and Berlin communities refused to make any such lists because they realized that the purpose of this concentration was, not to create an independent Jewish center, but to simplify the destruction of European Jewry. Only the head of the Austrian community proved to be amenable.

In view of the Jewish refusal to cooperate, the Gestapo made their own lists; and the first transport of Jews from Germany, Czechoslovakia and Austria left for Poland in November, 1939. When this transport arrived in Lublin, no housing had been provided, though winter was at hand. The Jews were dumped into the mud and cold and informed by one of Eichmann's assistants: "Here you can have typhus, pneumonia, or even cholera. It makes no difference to us if a Jew dies or emigrates. All we care about is that there be fewer of them."

The significance of this statement was fully appreciated by those who relayed it to the Jewish Agency. It meant two things: first, that the Germans were in earnest about their extermination program; second, that there was, however, a scant possibility that Jews might be allowed to emigrate.

In order to understand this situation, one must realize that in 1939, and for some time thereafter, a division of opinion existed among German authorities in regard to their Jewish program. The Wehrmacht was not in favor of immediate total extermination. The generals believed that Jews could be used for labor and, if fed very small rations, would die off gradually through a combination of excessive toil and famine. This method had the advantage of using Jewish work at a minimal expenditure of the German food supply and, at the same time, of liquidating the Jews without resorting to outright murder camps. America was still not in the war, and the Wehrmacht was chary of introducing such Nazi innovations as extermination factories for human beings. The Gestapo, on the other hand, was set on the annihilation of all the Jews in Nazi territories and wished to use the war for this purpose. A compromise was temporarily reached by these two contending groups: Jews would be permitted to emigrate. In 1939 and 1940, the passionate Nazi desire for a _Judenrein_ German Reich could be partly stilled by the departure as well as the murder of Jews.

When this became clear, the Jewish leaders started to negotiate with Eichmann about the conditions he would set to let Jews out of Germany. At that time Eichmann replied that if a large stream of Jewish emigration commenced, he would stop the deportations to Poland. Great Britain was approached at once and informed of the necessity of getting Jews out. The Allies were told that if the Jews of Germany were to receive certificates to Palestine, or visas for any other country, they could be saved. Although for Jews to remain in Germany meant certain death, the pieces of paper needed to save human lives were not granted. The Jews of Germany were, curiously enough, classified as "enemy aliens" and no move was made to take advantage of the murderer's temporary readiness to let his victim escape.

As legal possibilities to flee from death vanished, "illegal" flight took fresh impetus. _'Aliyah Beth_ (the key term for unauthorized immigration into Palestine) had been in progress since the advent of Hitler. As the situation became more acute, its scope increased. Organization and leadership came from Palestine, first through individual emissaries and later through the Istanbul office. One of the chief functions of the Istanbul bureau was the development of '*Aliyah Beth*. The work of rescue was not complete till departure from the European continent had been assured. And for the young men in Istanbul, final success was measured, not by the closeness of the links forged with the ghettoes, but by the number of boats laden with refugees for which they waited on the Bosphorus.

Even before the Istanbul office had been opened, while negotiations with Eichmann were still under way, transports of boats had been organized to go down the Danube to Constantza on the Black Sea. The first of these transports started down the Danube in 1939 in ships hired from the German Danube company. Eichmann had agreed to let this boatload try to reach Palestine. The alternative was death in Poland. Once these ships reached the Black Sea, however, neutral ships had to be found to transport the passengers across the Mediterranean.

Here another infamous chapter begins. The English consulates in the neutral countries, where attempts to hire ships were made, consistently interfered with these efforts. The Greek Government forbade the chartering of boats for "illegals," as the result of British intervention, and the situation worsened. In addition, the representatives of the Jewish Agency were hampered by lack of funds. Enormous sums of money were required for the hiring of ships and the transportation of groups of some thousand destitute human beings. These sums were not forthcoming. Nevertheless, the Jewish organizations engaged in this task managed to get Yugoslavian river boats to transfer refugees from the Danube boats. Several such transports sailed.

One of these ships was caught in the Danube in January, 1940, when the river froze. Laden with more then a thousand people, the boat remained in the icebound waters off the coast of Yugoslavia, near Kladova. The Yugoslavs refused to permit the passengers to find housing on Yugoslav territory, and the passengers stayed imprisoned aboard the boat throughout the winter and summer. In the autumn of 1940, they were placed in a detention camp where they were kept till Yugoslavia was attacked by the Germans in 1941. The Nazis found them in their pen when they invaded Yugoslavia and killed the majority.

Despite these calamities, the attempt to organize emigration continued. Three thousand people succeeded in leaving Germany at the end of 1940. They reached Palestine in three "illegal" boats: the *Atlantic*, the *Pacific*, and the *Milos*. They were caught by the British who transferred one contingent to the ill-fated *Patria* for deportation to the Island of Mauritius in the Indian Ocean. Every man in Palestine knows what happened to the *Patria*. Shortly before it was to set sail for the distant exile of the Indian Ocean, those aboard blew up the ship. It exploded in the harbor of Haifa with the loss of over two hundred lives. The survivors who were pulled out of the Mediterranean were permitted to remain in Palestine, but those who had not been placed on the *Patria* were shipped to Mauritius where they were kept till August, 1945.

When I came to Palestine, in September, 1945, celebrations of welcome for those who had lived through the five years of banishment in the remote island were being held. I saw children who had grown up in Mauritius as well as men and women who had withered there. The government of the great British Empire had been unable to conceive of any fitter disposition for those of Hitler's victims who had finally made their way to the Jewish homeland than expulsion to Mauritius. Of course, the privilege to die had not been denied. The refugees could have remained unprotestingly in Europe, waiting for the moment when they would be shipped to the extermination camp, or they could have committed suicide in the harbor of Haifa, in sight of the hoped-for land, as so many on the *Patria* did. Those who presumed to seek life had had to expiate that presumption in Mauritius. The returning exiles, who were admitted to Palestine after five years, were grateful neither to the British nor to the world. Mauritius was as incomprehensible to them as Treblinka. As far as they were concerned, the so-called civilized world was a zoo in which the British lion, the American eagle and the Russian bear had all been bitten by the Nazi mad dog.

Later, I met one of the survivors of the dynamited *Patria*. He had been a child at the time of the explosion. When I saw him, he was a youth, stalwart and proud like all the youth of Palestine. I saw him on a happy day. The night before, he had been one of those who had helped to bring in an "illegal" ship to the same harbor of Haifa where his family had perished five years before.

Another "illegal" boat, with an even unhappier fame, was the *Struma*. More than any other ship, its fate exemplified the slaughter of the innocents for which no nation can waive responsibility. The murder was committed by all who refused either to give shelter or to let the ship reach Palestine.

The facts are few and a commonplace of the Hitler era. The *Struma*, with seven hundred and sixty people aboard, succeeded in reaching the port of Istanbul. At that time, Turkey had agreed to give transit visas to those who held certificates for Palestine. People without certificates could not land. The *Struma* remained off the shores of Turkey for two months. Those aboard lacked food and the most elementary hygienic requirements, since no provision for a journey of this length had been made. The craft was no longer seaworthy. When all appeals for help failed, and it was obvious Turkey would not permit the passengers to land because Great Britain would grant no certificates, the captain of the *Struma* turned back. When the ship left the territorial waters of Turkey, it was torpedoed. There were only two survivors. Girls born that year in Palestine were named "Struma." The *Yishuv* was determined to remember.

Not all the journeys ended so disastrously. Some small boats managed to thread their way among the mines of the Black Sea and reach their destination. But the difficulties kept increasing. *Between 1939–1940, the chief obstacle to rescue had been the lack of ports of entry. The Germans had permitted their victims to escape — if they could.* By the end of 1941, however, the Nazi temper changed. An order was issued by the Gestapo forbidding Jews to leave Germany or German-occupied territories. This meant that Germany, Poland, Austria, the Protectorate, France, Holland and Belgium were sealed. Emigration could only proceed through the Balkans.

The Istanbul office did not give up. When Rumania declined to let its boats be hired, attempts were made to get Turkish or Bulgarian craft. When these governments declined to rent any of their shipping for transporting refugees, boats were secured from what may be described as "unofficial sources." The important thing was to save lives, and legal niceties could hardly be observed in the process. Besides, an English consul had objected to the chartering of one of the ships that was available with the classic words: "I don't like to save people by barge." So much for the sympathy and understanding of the proud owners the world's greatest navy! The young men who worked in the heartrending business of organizing these transports told me with what agonized expectation they would look out toward the Bosphorus when a boat was expected and would wait to see from their vantage point what the fate of the passengers would be. Would they be permitted to disembark in Turkey, or would the boat be turned back? Each boat involved an immense amount of political negotiations with the Turks and with the British. A perpetual battle had to be fought for the privilege of letting those who had already evaded the Nazi murderer remain in the precarious shelter that they had reached. The numbers on the boats became very small: seventy or a hundred men and women. But each craft that was not turned back represented a major campaign for the Istanbul office.

Britain had a change of heart in December, 1942. In that month Parliament magnanimously declared that any Jew who managed to reach a neutral country would be permitted to enter Palestine This announcement was made after the extermination of the Jews in Poland was already a matter of public knowledge and when it was impossible to pretend to misunderstand Germany's intentions in regard to any Jew left in her grasp. However, and this is a very serious "however," the Turkish government was not *officially* informed of the new situation till six months had elapsed after the British Parliament's compassionate decision. Therefore, the organization of transports could not be resumed on a larger scale till July, 1943. This method of trying to get Jews out of Europe continued till the Balkans were occupied by the Germans in March, 1944.

3

Negotiations with Wislitzeni

❁

THE attempt to negotiate with Eichmann about emigration during 1939 and 1940 was the first of such endeavors. It was the most promising from every point of view and, had the Jewish representatives not been thwarted at every step, the entire fate of European Jewry might have been a different one. The six million might not have been murdered. As it was, even the abortive and small-scale efforts to organize emigration slowed up the deportations to Poland. As long as there appeared to be any realistic prospect of getting Jews out of Germany, the sealed trains were temporarily held up. Each transport that left German-occupied territory saved the lives not only of those comprising it but of the far greater numbers whose deportation was being deferred. Each phase of the negotiations was a play for time — and time in this case meant human lives.

The second attempt to come to terms with the Nazis took place in Slovakia in 1942. The chief figure in these negotiations was Gisi Fleischman — another name to be remembered in the history of the time. Something of Gisi's background and her activities must be given in order to make the role she played comprehensible.

Gisi Fleischman was a middle-aged woman, the wife of a prosperous coffee importer, who had been active in WIZO (Women's Zionist Organization) before the war. In 1939, her two children left for Palestine. She remained in Slovakia to organize the escape of Jewish children from Poland, where conditions were worst and danger most immediate. As one surveys the various types of rescue activities and the countries where they took place, one must bear in mind that the focus of the terror was in Poland. From this center the catastrophe steadily progressed outward. The rescue operations involved the constant effort to escape beyond the fatal radii which finally extended over all Europe. In the beginning, Jews fled primarily from Germany and Poland. Gisi's first work was then dedicated to smuggling children across the Polish borders into Slovakia. A technical term, *tiyyul* (hike), was evolved for the task of crossing the border. But, despite the agreeable name, the process bore few resemblances to hiking. It always involved deadly danger for those engaged in it, children and smugglers alike. And it was a process which was apparently endless. A child that had been smuggled out of Poland to the comparative safety of Slovakia had to go through the same procedure again and be smuggled into Hungary, when the situation in Slovakia deteriorated. That was why no venture appeared too fantastic to those who understood that only an exodus from Europe could mean salvation.

In the desperate game of trying to foil the Germans, Gisi was ingenious as well as brave. All kinds of schemes had to be devised to conceal the children. Not all could be trusted to cross the frontier secretly at night with a hired smuggler. Smaller children, unequal to the "hike" across mountain passes or through woods, had to have other types of conveyance. Gisi's children were smuggled to safety in coal-carts and hay wagons and lived to tell the tale. If a child was too young to remember its name and antecedents, Gisi would send a separate report to Istanbul describing the child's history accurately, so that if the child should succeed in getting out of Europe the links with its past would not be completely severed and, if any relative by some miracle survived, a reunion could take place. I have seen such reunions in Palestine.

At the same time, while trying to get children out of Poland into Slovakia, and from Slovakia into Hungary, she and her associates were constantly seeking to send money and food into the ghettos of Poland. As soon as the Istanbul office began to operate and establish contact with Bratislava, where Gisi worked, it began to supply her with funds which she used both for the job of smuggling people out and of smuggling food and money in.

When the first letters from Istanbul reached Slovakia, the effect was one of bewilderment. One of the chief Slovakian workers in rescue, whom I met in Jerusalem in 1945, told me that when he received the note with the electric words: "*Moledeth* (homeland) greets you and family," he assumed it was merely an opportunity for personal emigration. When he answered, later replies clarified the situation. There is a moving letter from Gisi in the Jerusalem archives which shows what the contact with Palestine through Istanbul meant to those struggling within the Nazi prison. The letter is dated July 13, 1943, Bratislava, and consists of a long, detailed account of her work, written after regular correspondence with Istanbul had been in progress for some time. She concludes the factual record of her recent activities with the words:

Comrades, in my many years of activity for *Eretz* (Palestine), as well as for the whole *Klal* (community), I have met with much beauty and dignity, but I have also experienced many disappointments. This last terrible year, which took sixty *Alafim Korbonoth* (60,000 sacrifices), made me feel that all which mankind in general, and Jewry in particular, had striven for and attained is senseless. All that creation formed so fairly, all that art and technical knowledge brought to greater perfection, have become meaningless to me, for extermination has been conceived in human brains and performed by human hands. Daily I hear of the terrible extermination and destruction in Zivia (Poland) and, more than once, I have asked myself, why all this? This reaction was, I suppose, natural because we are so hemmed in here and see only uncrossable mountains around us. No light, no sun, and no horizon beyond!

Yet, we comrades, who carry *Eretz* in our hearts, always believed that difficulties existed only to be overcome. When my work with Nathan, Dr. Solboda and Saly began (Joint Distribution Committee — Geneva), I saw that we were not alone and abandoned, and that our cry had found an echo in Jewish hearts beyond the border. But when your first letter came, and we heard the heart of the *Yishuv* (Jewish settlement in Palestine), I felt like a mortally sick man who is saved by a transfusion. The young, fresh blood of *Eretz*, brought to us through you, has given your dying comrades strength and courage to go on.

THE UNDERGROUND NETWORK

I thank you for this, comrades. Through your expression of solidarity and timely help, you have fulfilled a historic deed. Our common effort must help in checking the horror, for in our unshakable will we are aware of a great mission to maintain the Jewish people. We must master destiny. That this be possible, I await word from you, comrades.

How hard this woman tried to "master destiny!" One senses this in every one of the numerous letters she found the energy and time to write and despatch in the midst of her rescue work. Mostly she wrote of children, *yeladim*. Discussing a children's "action" which she is preparing, she says:.

The children range from infancy to 14, 15 years. This work seems to us most important, for of children something great from the human and Jewish point of view can be made, no matter who their parents were. I should also like to mention that these are children whose parents already have become sacrifices, or whose parents are already in the concentration camps and had to leave their children without care and therefore bound to perish.

This phase of Gisi's work went on till her death. But there was still another way in which she strove to "master destiny." When the deportations from Slovakia to Poland began in 1942, she realized clearly that all that she and her devoted handful of associates were accomplishing was a pitiful trifle beside the immense need. The food that was sent to Poland only prolonged life for a few days or weeks. For one child saved, thousands more perished. Each one rescued was precious and irreplaceable, but Gisi could not free herself from the dream that perhaps it would be possible to stop the entire murder, perhaps it would be possible to save, not several thousands, but hundreds of thousands, a million!

This dream of Gisi's inaugurated the second attempt to negotiate with the Gestapo, which took place towards the end of 1942. Gisi managed to establish a contact with the Nazi leader, Willy von Wislitzeni. This meeting was the climax of less ambitious negotiations with Slovakian authorities who in turn negotiated with the Germans. The purpose of the discussions with the Slovakians had been to win the exemption from deportation of certain categories of Jews, such as those with emigration certificates, families of war veterans, and those of special economic usefulness. These attempts met some slight success, but the crown of the endeavors was the direct meeting with Wislitzeni.

Gisi asked: Under what conditions would the deportations and executions of European Jews be stopped?

Wislitzeni's answer was: For two million dollars, deportations and executions would be stopped in Europe with the exception of Germany and Poland. There the process of extermination could not be halted; but the Jews of Slovakia, Bulgaria, Rumania, France and Belgium would be safe. That is to say, the lives of close to a million Jews could be purchased for two million dollars. As one can see from the figures, the Wislitzeni offer made it possible to ransom a Jewish life for a little over two dollars.

Geneva and Istanbul were informed of this proposal. Istanbul replied that Palestine was prepared to raise the two million dollars, but that this would mean the stoppage of all other rescue activities in Europe financed through Istanbul. No further funds could be found. As an earnest of their intentions, they were prepared to send $100,000 at once.

Geneva replied that the Joint Distribution Committee would be willing to pay the two million dollars after the end of the war. Payment would be made in the United States. The agent bearing this answer was intercepted and the Germans learned how scant were the chances of raising the two million dollars immediately. Obviously the Nazis were not prepared to view promises of payment at the end of the war in America, of all places, as worthy of serious consideration. The negotiations broke off at this point.

During the months in which the negotiations were conducted — for Gisi played for time all along and kept assuring the Germans that satisfactory replies were bound to arrive from responsible Jewish bodies — deportations were suspended in Slovakia. That much Gisi achieved. When Wislitzeni became convinced that nothing would come of the discussions, the sealed trains resumed their regular trips to the extermination camps. Wislitzeni returned the initial payment of $80,000.

The arguments which prevented Jewish organizations, or for that matter non-Jewish bodies, from ransoming nearly a million human beings are familiar. To give the Nazis currency would have meant aiding the enemy. When one bears in mind, however, that two million dollars was just about enough to finance the war for less than a day, that it was a negligible sum in the total war budget of either the Germans or the Allies, one must presume to question the wisdom of the decision taken. Purely in economic terms, was not the usefulness of hundreds of thousands of potentially productive workers

and fighters worth more to the Allied cause than the pitiful figure of two million dollars? In any other terms —
those of humanity, or morality, or justice — there can
be no debate; from that aspect, it becomes indecent to
weigh the relative worth of a million human beings to
the world or two million dollars to the Nazis.

Perhaps the Germans would not have kept their word,
perhaps Wislitzeni was unreliable. The fact remains
that for a while there was a respite from the journey to
the gas chambers. As a result of this respite it is estimated
that some 20,000 Jews were not deported. It is, however,
impossible to state that all these Jews were ultimately
saved, for deportations were resumed in 1944, after the
long-drawn-out discussions had finally collapsed. As
has already been pointed out, every rescue which did
not result in emigration from Europe could only be
viewed as a delaying action whose success could not be
assayed till the very end. But without these delaying
actions no one could be saved.

Even after the vision of a great mass salvation failed,
Gisi never abandoned her less extensive efforts at rescue.
By this time the smuggling of Jews out of Poland
into Slovakia had to be extended. Slovakia was no
longer a possible haven. Jews had to be smuggled
on into Hungary, where conditions were temporarily
better.

In September, 1944, an abortive revolt against the
Germans took place in Slovakia. The last deportations of Slovakian Jewry began in October, 1944. Gisi
was summoned by the Germans and told as follows:
since the Jews had taken an active part in the resistance against the Germans, they were all to be placed in
concentration camps. The existing camps had to be

enlarged and new ones built so that all the Jews could be lodged. Gisi was to raise the money for this purpose, otherwise deportations to death-camps would start. She was given two weeks to make the necessary arrangements.

This was a typical Nazi trick. The very next evening after the order had been issued, all the Jews of Slovakia, including Gisi, were collected and deported. The Germans knew that if word got around that deportations were being resumed on a large scale, there would be a tremendous effort to flee or to hide. Thousands might escape the round-up. At any rate, a round-up would be troublesome and might even involve armed clashes if the Jews had any inkling of what was coming. To dissipate all suspicion, Gisi, the known leader of the rescue movement, was the ideal person to be told that two weeks would elapse before imprisonment in camps would begin. The ruse worked. The Slovakian Jews and Gisi were caught unawares and were unable to plan either active or passive resistance. Gisi was shot while jumping from the train which carried her to an extermination center.

Gisi's co-workers described Gisi in terms as lyrical as those used by the young parachutists in regard to Hanna Senesch. Certainly, the two Jewesses were unlike in every respect except courage. Of the middle-aged woman, her friends said: "She was brave, but cautious." Of the romantic girl, her associates lamented: "She was brave, but so reckless." Hanna sacrificed all that she might have had and might have been. Gisi gave up what she already had: her children, from whom she was separated, the personal happiness which was already realized. One cannot measure the extent of these sac-

"the vast machine of evil"

rifices. One can only reverence the love of mankind, the sense of responsibility towards others, which drove both the poetic girl and the clever, energetic woman to pit themselves so heroically against the vast machine of evil which crushed them and their people.

4

Eichmann's Last Offer: "Goods for Blood."

⚙

T HE attempts to negotiate with the Nazis still did not end. The third and most ambitious of these efforts took place in Hungary. The same villains appear in the cast, but there are new heroes. Before relating this phase, the situation in Hungary must be described.

The Germans occupied Hungary in March, 1944. Up to that time, the condition of Hungarian Jewry was incomparably happier than that of the Jewries of other European countries. Their better fortune consisted in the fact that, though Hungarian Jews suffered discrimination and persecution, they were not being exterminated. When the Nazis marched in, there were about 800,000 Jews alive.

Because of its comparatively privileged state, Hungary had been an active rescue center for German and Polish Jews since the rise of Hitler. From 1933 on, a steady stream of refugees had poured into Hungary. It was one of the last way-stations in the outward trek of Jews seeking to leave the continent. This influx of refugees was directed and assisted by the rescue office in Budapest. Furthermore, the Budapest office was in secret contact with Gisi Fleischman's rescue cell in Bratislava, Slovakia. Both groups cooperated in smuggling people out of Poland. After 1941, when the Istanbul office was established, a threefold contact was achieved.

Among the leading figures in the rescue and resistance movement in Hungary were Rezo Kastner and Joel Brandt. (Their names were mentioned in the proceedings of the Nuremberg Trials in connection with the evidence concerning Nazi crimes against the Jews.) Joel Brandt worked with Kastner. He became the hero of the most grandiose rescue scheme of all that were contrived by the stubborn handful of men and women who refused to resign themselves to the idea that the Jews of Europe were to be wiped out with not a finger lifted in their behalf. Nothing came of Brandt's manoeuvers; the web tore; but there was a brief moment when it seemed as though ultimate salvation was at hand.

I saw Brandt in Tel Aviv where he was staying after the collapse of the extraordinary campaign he had initiated. He told me the details of the fabulous story, and together we meditated on the terrible "if"'s and "but"'s with which it abounded. History will judge whether the "but" should have outweighed the "if." Brandt still had no doubts; the chance should have been taken, despite the fearful doubts and alternatives.

Something must be told of Brandt's background to make the role he played intelligible. He had been one of the leaders of the Socialist-Zionist movement in Hungary, and, as such, one of the chief organizers of the Jewish underground. In 1941, when reports of extermination started to arrive, the Zionist Youth groups began to create resistance units which were active in sabotage against the Nazi. The Budapest office developed an extensive network of agents and couriers who managed to penetrate into the ghettos of Poland and aided in the escape of some 50,000 Polish Jews into Hungary. This was an enormous number in view of the difficulties. Besides, one must bear in mind that the successful crossing of the border was only one phase of the enterprise. Once the refugees were in Hungary, they had to be provided with false documents, lodging and food. All this involved the functioning of an intricate underground machine. The Istanbul office aided in the provision of funds. Except for its scope, this aspect of the rescue work of the Budapest center differed little from that of Bratislava, Bucharest, or Geneva. But in Hungary the development of contacts with government officials had reached a much higher stage than in other places. With the passage of time, those who directed the rescue campaign had acquired a number of extremely influential acquaintances able to reach Hungarian and Nazi government circles. The individuals in question were influenced through bribery and through intimidation. After Stalingrad, it was possible to appeal to the fears of the governing classes. The Jewish representatives argued: "The war is lost; if you let us save Jews by not insisting on too strict a check of papers, and by not shipping back those who manage to cross the border, we will some day testify that you opposed the extermination program."

This argument, reinforced by cash payments, was not without effect. There were many officials among the Hungarians who were becoming increasingly dubious of Nazi victory. They wanted to have a foot in both camps, and permitting Hungarian Jews to rescue other Jews seemed to be good strategy. There were also German Nazis who were no longer confident of ultimate success. All these states of mind could be exploited, provided one had the necessary connections. These the Budapest office had succeeded in obtaining. The stage was set for attempt number three.

Though Gisi's negotiations in Slovakia had foundered in 1943, the Budapest office was familiar with them and had participated in the discussions. In January, 1944, there took place a prelude to the final offer made by the Nazis. Dr. Schmidt, of the Wehrmacht, informed Brandt and Kastner that the long struggle between the Wehrmacht and the S. S. as to the extermination of the Jews had been decided in favor of the former. The Wehrmacht proposed that the killings be stopped and that all remaining Jews should be concentrated in camps which could be inspected by the Red Cross. The responsibility for feeding and maintaining these camps should be borne by Jewish organizations. The scheme was to apply to all occupied countries except Hungary. In return for this, the Allies should be informed of the names of the chiefs of the Wehrmacht who were responsible for the cessation of the mass slaughter. That was the only stipulation made in addition to the provision of funds for the support of these Jewish camps.

Assuming that this offer was made in good faith and merited consideration, we may be certain that it was not motivated by a sudden burst of humanitarianism on the part of the generals. They were as ruthless as the S. S., but more calculating. As soldiers, they objected to the extensive use of railroad equipment for the deportations. No matter how many human beings were choked into sealed trains, the sheer physical process of transporting several million people required more engines, rails and time than the military wished to give to purposes other than those connected with troop movements. The shipping of huge numbers of civilian Jews for the purpose of murdering them was a luxury in which the Wehrmacht did not feel justified in indulging for the time being. In addition, as soldiers, they had by this time a fairly realistic view of the possibility of a German victory, and the notion of avoiding trial as war criminals was tempting.

While these discussions went on, the balance of power shifted again. Hungary was occupied and the S. S. took charge of the country. The Wehrmacht generals who had conferred with the Jewish leaders were imprisoned, and large-scale deportations of Jews were resumed. While, however, the situation of Hungarian Jewry deteriorated rapidly, the S. S., curiously enough, began to negotiate with Brandt.

We encounter the same cast as in the previous act. Willy von Wislitzeni, who had been the chief protagonist in the discussions with Gisi Fleischman, reappears. His behavior in the Slovakian affair had been such as to inspire confidence. He had permitted the negotiations to drag on while replies were awaited from the bodies who were expected to provide the ransom. This had meant that Jews had been saved from murder during a given period. Wislitzeni's return of the initial installment, after the failure of the project, also served to make those who dealt with him feel that his offers, even if not trusted too naively, should at any rate be seriously weighed.

Wislitzeni, a brother-in-law of Himmler, claimed to

be concerned for the rescue of the Jews on humanitarian grounds. The merits of this contention are, at present, a purely academic issue, though it provided a basis for the negotiations. Kastner and Brandt had their first meeting with Wislitzeni at the end of March, 1944, approximately one year after the Slovakian fiasco.

The negotiations involved all Jews in German hands; that is to say, about two and a half million Jews who still remained alive. Up to the spring of 1944 the Germans had murdered somewhere between three and four million. It is impossible to give the exact figure despite the astronomic size of the carnage. The Jewish representatives suggested that the originally mentioned two million dollars ransom be the basis of the talks. They offered to raise the sum provided four conditions were met: 1) that killings of Jews stop, 2) that Jews be not concentrated in ghettos, 3) that there be no further deportations, 4) that emigration be permitted.

Wislitzeni discussed each point at length. He declared that he was in agreement with the stoppage of executions, but he could not guarantee absolute success in the carrying out of this order. In a time of war, many "actions" went on of their own momentum. With such a large territory affected, one could not expect a hundred per cent cessation of the slaughter, but it could be substantially checked.

As for point 2, he was not in favor of the creation of further ghettos. But local sentiment in Hungary had to be considered. Jews would have to be evacuated from towns of less than 10,000 inhabitants, since there would be too much hostility from the local fascists if such "purges" did not take place.

Point 3, the question of deportations, was purely in

German hands, and, for the time being, the Germans were not interested in continuing the deportations. But consideration had to be given to the fact that Hungarian anti-Semites would press for deportations. The Nazis could hardly assume the role of the champions of Hungarian Jewry. Therefore, it was essential that concrete proposals be made involving point 4, emigration. Wislitzeni, however, was not interested in a small trickle of emigration to Palestine, such as might be possible under present conditions. He wanted a mass evacuation of the Jews from German-occupied territories. Even if the Jewish Agency removed 50,000, or 60,000, Jews to Palestine by using up the remaining certificates* and other means, he did not view this as a solution of the problem. Furthermore, such emigration would take five or six months. In addition, he wanted no complications with the Arabs, who would object to such a plan. He demanded an immediate mass migration of the Jews to North America, including Canada, to South America, Australia, to North Africa, west of Tunis, and to South Africa.

This in brief was the Wislitzeni reply. He refused to commit himself as to whether two million dollars would be acceptable as a ransom. This question required further discussion.

After several more meetings, the negotiations began directly with Eichmann, the head of the Jewish section. Eichmann was one of the top Nazis, very close to Hitler and Himmler. He had been born in the German colony of Sarona in Palestine and spoke perfect Hebrew. He was accurately versed in all Zionist questions, keeping

* Certificates of immigration issued by the British government.

abreast of the proceedings of Zionist congresses and political developments within the various Zionist parties, to the minutest detail. With this equipment he was therefore a natural candidate for the post of chief of the Jewish Department in Nazi Germany. The task of organizing the extermination of Polish Jewry had been entrusted to him, and he was the notoriously successful executor of the "action." Just as he was the principal figure in the first attempts at negotiations in 1939, so he emerged again in the somber finals.

In the middle of April, Brandt received word that Eichmann wished to see him: Brandt was to stand in front of a well-known café in Budapest; he would be fetched to the meeting place. The arrangements were carried out and Brandt found himself face to face with Eichmann, the butcher of several million Polish Jews, with whom salvation had to be discussed. A stenographer and an S. S. officer were present throughout the interview. Brandt believes that an official record of the conversation was made.

Eichmann made no bones about his history. He announced without further ceremony: "You know who I am? I carried out the actions in Poland, in Slovakia and in Germany. I have been assigned the task of solving the Jewish problem here. I called you to do business with you. I have investigated and decided that the Jews of the Joint* can still raise something. I am ready for business. Goods for blood; blood for goods (*Ware für Blut; Blut für Ware*)."

These words are taken from Brandt's notes made immediately after the meeting. They are probably as

* American Jewish Joint Distribution Committee.

accurate an account of a conversation as can be had short of a stenographic report.

Brandt replied that what goods Jews owned had been confiscated long before. Money could only be raised outside of Europe, but then the four conditions made to Wislitzeni would have to be met. Eichmann continued: "I am ready to sell you your Jews. I'll hand them over to you wherever you wish, except in the Balkans. I can't allow emigration into Palestine. They can go to America, South Africa, or North Africa west of Tunis. What kind of goods you will deliver, you'll have to consider. For instance, I would be interested in trucks."

Brandt reported the conversation to other leaders in the Jewish rescue group in Budapest, and all agreed that it was essential to continue the talks as long as possible. Whatever happened, time might be gained in the course of which more "hikes" could be organized, the resistance cells could be strengthened, and more people could be hidden in bunkers.

The next day Brandt was again summoned to Eichmann. Brandt told him that he had been selected to go to Istanbul to make the details of the negotiations known and to see what could be done about getting funds to meet the terms. He asked that the journey to Turkey be permitted.

Eichmann agreed to let Brandt leave Hungary for this purpose, but demanded that Brandt's family, consisting of his wife and two children, be left as hostages. When Brandt accepted this condition, Eichmann developed his ideas more explicitly. He urged Brandt to expedite the fulfillment of his mission, for the S. S. extermination policy would soon be resumed. There was not enough money and goods to ransom all of the Jews; but he was prepared to let a certain number be bought off. Eichmann then asked Brandt which Jews he wanted to save: those in Hungary, Theresienstadt,* Poland or elsewhere. He also wanted to know which categories interested Brandt most. He assumed it would be men still able to procreate, and women of child-bearing age. To this Brandt answered that all Jews were equally precious to him and that he was in no position to designate which classes were to be exempt from slaughter.

There were several further meetings with Eichmann, in the course of which the following tentative offer was made: Eichmann would permit the emigration of a million Jews chosen from every German-occupied country. In return for this he wanted 10,000 trucks and some tons of food and soap. These trucks, Eichmann informed Brandt, would not be used on the Western Front, but exclusively on the Eastern Front. Eichmann was prepared to implement the agreement in installments. After 100,000 Jews had been permitted to leave German-occupied territory, 1000 trucks and 10% of the food was to be supplied. After the next 100,000 Jews had left, the next batch of trucks would be delivered, etc. Eichmann warned against the delivery of defective trucks; he would not let himself be fooled.

The strategy of Eichmann's offer is clear; but before its obviously vicious intent is analyzed, it is necessary to complete the history of this episode. Then the "if"s and "but"s can be considered.

While the terms were being drawn up, and while Brandt was waiting for an opportunity to set out on his

* A concentration camp in Czechoslovakia.

journey, deportations and executions continued. To Brandt's remonstrances Eichmann replied that, though the deportations were taking place at the rate of 12,000 daily, the individuals deported would not be exterminated pending the return of Brandt. But Eichmann warned: "See that you hurry back with a satisfactory answer. I cannot keep your Jews on ice. (*Aber ich mache sie darauf aufmerksam dass ich ihnen ihre Juden nicht auf Eis legen kann.*) The young and healthy can work, but the old, the sick, and children have to be fed."

At the same time, Eichmann announced that he and Brandt would have to fight each other again in the future, for he was an "idealistic German" and Brandt was an "idealistic Jew," and as such they were natural antagonists. For the present they could cooperate. To this characterization Brandt replied that he was an ordinary Jew concerned only with doing his utmost to save his brothers, and that, far from considering Eichmann an "idealistic German," he viewed him solely as the murderer of the Jewish people. However, in view of the stakes, he was prepared to "do business" with him in the question of rescue. This blunt rejoinder in no way affected Eichmann. He concluded the conversation by again counselling haste in the fulfillment of the terms.

Brandt was enabled to leave for Istanbul to acquaint authoritative bodies with the offer. From there he went to Cairo. As soon as the facts had been made known, the Jewish Agency at once informed the Allied powers of Eichmann's proposal.

From this point on, the dénouement of the whole scheme was rapid. In Cairo Brandt was detained by the British for investigation. He was imprisoned in great elegance in a pasha's palace, while his story was being examined, and was only released after a prolonged hunger strike.

Ira Hirschmann examined Brandt in Cairo.* Washington had been informed that a "Nazi agent" had arrived with a suspicious proposal. President Roosevelt was anxious to acquaint himself with all the features of the offer, and Hirshmann consequently flew to Cairo for the express purpose of questioning Brandt. It was not easy to get access to him. The British suggested that Hirschmann leave at once for London where the question of the Nazi offer was going to be discussed between Moshe Shertok of the Jewish Agency and Anthony Eden. But Hirschmann insisted on being permitted to carry out the instructions of the United States Government, and he was finally allowed to see Brandt. After questioning him exhaustively, he concluded that Brandt was exactly what he claimed to be: a Jew who had made a desperate effort to save his fellows. After the interview, Hirschmann sent a report "underscoring my (Hirschmann's) belief in Brandt's integrity." This testimony from an American is important, because it confirms from another source the evidence available in the offices of the Jewish Agency in Jerusalem. The most compelling internal testimony of the truth of Brandt's claims comes from the British themselves. They would not have released a "Nazi agent" in the course of the war.

The Eichmann proposal was quickly rejected. While Brandt was imprisoned, the B. B. C. radio announced the Nazi overtures and officially refused this "blackmail"

* See *Lifeline to a Promised Land*, by Ira A. Hirschmann, Vanguard Press, 1946, pp. 117 ff.

offer. This public rejection put a summary end to the negotiations. Eichmann at once followed up his threat that he would not keep the Jews "on ice." The deportations and executions were resumed, and the Nazis gassed and shot another million Jewish civilians before they were vanquished. When the Germans were finally defeated, a million and a half Jews remained alive in Europe — a million less than in the summer of 1944 when Eichmann demanded 10,000 trucks.

No extraordinary analytic faculties are required to perceive the many suspicious features in Eichmann's offer. First of all, his promise that the trucks would be used exclusively against Russia could only be viewed as an obvious manoeuver to split the Allies. Secondly, there was no denying that trucks, food, or soap, wherever used, would strengthen the Nazi war machine. Finally, his demand for the mass evacuation of the ransomed Jews to territories other than Palestine was a bombshell which placed the question of finding immediate asylums squarely before the democracies.

Each of these terms — if it became a question of debate — constituted an insurmountable obstacle to the scheme. The entire proposal could only be discussed on the basic assumption that the saving of one million human beings from certain murder was important enough to cause the democratic world to examine the obvious pitfalls in the offer and to agree on ways of minimizing its dangers. In the first place, the agreement of Russia to such a scheme was essential, for no step that might jeopardize the unity of the Allies could be considered. Russia would have had to decide whether the presence of an additional 10,000 trucks on her front, to be delivered in installments of 1000, would constitute a serious menace, so serious that it outweighed the merit of saving one million people. The United Nations as a whole would have had to consider whether the Nazi war machine would be substantially strengthened if Eichmann received assistance to the extent mentioned. And, of course, the democracies would have been obliged to find room for the refugees in the vast continents at their disposal.

Those who urged the acceptance of the offer contended that the total amount requested represented less than a day's expenditure in the war budget; they argued that, though it was admittedly unfortunate to give the Nazis as much as a penny, so immense a disaster could be averted, that the claims of humanity warranted "doing business" with the Nazis to this extent. They insisted that the outcome of the war could be neither affected adversely nor delayed by such an agreement. Too little money or goods was involved to affect any issue save that of the rescue of the Jews.

A natural objection to this reasoning arises. If what Eichmann wanted in the way of "goods" was really so trifling, why should he have been willing to deliver the Jews for it. It seems too poor a bargain. Several explanations occur to one's mind: Eichmann might have hoped that, by presenting this project, he would succeed in embroiling the United Nations in disputes among themselves. Perhaps England and America would consent without securing Russia's agreement, and the result would be the long-desired clash. Since the Germans spared no energy and cunning in attempting to create a rift between the Soviet and the democracies, this element may have played a part in the offer. No possibility, no matter how far-fetched, was likely to be disdained. We must remember, however, that ransom negotiations with the Nazis went through various phases, beginning with 1939, and that the question of trucks for the Eastern Front appeared only at the very end. Therefore, the prospect of creating trouble with Russia could not have been the decisive factor, though it was probably one of several motives.

Another possible explanation, and a very plausible one, is that Eichmann and the government he represented were anxious, not so much to embroil the Allies with each other, as to make them partners in Nazi guilt. He wanted to be able to state for the record: From 1939 on the Nazis were ready to let the Jews be ransomed for sums which could have been raised, provided other countries were prepared to admit them.

One of the favorite German defenses against the outcries of an outraged humanity has consistently been that the same outraged world was never willing to open its doors to the victims of the Nazis. This charge does not lessen Nazi guilt by one iota, but one can see that the Germans would take pleasure in twitting the democracies on this score. They probably believed that by an offer such as that of Eichmann they were bolstering their case before the bar of history.

Then there is reason to assume that Eichmann, like Wislitzeni and other Nazis, believed that, in case of defeat, their individual positions would be more secure if they could point to some act of mercy to mitigate their black record. There is no doubt whatsoever that, as German fortunes fell, many minor officials sought to ingratiate themselves with the Allies and, since some of them had come to trust the legends of their own creation, they might have thought that "Jewish influence" would save them from trial as criminals if they added a ransom "action" to their roster of good deeds.

The breath-taking schemes of mass salvation plotted by such optimists as Gisi Fleischman and Joel Brandt never materialized. But the loss was not total. Just as Gisi's negotiations in Slovakia managed to stave off the day of extermination and so won a permanent reprieve for some thousands of the hundreds of thousands involved, so the Brandt-Kastner discussions had some tangible results. As an earnest of his good will, Eichmann had authorized the sending of 15,000 Jews to Austria instead of Oswiecim; these lived to see the day of liberation. Some other thousands were shipped from Bergen-Belsen to concentration camps near Switzerland. They too survived. It seems a small number when one thinks of the vastness of the original scheme, but in the total of Jewish survivors even those thousands play an appreciable part.

In Tel Aviv I met one of the men who was saved by virtue of the abortive negotiations with Eichmann. The occasion was one which drew many of the threads in this story together. There had been a memorial meeting for the lost parachutists, attended by those of the group who had lived to return to Palestine and by the relatives of those who had perished. Afterwards, some of us had dinner together: Joel and Reuben, the friends of Hanna and heroes in their own right, were there. Present also was a middle-aged Hungarian Jew recently arrived in Palestine, the father of Perez, the youngest of the parachutists, who had been executed by the Germans after his capture in Hungary.

When I inquired how the father had escaped from Hungary, I was told that he had been a member of the transport which had been sent to safety instead of extermination because of the Brandt negotiations with Eichmann. The son had flown from Palestine to perish in Hungary in an attempt to bring help. The father had been saved through ransom. Now he was in Palestine, like the mother of Hanna, while their children lay buried on the continent to which they had insisted on returning.

I mention this circumstance because the only way the pitifully small or catastrophically large numbers, which one employs when discussing European Jewry, acquire meaning is in terms of actual individuals. The few thousand Hungarian Jews who escaped slaughter, thanks to the obstinate will of "madmen" or "simpletons" like Brandt or others, loom large after one has met face to face any of the human beings who were saved. Before such meetings some may presume to ask: "Was all the excitement worth while in view of the slight result?" Afterwards, one shudders at the brutality and the lack of imagination implicit in the question. The question was put often by those who decried Brandt's efforts. Those, however, who sat with the father of the young parachutist whose memory we had gathered to honor in Palestine can never think of the effort as vain or of the outcome as trivial.

To save these thousands a ransom of nine million Swiss francs had been collected and given, as a first installment, to Kurt Becker, an S. S. man. In addition to the cash, jewels and gold had been gathered. The fate of this ransom has been a curious one and indicates something of Nazi mentality.

Just before the German collapse, one of the leading Hungarian Zionists, Dr. Moshe Schweiger, was summoned by Becker to a *Jagd Schloss* (hunting lodge) where General Winckelmann, chief commander of the East, was staying. There Becker returned the total sum to Schweiger with the statement that the money had been taken to save Jews and, since the promise had not been kept except in a small measure, he wished to return the amount given. The money was turned over to an American captain in Switzerland, a member of the American counter-intelligence, who up to the date of writing has been waiting to hand it back to its rightful owners, the Jewish organizations which provided the funds.

This Arabian-Night twist to the black tale indicates how much some of the Nazi hierarchy banked on a last-minute gesture of good will to the Jews to save their skins. Becker no doubt felt hopeful of escaping trial as a war criminal if he returned the murder ransom.

Brandt did not get back to Hungary during the course of the war. After his release from his Egyptian bondage, I saw him often in Tel Aviv, waiting for word from the family he had left as hostages to the Nazis.

Some sanctimonious individuals, many Jews among them, will probably feel that the whole attempt to negotiate with the enemy was improper. All official Jewish bodies took this stand when the hope of saving a million Jews flashed on the horizon. The reasons for and against the proposal have already been discussed. Nevertheless, it is hard to free oneself from the feeling that no consideration, save the actual outcome of the war, should have weighed against the possibility of large-scale salvation. There were many "but"s, yet how immense was the "if"!

The final summary report of the executive director of

the War Refugee Board (September, 1945) explains why American organizations could not afford to be implicated in ransom parleys with the Germans. The Nazis had repeatedly attempted to approach the Joint Distribution Committee directly. Naturally, the United States government was kept informed of all such overtures. The American government took the position that no American citizen could be involved in such negotiations. In view, however, of the possibility of gaining time, the War Refugee Board agreed to permit Saly Mayer, a Swiss citizen and a representative of the Joint Distribution Committee in Geneva, to discuss terms for the release of Jews. It was specified that Saly Mayer could act only as a Swiss citizen and not as a representative of an American organization. Saly Mayer's protracted negotiations were instrumental in saving thousands of Jews. But the efforts of individuals like Mayer or Brandt could not bring significant results without explicit government backing. Though America, through the War Refugee Board, was sympathetic to all rescue attempts, the Allies officially opposed any form of "traffic with the enemy."

Nor can one escape the suspicion that some statesmen were embarrassed at the prospect of a mass exodus of the Jews of Europe. It is a matter of solemn record that one high British official, when discussing the Brandt proposal with a member of the Jewish Agency, so far forgot himself as to exclaim, "But what will we do with them?"

The Germans were the murderers. That is their special distinction. But those who preferred to let the slaughter continue, rather than permit the victims to enter their territories, are not without stain. I do not presume to estimate the measure of their sin. It is foolish and dishonest to pretend that there is no difference between their guilt and that of the Nazis — a conclusion for which the Germans angled. No one can deprive the Nazis of their monstrous preeminence in crime. But there are rungs lower down on the ladder, on which the gentleman who inquired, "But what will we do with them?" surely merits a place.

And while the bubble burst, the digging went on uninterrupted — here a small boat, there one of those "hikes" across freezing mountain passes, or else the long immolation in a bunker.

IV. The Ghetto Battle

1

The Witnesses

◎

IT IS not to be avoided — this entrance into the ghetto, behind the brick wall, and into the murder-factory, behind the barbed wire. We who were not within the gate can only see the horror as it is mirrored in the eyes of those who emerged. They have come out — the Lazarus men and women, and each one knows that he has been miraculously saved. "It was a miracle," they say to explain the fact that they remained alive. But after they pronounce these words, one realizes that they do not view themselves as resurrected. Alive, yes; but not alive as before, not whole, not new. They belong to the world of death as much as to that of life. I have spoken to so many of them, and even when they looked healthy and cheerful, as they frequently did, the moment always came when we both knew that no true miracle had taken place. There had been a lucky chance. The Russians had come; the Americans had come; here and there an escape route had offered itself to courage and ingenuity; but no one had risen from the tomb really alive.

No, you cannot tell by looking at them. The pretty blond girl who serves me coffee and hot buns in a Tel Aviv bakery seems fresh and merry. There is nothing in her appearance to indicate that on her breast is tatooed a number with a yellow sign indicating that she had been reserved as a prostitute. That is why she had survived. My breakfast companion, who is a social worker and who had been assigned the case when the girl first came to Palestine some months earlier, whispers this information to me. A grafting operation is possible. There is a woman in the Hadassah hospital in Jerusalem on whose bosom the words, "officers' whore," are tatooed in German. She is being given a new skin. But the girl who serves my coffee is penniless. Besides, on her breast are only telltale numbers, and numbers are too common among the survivors to be cause for surgical intervention. The concentration-camp numbers tatooed on the inmates' arms in blue ink — after a while one hardly notices them. The figures are almost all high — in the hundred thousands — because those with the lower numbers had been liquidated long before. The Germans were orderly and methodical in their extermination, so that the survivors, for the most part, have six digits on their arms.

You sit down at a table in a *kibbutz** and the bare-armed youth or girl who passes you the bread, or pours your tea, is branded with the neat, close figures. "Oswiecim," you may hear in explanation, or "Maidanek," or "Buchenwald," or any of the other dread names. Sometimes you hear a combination: "I was in Maidanek and Oswiecim."

* Communal group of workers.

134

The first time you hear the fearful words: Maidanek, Treblinka, Oswiecim, you are afraid to look at the being who claims to have been within those walls. There is Mashka, for instance. Her experience includes the Warsaw ghetto, Maidanek and Oswiecim. She is a small, dark girl — one of the few non-Aryan appearing survivors that I have seen — and she tells me her story as we sit over a dairy lunch in Tel Aviv. She talks quickly and brightly, but she has to be careful about her diet. Something happened to her internal organs in Oswiecim. She is ill, though the outer appearance is that of energy and well being. She relates various episodes briskly, without any apparent emotion. When she describes how the Germans would seize babies from their mothers and dash their heads against a wall, and how women would go mad and choke their children, she speaks without any special emphasis or display of feeling. These are the routine details of the past five years. She has witnessed scenes like these too often to be able to endow them with a special aura of horror or agony. That is one of the terrible features of the narrative — the matter-of-fact, business-like tone of the teller.

I say to her: "You know, I find this hard to believe."

And she answers me sensibly: "Of course, you can't believe it. I would not have believed it either, if I had not seen it."

Why do I mention Mashka? There are a dozen others ot whom I could speak. Ruth, who unlike Mashka looks so Polish that one wonders why she ever got into Treblinka in the first place — she could have posed as an "Aryan" from the beginning — relates her adventures and her escape from the death camp in the same characterless way. There is only one moment when the memory overcomes her. That is when she describes her journey in the sealed train to Treblinka. Many of her companions in the train, including her mother and sister, had already died for lack of air. The survivors found themselves standing on corpses, and when Ruth tells of how her feet stubbed against dead faces and bellies, she makes a gesture of revulsion. The sheer physical horror of the contact is still with her; she explains with a renewed sense of shock: "My toe would get into an open mouth." But she collects herself and continues the story.

The story is familiar. Every survivor tells all or part of it. It is unbelievable and it is never really believed. Yes, you know the facts are true. The eyewitness accounts have piled up. The testimony is incontro-vertible — the mute testimony of the ovens and the gas chambers, and the charred piles of bones and human ash, the circumstantial accounts of the survivors, the documents seized from the Nazis. So many of these narratives have been heard in Palestine. Every boat, legal or illegal, brings its quota of refugees from the death camps. Already people say: "He was in Treblinka," without any special awe. I have heard the phrase, "Oh, he's been everywhere," and "everywhere" turns out to be a sojourn in Buchenwald and Oswiecim and one or two of the ghettos. The names trip lightly from the tongue, almost as though one were describing a tour.

It is at this point that one realizes that no one except the survivors can have a true faith in the reality of the experience, and even they occasionally find themselves recalling it as an evil nightmare rather than as an actuality. And the eagerness to hear the story is, already, less intense. Interest flags. The first ones who arrived were heard with every nerve of apprehension taut. Their words were recorded; their message spread. But now, as the later survivors come, the impulse to listen grows slighter. One knows the steps of this progress through hell too thoroughly. It begins with the moment when the man, or woman, or child, before you was immured in a ghetto. It may have been Warsaw, or Vilna, or Bendin. Then there is the deepening misery till the summons to the transfer-point comes and the journey in the sealed train starts. You already know how they will describe the choking horror of the train in which a large number of the transported perish. Then comes the death camp, and for each the special circumstance which caused him to be rescued at the door of the gas chamber. You have heard the story with its macabre variations so often that you can almost supply the details yourself. You no longer feel that you have to hear it again. You steeled yourself once in the beginning, for the sake of historic truth, for the record. But now, you feel like Ruth. You don't want to stub your toes endlessly against corpses and feel your foot press into a human mouth or eye.

And terrible questions occur to you. "What kind of a person are you?" you want to ask the being before you. "You saw the trains with their cargoes of corpses, you watched the long lines being driven into the gas chambers. Your friends and relatives were murdered before your eyes. And yet you sit in front of me, and eat and drink, and plan some kind of future."

In your innermost heart you feel that you are different. You would have died long ago with the six million. You would not have retained your sanity, or had the

physical endurance to crawl out into the light of day
from the charnel house which the Germans fashioned.
You would have been among the martyred dead, or
among the mad, driven by the furies of remembrance.
And you pat yourself on the back, secure in the conviction of a more delicate nature, a more sensitive
organism.

There are some things that you hear which increase
your sense of virtuous recoil. That man was a sorter of
clothes in Treblinka. The neatly catalogued piles of
shoes and dresses and false teeth and toys belonging to
the murdered, which the Germans demanded, had to be
arranged by Jews who were taken out of the death
transport for this purpose. Afterwards they would be
sent with a later group into the gas chamber. But in
the meanwhile time had been gained — time in which
to escape or to wait for liberation. So you look at
Lazarus who sorted the clothes of his murdered brothers,
and you shudder. And of this one it is whispered that
he had actually worked at the ovens. That is a technical
term — "working at the ovens." It means stoking them
with the corpses that were taken out of the gas chambers.
When you see such a being — I met one — you are
utterly sure that you would have broken into the lines
being driven to death rather than have gained additional
weeks of life through the performance of such a task.

All those who stood on corpses to survive — they
puzzle you, and you cannot overcome your sense of
bewildered virtue. And if you have the impertinence
to ask: "How did you stand it?" — they answer
simply: "I don't know."

But sometimes one meets accusing eyes. The victim
does not look apologetic for being alive. He offers no

excuses for what he has been obliged to endure. He does not feel inferior to you because you have not waded in blood nor lain among the putrifying dead. He looks at you and demands: "How did *you* stand it?"

Sometimes you find yourself shrewdly scanning the man (or woman) telling his tale, and you catch yourself thinking at some point: "He is probably lying or exaggerating here. Such things could not have happened." And later, when you have spoken to people from other camps, you are ashamed because, after you have heard the same gruesome detail from a number of entirely independent sources, you not only understand that it was all part of the same Nazi pattern — like the lampshades made of tatooed human skin — but you have also become accustomed to the narrative, just as you have finally become accustomed to the idea of the gas chambers and the ovens. But that does not prevent you from again playing the detective the next time you hear some new variant — mostly unprintable — of German ingenuity in devising methods of torture. Whenever you have the new abomination confirmed, it is borne in upon you how vast a gulf separates you from the beings whose experience you strive to understand.

Not all of them want to talk; many want to leave the pool of memory unstirred; but there are some who are vocal. They are the ones with the sense of a mission, who long to inform the universe of the crime that has been perpetrated against them and their people. The more articulate ones are writing memoirs. How often, when I have gone to interview some freshly escaped refugee from Buchenwald and Oswiecim, have I discovered that he is either writing, or is about to write, an account of his experiences. And you hear the words: "Perhaps

I was saved for this — to tell the world." Or else you hear the even darker explanation: "Perhaps I was saved for this — to warn the rest of the Jews — the Jews of America, of Russia, of England, that they will be murdered as we were." And when you start back in anger, saying: "Not in America" — or England, or Russia, according to your taste, the man across the table looks at you somberly, and with a terrible assurance answers: "We know the Gentiles. If the Germans and the Poles could do it, so can the rest of them."

It is hard to hit on the right rejoinder. For when you say, with the love and faith of your American upbringing: "I know America and Americans," the bitter answer is always: "I knew Germans. I lived among them. If it happened there, it can happen anywhere." The vision of a Maidanek near Washington, of a Treblinka near Moscow, obsesses them, and they disregard your protests as the babblings of the blind. They have seen. They have tasted the truth in the heart of the fiery furnace which consumed everyone they loved and from whose flame they barely issued, and they no longer believe in any other truth. They are sure that, sooner or later, the moment comes when the victorious evildoer celebrates his heathen rites with the blood of Israel and makes the human sacrifice to Moloch. They are equally sure that even those who take no part in the murder will watch the spectacle with acquiescence or indifference.

No argument shakes this conviction: "You will see; when it will be too late, you will understand." And because they want me "to understand," they are ready to speak, to write, to cry out the terrible tidings.

There is another group which is ready to speak. It is

that of the mothers. I think of three women whom I met in Palestine. I came upon the first one unexpectedly. She had just accepted a post as teacher at a girls' training farm which I was visiting, and when I saw her delicate, blond beauty, I did not have to be told that part of her experience had included life as an "Aryan" with forged papers. But that had come later, after she had been smuggled out of Treblinka. At first she had been shut up in the Warsaw ghetto, where her three-year-old daughter had been "liquidated."

Treblinka had been survived through one of the gruesome "miracles" to which those who emerged alive so unjoyously refer. A quota for extermination was being chosen daily, the number increasing as time went on. Helena had been permitted to live because she was a skilled and competent worker. But her turn came. As the war progressed, everybody's turn was bound to come. The morning that Helena was "chosen," her group was being shot, not gassed. She was already standing in line before a freshly dug trench, waiting for the moment when the bullet would strike her. Then a Nazi guard noticed her. Helena had knitted woolen gloves for him; he had been so pleased with her handiwork that he had ordered a sweater. When he saw Helena in the line, he demanded: "Did you finish the sweater?" And when she told him that the sweater was only half done, he pulled her out. There were plenty more to fill the quota, and she might just as well finish the sweater. Besides, he may have taken a fancy to her pretty face and trim figure. But the decisive factor was the half-knitted sweater.

Of this scene at the mass grave the young woman spoke with that curious apparent lack of emotion which

I had already remarked. Even the Nazi's reason for saving her did not seem to impress her. What reasons could a Nazi have which would seem reasonable in accepted human terms? Her clear grey eyes, luminous and intelligent beneath delicately arched eyebrows, filled with tears only when she spoke of her child. That was why she had come to this training farm for young refugees. She wanted to devote herself to children who had been saved, in memory of the child that had been murdered.

We sat in a garden blooming with chrysanthemums of every shade of yellow, russet and gold; we could look out toward Masada, where the last fortress of Judea had stood. The children of the farm, some recently from Teheran, some from Transnistria, were celebrating a great moment. They were beginning to clear a newly-acquired stretch of land farther down the hill. First, the rocks had to be removed from the stony, arid soil which began at the base of the vineyard. The boys and girls laughed as they lifted the rocks. Another bit of the homeland would be recovered from desolation through their labor. The mother of the murdered child, who was to become their teacher, smiled sadly and affectionately as she watched. I wondered if being among children would be good for her, but, as if in answer to my unspoken question, she said: "I want to work with children in Palestine. What else is left?"

The second mother had been luckier. Her child had been seized, but she had recovered her. She had fought her way back into Poland to find the little girl and had succeeded. This, at last, was an authentic miracle — a miracle of maternal passion. But the months of search for the lost child, as well as the totality of the experience, had left a more visible mark upon this woman than upon most of the others whom I had met. She was viewed as "unbalanced" because she felt the urgency of the message she had to deliver. She had to preach righteousness, the return to God. So, sensible people objected to her eloquent harangues and her fiery intrusions upon their peace.

This woman was no youthful blond beauty, but dark, stocky and middle-aged. She had been a practicing physician. Her experience with the Germans had been more favorable than that of the other narrators. She had known nice, kind Germans whom she had treated in her capacity of physician. (In her town Germans had been using the services of Jewish doctors.) These Germans were genuinely sorry that they would be obliged to "liquidate" her and her children when the order came.

She described a scene which illuminates the mentality of the "decent" Germans. When conditions became threatening, she escaped from the town in which she had been living, but was caught in the neighboring woods and brought back to the police station. The officials knew her well. The Nazi in charge was truly distressed. "*Ach, Frau Doktor!*" he exclaimed, "How could you mismanage things so. Now I will have to send you in a transport to Poland to-morrow." And when she pleaded: "Surely you won't send me and the children to be killed," he answered with regret: "I am very sorry, but everybody has seen you brought in. I must execute the orders."

Fortunately, however, an Austrian policeman, whose child she had cured, helped her escape in the course of the night. Finally, after months, she reached Palestine, where I met her walking about and urging the world to bethink itself of its sins, and consequently acquiring the reputation of being a bit deranged.

When she clutched my arm and said fiercely: "Why did I remain alive; why did I find my child, if it was not a sign — to tell the world?" — she seemed to me a more rational being, actuated by more explicable motives, than the "nice German" who had declared: "*Frau Doktor*, how could you so mismanage affairs. Now, you will have to be liquidated. I am so sorry."

The third mother who wanted "to tell the world" came with a poem written by her little girl a few days before the child had been removed for extermination. Mother and child had been in the Kaiserwald camp near Riga.

The poem is such as a bright ten-year-old child might very well have written. The Yiddish original has simplicity and pathos — the inevitable pathos of the subject matter. The verses consist of a series of questions:

> *Ich hob dir, mein mame, asei fil zu fregen,*
> *Es is altz unfarstendlich far mir*

("I have so much to ask you, my mother; I don't understand anything.") The child asks why the whole family has been killed with the exception of herself and her mother; why do they have to live in a concentration camp; why were they separated into "right and left" in the Vilna ghetto. The last question is a reference to the Nazi custom of lining up a given number and ordering them to go — "to the right," "to the left." One group would be reserved for further labor, and the other would be sent for immediate extermination. Nobody knew which line was destined for death, and I have heard numerous accounts of the attempts, among those waiting, to discover the Nazi's intention. Mostly chance, very occasionally ingenuity, would determine the choice which meant life. This hour of sorting became so much part of the experiences of the ghetto and the camp, that the child asked — without further explanation — why were we divided "into right and left." The child's last question is: "<u>Why is there so much evil?</u>" The concluding stanza is unexpectedly mature:

> *Nor wen ich derseh deine traurige eigen,*
> *In welchen es glanzt noch a trer,*
> *Dan will ich shein, mame, bei dir gor nit fregen,*
> *Un wart auf kein entfer nit mehr.*

("But when I see your sad eyes in which a tear shines, then, mama, I don't want to ask you any more questions, and I wait for no answer.")

The little girl was pretty, clever, and the camp's darling. Even the Nazi commander liked her. He was another "nice" German. Once he came in unexpectedly, when the precocious little girl was reciting a poem of her composition to a group that had gathered secretly, and, instead of ordering her to be lashed, he applauded. But three days later, when the order to liquidate the children, as useless mouths, came through, the little girl went to her death.

The mother, who belongs to a distinguished Jewish literary family whose name everyone would recognize were I to give it, described the scene in which the child was seized from her. "<u>Even a cat,</u>" she said, "<u>is led away before her kittens are taken.</u>" The Nazis showed no such concern for the feelings of the Jewish mothers. The children were wrenched from their arms and piled

145

into the fatal trucks whose function everyone knew. When the mother tried to rush in after her child, the little girl kept waving her back and calling: "Stay, mama; take vengeance."

The next morning, as she lay in her bunk, the mother heard two women near her discussing a possible exchange of provisions. One had a piece of herring; the other a piece of bread. They were striking a bargain; and, in the midst of the talk, one asked casually: "Who was taken yesterday?" and then went on again with the talk about the relative merits of the crust of bread and the bit of herring.

The woman who was telling her story voiced neither astonishment nor bitterness concerning the dialogue she overheard the day after her daughter's murder. Such was existence in the camp. She herself had uttered the same words on many previous occasions — "Who was taken yesterday?" — and had then gone on to the wretched business of trying to live somehow as long as she was permitted. But after the child's seizure something happened: "Mama, take vengeance." The cry did not stop ringing in her ears. When she was saved by the arrival of the Russians, she carried the cry with her. Now, she goes about reading the child's poem to those willing to listen. It is a way of resurrecting the eager, pretty little girl, of making her live again in the imagination of others. Like the other mothers whom I have mentioned, she wants to talk — about the child, about the crime, about vengeance.

2

Why They Went:
Hopelessness and Hope

❁

WHEN you hear the word "vengeance," or "punishment," on the lips of the survivors, another question inevitably occurs. Why did the Jews of Europe begin to resist so late? Why did the Warsaw ghetto fight back only when a mere 30,000 were left and over half a million had been massacred? Why was there an uprising in Treblinka when only a few hundred were left? How explain this obedient pilgrimage to the extermination center in which six million human beings took part? The answer lies only partly in the fact that unarmed civilians, among them a large proportion of women, children and old people, were physically helpless before armed thugs who shrank from no form of violence. One still wants to know why these very women and men did not perish clawing with their bare hands at the Germans and their Ukrainian, Polish or Lithuanian henchmen? Why did they not make the job of "liquidation" more difficult?

I asked this question of ghetto fighters, of partisans,

and of ordinary refugees who escaped without participating in any organized resistance. The answers, even when not identical, are not contradictory; they dovetail. It is possible to reconstruct the picture of what happened. When we remember that we view the events in the light of a knowledge that could not have been had beforehand except through a tragic intuition, the phenomenon becomes more intelligible.

The murder of the Jews of Europe was a chief plank in the Nazi master-plan from the beginning of their rule. There were disputes between the Nazi hierarchy and the Wehrmacht, and there were periods of vacillation when changes of policy seemed possible, but the line as originally laid down, and finally pursued, required the physical destruction of every Jew within German reach. Consequently, the entire Nazi Jewish policy was shaped to facilitate this purpose. The same careful technical preparation and adroitly planned psychological warfare which had gone into all phases of the Nazi attack on civilization were employed for this aspect of their program. The Nazis were aware of the danger of letting the Jews realize at once that they were doomed *en masse*. An immediate perception of their hopeless position might well have aroused large-scale resistance, which, even if unarmed, would through the sheer weight of numbers have immensely complicated the Nazi murder enterprise. Therefore two objectives had to be attained: the Jews had to be subdivided and separated into conveniently manageable groups; and the knowledge that they were to be murdered had to be kept from them to the last moment so as to forestall a desperate last effort to resist.

The formation of the ghettos achieved the first

purpose. The Jews were not only concentrated by this means. They were also split up. In this fashion the Jews were systematically segregated into pre-extermination centers, and were at the same time subdivided into groups which could establish no contact with each other or with the outside world. Three and a half million Jews scattered through Poland might have proven a formidable obstacle to the easy execution of the Nazi scheme, but herded into ghettos, of which the Warsaw ghetto with its shifting population of some 400,000 was the largest, they were in readily controllable groups.

Furthermore, the ghetto walls achieved still another purpose. The brick barrier segregated the Jewish communities not only from each other but from the world. It withdrew the Jews psychologically as well as physically from any contact with their fellows which might have resulted in sympathy or help. Their isolation became complete. The ghetto was a place for lepers into which no one except a saint would venture of his own free will, and its inmates were sufferers about whose fate apparently no one except saints were troubled. The Nazis knew from experience that round-ups of Jews in localities where no ghettos had been established provoked popular protests and indignation. The job was more troublesome. But once the Jews had been sealed in ghettos, they had been placed more readily out of the reach of the compassion and comprehension of the surrounding Christian world. They could be hunted down at will with a minimum of interference; they were free game.

After the Jews were immured in the ghettos another stage began — the calculated attempt to enfeeble and degrade the ghetto dwellers through physical and psychic oppression. The Nazis had proclaimed in the *Schwarze Korps* that they would so wear down the Jews through starvation and persecution that they would inevitably degenerate to the level of criminals. Those Jews who did not die in the process would rend each other like wild beasts. Perhaps the Nazis expected to be spared the necessity of building special extermination centers. But the Jews did not die rapidly enough, nor did they degenerate as required. This failure must have been an acute disappointment to the Nazis. Though truth was unimportant to the Nazi propaganda machine, and the veracity of an accusation was in no way essential to its use, Goebbels would probably have experienced a sense of added victory if his obscene lies had been transformed into realities. The Jews, however, showed an extraordinary inner and outer resistance to the regime to which they were subjected.

The mortality — as all ghetto statistics indicate — was enormous. Hundreds died daily of hunger, disease and sporadic violence. Shootings for sport or punishment were an always-to-be-expected occurrence in the ghetto streets. But one must bear in mind that Hitler had set himself the objective of murdering ten million people — the total Jewish population of Europe including Russia. Thousands, not hundreds, had to be killed daily in order to fulfill his plan. When it became apparent to the Germans that the Jews were displaying an unexpected capacity for maintaining life and resilience within the ghetto prisons, the death factory speed-up began.

I do not pretend that the Nazi scheme was in all details as logical and orderly as outlined. Life in the ghettos and camps was full of contradictory elements which make it hard to give a coherent explanation of the minutiae of Nazi behavior. But the broad outline was plainly marked from beginning to end. For instance, one of the curious features of existence in the camps was that, though it was generally fatal to appear sick and consequently incapable of work, because that meant immediate liquidation, there were, on the other hand, cases of people who owed their lives to illness. In some instances, the Nazi would send a sick inmate to the camp hospital — there was such an institution — to be cured before sending him on to be exterminated.

This paradox of sickness, which might result either in immediate death or the postponement of a sentence already pronounced, runs through the accounts of any number of survivors. When you ask them to explain the contradiction, the answer is generally: "The Germans are methodical." The routine of one camp might call for immediate extermination in case of illness, while the routine of another camp might demand that even a member of a contingent about to be sent to the gas chambers should first receive medical care. In each case the routine was observed. It is these variations in details of administration depending on the camp, or even the particular camp commander, which confuse the picture if one seeks to put the pieces together in an orderly pattern. One cannot discover a fully elaborated design into which each item of information falls harmoniously. Time and again the lines go awry or crisscross back and forth. But only in detail. Even if an observant eye sees a snarl here and there, a total symmetry springs from the original concept.

The major purpose of the ghetto was segregation for extermination. There were also subsidiary purposes which temporarily seemed to deflect the Nazis from their primary goal. Since not all the Jews could be murdered at once, even with the best efforts of German efficiency and ingenuity, Jews might just as well be used for labor while waiting. This involved a selection in the order of the killings. Here again no strict adherence to a given system can be seen. In one ghetto children would be among the first to be liquidated. In another place, an older age group would receive the preference. Sometimes, there would be different phases in the same locality. We know, for instance, that there was a period when word went around that orphans would be permitted to live. This at once resulted in large numbers of suicides among mothers who hoped by this act to ensure the lives of their children. On the other hand, we also know that at a later period, when all children were being killed as useless to the war economy, mothers who stayed with their babies would be sent with them into the death transports. And just as there are many reports of women who jumped from windows to save their children, so there are occasional grim tales of mothers who abandoned their babies rather than follow them to death.

Variations in the master-plan were also introduced by the sadistic caprices of the various Nazi chieftains who were in charge. A guiding principle, however, can be discovered in the fluctuations of the administration of the camps and ghettos: those best able to work were last to be killed. This accounts for the fact that only about 150,000 Jewish children have remained alive in all Europe; the survivors belong for the most part to age groups that were capable of hard physical labor.

In retrospect the ultimate objectives of Nazi policy are unmistakable, but they were not so clear to their victims. That is what must be understood if we try to answer the question why mass resistance came so late. Had there been general comprehension, at the very outset, of the fate reserved for the Jews, a far greater measure of militancy would have arisen. But despite the candid declarations of policy by Goebbels and Hitler, very few believed that these pronouncements were more than threats. Jews expected to be hounded, to be tortured, to be decimated, but the reality of the extermination center was something to which they could not give credence.

The Nazi program was implemented step by step. By the time Jews were driven into ghettos, they had already been weakened and terrorized by years of persecution and discriminatory legislation. To some the ghetto even appeared as a shelter where, despite all physical privations, Jews might lead some kind of autonomous existence; the walls would shut them in from enemies as well as from friends.

When stories began to circulate in the Warsaw ghetto that the Nazis had begun a systematic extermination of Jews and that hundreds of thousands of Jews from all parts of Poland had already been murdered in especially constructed death camps, the reports were received with incredulity. It was as hard for the intended victims to believe the truth as it was for the peoples of the United States or England. Even Jews who had suffered Nazi outrage since 1933 at first dismissed tales of the murder factories as "atrocity stories."

"Even the Germans wouldn't do this," people kept assuring each other, although each one of them had daily cause to understand just what the Germans were capable of. A mother whose child had been clubbed to

153

death by a storm trooper, or whose husband had been shot down as he crossed the ghetto street, could not bring herself to believe that the remaining children were to be asphyxiated by government decree. It was easier to blame an individual storm trooper, or a particular official, than to face the fact that no act of savagery was an accident, that no German official was more or less barbaric, and that, whether he was a "gentleman" or a Streicher degenerate, the result would be the same. The Nazis naturally did everything in their power to foster the illusion that, despite the rivers of blood that were being continuously shed, some Jews would be permitted to remain alive.

When deportations started, the ghetto inhabitants would be assured that the purpose was to provide forced labor in Russia. Rumors were carefully spread by the Germans to the effect that "the workers" would be settled in agricultural communities. As a result, the deportation order began to appear to some as a promise of a less insufferable existence, and many volunteers would report to the transfer-center in the hope of bettering their lot. Besides, the Germans would distribute a chunk of bread and marmalade at the railway station. This bread and marmalade figures prominently in the accounts of the ghettos. It was a bait which famished people found hard to resist and the sweet jam seemed to augur better things. Why should the Nazis hand out the precious substance unless their intentions had grown kindlier? Perhaps they would really let Jews work and live in some region of Eastern Europe, far from Germany, where their existence would not offend Nazi racial sensibilities!

To keep suspicions stilled, postal cards would come

to the ghetto, presumably from the deportees, indicating that the writers were alive and working. This was further bait, the more readily swallowed because few people could bring themselves to believe the truth.

The Nazis were aware of their advantage. Whenever necessary they kept baiting the trap with bread and marmalade — very little bread and just a taste of marmalade. They were suspicious of Jewish "cunning." Some Jews might be "tricky and dishonest" enough to attempt to conceal themselves even in the ghetto. It was necessary to bring them out of hiding, should any be seeking shelter in some undiscovered cellar. Schemes were devised to make certain that every man, woman and child would be registered with the authorities. Ration cards, even for the starvation fare allotted, were one method. But there had to be other ways to catch the wary.

One day an announcement appeared in the Warsaw ghetto that all Jews who wished to go to Palestine should register with the authorities. Again stubborn hope arose. Perhaps the Germans had grown tired of their own savagery and would let a number of women and children go. It was assumed that no men physically able to work would be released as long as they might be able to slave for the Germans, but there was a momentary renewal of faith in the possibility of escape for the very young or the very old. And the Jews of the Warsaw ghetto rushed to offer their names for placement on the fatal lists which added to the accuracy of the German records. More than 150,000 of the inhabitants of the ghetto expressed their desire to go to Palestine. Naturally, some wiser and soberer spirits warned against the new trap. But though there was no genuine conviction in the hearts of many of the registrants that they would ever actually be able to leave the ghetto and sail for Palestine, the horror of the present was so great that any shadow of hope had to be seized as if it were substance.

The Germans combined business and pleasure in these games. Taunting and harassing their victims with useless expectations were part of their amusement. Besides, the Nazi officials might be able to extract a last hidden coin or trinket in return for a promise to give special consideration to an applicant.

There was still another game the Nazis played with the helpless Jews in their grasp. After the fateful July 22, 1942, when the deportations from the Warsaw ghetto started, word went round that Jews who were working for German firms or "shops" would be spared. German civilians appeared who offered to establish shops in the ghetto with Jewish assistance. If the Jews would manage to raise some more money, or discover some overlooked goods or supplies of any kind — something might be done and deportation would be avoided for the lucky individual's family. Again the purpose is at present plain. The Germans were afraid that some Jewish possessions might have eluded their rapacity despite Gestapo searches. They wished to make certain that the Jews had been drained absolutely dry before they were dispatched to the *Vernichtungsstelle*. The Germans were as economical before their murders as after them. We have all seen the pictures of the neatly catalogued belongings of the victims of Maidanek — piles of shoes, spectacles, clothes, toys — of which the victims had been stripped before they were led into the gas chambers. That was merely the final stripping of the effects actually used on the journey. The preceding stages of spoliation were equally complete and systematic.

This process was not limited to Warsaw or to Poland. Wherever Jews existed in countries occupied by the Nazis the same thing went on. There was no limit to Nazi ingenuity when it came to making certain that no Jews would escape their dragnet. Their propaganda machine worked as actively for the purpose of duping Jews who might otherwise manage to avoid detection as it did to instigate the non-Jewish population of every country against its Jewish citizens. When the Russian armies retreated from Poland, the Nazis feared that the Jewish population of Russian-occupied Poland might seek to flee in the wake of the Red armies. Many Jews attempted to do so, although the advance of the German troops was too swift to enable more than a small number to escape. But, strangely enough, some Jews returned to the Warsaw ghetto of their own accord. They had heard that an autonomous Jewish community had been set up in Warsaw, where Jews could exist after a fashion behind the supposed protection of the ghetto walls. Rumors of this idyllic life had been skilfully circulated by the Nazis in those parts of Poland where no knowledge of the actual conditions of the Warsaw ghetto had as yet penetrated. The Goebbels technique had scored another success.

In countries like France, where no ghetto had been established, other devices had to be used to lure Jews out of hiding. It was much easier for Jews to merge with the local population in a Latin country, where the predominant physical type was brunette, than in countries like Poland where differences in appearance were more obvious. In France round-ups of Jews might net the Nazis one member of a family, whereas the Nazi purpose could not be served until every last representative of a Jewish stock had been extirpated. Consequently, Nazi knavery again had to be invoked to supplement Nazi ferocity. When men were seized for deportation to the dread camp of Drancy, it was incumbent on the Nazis to discover whether a wife or a child had succeeded in evading capture. Therefore an apparent shift in policy took place. For a while, in 1943, a new regime was introduced into Drancy. Food was distributed. Brutalities were mitigated; and, finally, the Nazi officials began to assure the men in their grasp that they had no desire to separate families. "We are not unreasonably cruel," they would say. "We have our Jewish policy which requires the segregation of Jews, but we are willing to let you lead a normal existence in these surroundings. Let us send for your wife and children. You will all be together." And many unfortunates were unable to withstand this siren song. They would communicate with their families, and the clever Nazis could chalk up another victory against a few defenseless human beings. The "tricky" Jews had been outwitted.

Or else a Nazi official would sympathetically urge a prisoner to send a parcel of food out of his store to his starving family. This bait was hardest to refuse. Bread and marmalade again! And another address fell into the hands of the Nazis. German thoroughness was used to the full in tracking down every individual of the proscribed people.

In order to combat any doubts that might be developing among the Jews who were being urged to report voluntarily for deportation, the Germans would occasionally show motion pictures of life in one of the supposed "work camps." Old people would be shown reclining comfortably in armchairs, whereas the young would be seen cheerfully working in factories and fields. After such a showing, weak or gullible souls were to be found who would protest: "Why should we keep on suffering in the ghetto? The work camp is better." And the attempts of the youth groups to explain the true character of the "work camp" would be dismissed as alarmist propaganda. When deportations took place from localities where there were no ghettos, instances are reported of people who paid rent for their dwellings six months in advance. They were certain that within that period of time they would return; and they wanted to make sure that their homes would be waiting for them — the familiar homes with the familiar furniture and photographs.

To add to the chaos, Jews in one ghetto would be deluded by rumors that conditions were better in some other ghetto. There was a period when the Warsaw ghetto seemed a desirable refuge to those shut up in Lodz or Bialystok, and one reads of the pathetic efforts of some "lucky ones" to bribe their way into the Warsaw ghetto. Perhaps it would be easier to get food in Warsaw. In Lodz, people were dropping dead from hunger at an increasing rate; in Warsaw, a scrawny child could slip out at night under the gate, past a guard, and, if unseen, might return with a scrap of food. Of course, the child would be killed, if spotted, unless the guard were exceptionally generous. At any rate, it was a chance to be taken, and the chance came more easily in Warsaw than in Lodz. Such was the reasoning. The man or woman who had escaped from Lodz to get behind the walls of the Warsaw ghetto was under the impression that he had won a reprieve. The Nazis played the game. They took bribes to let Jews out of Lodz into Warsaw or vice versa. What was the difference?

Another means of harrying the ghetto and of preventing the inhabitants from reaching some stable equilibrium, no matter on how abysmal a level, was the Nazi practice of constantly changing the rules. No sooner had families established themselves in some wretched room and begun to try to adjust themselves to the conditions in which they found themselves, then the Nazis would announce that the limits of the ghetto had been changed. Certain streets had been cut off, and those living in them had a few hours in which to discover dwelling places within the new confines. The penalty for being found outside the ghetto was death. So again there would be a desperate scurrying about to find a corner in which to hide. This perpetual upheaval was another instrument to counter the efforts of those concerned with maintaining morale and unity in the ghetto. The scramble for some kind of shelter, for a crust of bread, for a garment for one's shivering limbs, for the breath of life amid the stench of death, consumed whatever little energy remained.

A time came when it was finally impossible to dismiss the whispers about the Nazi extermination centers as lies intended primarily further to terrorize and torment the population. Too many reports of trainloads of Jews who had vanished and had not been heard from were beginning to circulate. Here and there an escaped eye-witness had returned to bring warning. Even then, the doomed sought sources of consolation. A curious psychology developed. The very evils endured began to appear as guarantees of eventual salvation. In Warsaw, people took comfort in the fact that a typhus epidemic was raging. Hundreds were dying daily of spotted typhus. The Germans were known to dread the spread of the disease. Surely they would hesitate to transport Jews from Warsaw into other parts of the country and so run the risk of contaminating other sections. We are told by many survivors that even the ghetto walls were viewed as a reason for confidence. Why should the Germans have built these walls, why should they have gone to the trouble of creating a special Jewish quarter, if within two years they proposed to murder all the inhabitants? Would it not have been cheaper and easier to kill all the Jews at the outset without first bothering to set up the elaborate inferno of the ghetto with its special council, its decrees, its quarters?

Human beings in this state of mind were easy prey for the Germans. It is characteristic that immediately before the mass murders of the inhabitants of the Warsaw ghetto began, on July 22, 1942, the official German paper in Warsaw started to emphasize the possibility of using Jews for productive labor on a larger scale than before. This was done to counteract any suspicions or apprehensions that might have sprung up as a result of information which had leaked in about the liquidation of the Jews in Lublin and in the death camps of Maidanek. And, of course, bleak comforters were to be found who assured each other that the Warsaw ghetto was too large for mass liquidation. The Germans would be unable to kill so many human beings. Perhaps it could happen in Lublin, but not in Warsaw where close to half a million people were segregated. All this made possible the spectacle of whole families appearing voluntarily at the fatal *Transferstelle* for deportation into the unknown. Bread and marmalade were still being doled out; a shelter in the sealed train was being offered.

Another element which must not be minimized was the paradoxical faith of a people with a long history of persecution. "We have survived other persecutors; we shall survive Hitler." A greeting in Lodz current at one period was: *Guten morgen, ich hob im in der Erd.* (Good morning, I don't give a damn about him!) The memory of Egypt, of Spain, of czarist Russia, served as a kind of obstinate solace. Jews were unwilling to believe that the droll-looking fiend with the small mustache should be able to accomplish what a Pharaoh, a Haman or a Torquemada had failed to do — not to mention the more recent massacres of a Chmielnitzki. The will to overcome the evildoer through national survival, and to exist when his creations would be dust, was an impulse nourished by Jewish history and by Jewish religion. It affected both the devout Jew who sang to the last the mystical ghetto song: "I believe in the coming of the Messiah," and the unbeliever who found present comfort and reassurance in the centuries of suffering that Jews had endured. Jews had perished on the pyre and at the stake for the greater glory of God — "to sanctify the Name" — time and time again in their long history, but they had always perished as individual martyrs; the people had remained as a living witness to the God of Israel and to the continuity of Israel. The desire to ensure the survival of the people as a whole must be accounted as a by-no-means-negligible factor in the readiness to be deluded by the Nazis.

This inability to believe that not only countless individuals but the whole people was doomed helps explain the sorry search for "rational" explanations for the executions when reports came which were incontrovertible. As has already been indicated, Jews were not exterminated in all places nor in all categories at the same time. When the accounts of the mass murders in Vilna became too numerous to be disregarded, an explanation arose that the Germans were killing Jews in former Russian-occupied territories on the charge that they had supposedly been communists and had supported the Russian regime. If this reasoning were correct, the Jews of Warsaw could consider themselves safe, particularly as large factories had been opened in Warsaw in which Jews had to work as slave laborers.

The Nazi attempt to maintain Jewish illusions went as far as the door of the death-chamber. Here, too, they sought to feed the faith that it was the individual who was being clubbed to death, or gassed, not the people. In the mad welter of Nazi blood-thirstiness, one general rule can be observed: *Whenever large numbers of human beings were involved, the Germans sought to get the maximum of cooperation from the victims themselves so as to insure the efficiency of the operation.* A description of Treblinka, compiled from many accounts of eyewitnesses and survivors, indicates the nature of the trickery:

As a rule, two transports arrive daily: one in the morning and one toward evening. At the height of the "action," several transports arrived daily. Each train consists of a few score freight cars. Part of the cars halt at the siding directly across from the arrival square, while the remaining cars are shifted to the side to wait until the first part is taken care of. The cars are quickly emptied. The tortured and greatly excited human throng breathe with relief when let out on the square. They are immediately taken over by the Jewish auxiliary guard, headed by the *kapos*, who give them orders in Yiddish. The women and children are told to enter the barracks immediately, while the men remain in the square. Looking around, they see a high pillar with a poster bearing a large inscription: *Achtung Warschauer* (Attention, People of Warsaw); despite the fact that transports of Jews from many other towns of the General Government, * from Germany, and the states of Western Europe are also brought to Treblinka. "Do not worry about your fate" — continues the poster — "you are all going eastward for work; you will work and your wives will take care of your households. Before leaving, however, you have to take a bath and your clothing must be disinfected. You have to deposit your valuables and money with the cashier, for which you will get receipts. After the bath and disinfection, you will receive everything back undamaged."

In the first period of murder in Treblinka, an S. S. officer with an angelic, confidence-inspiring face used to come to the square and deliver a speech along the same lines to those assembled. When, however, transports began to arrive from various parts and the crowds had to be liquidated quickly, the Germans cancelled that speech as superfluous.

To make the Jews believe that actual classification according to trades would take place at the arrival square, in order to assign occupational groups for labor, they posted small signs with inscriptions: tailors, shoemakers, carpenters, etc. It goes without saying that no such segregation ever took place.

The *kapos* quickly arrange the men in rows of ten, asking them to take off their shoes, undress completely and prepare for a bath. Everybody is permitted to take along a piece of soap and his documents. In the meantime the sorting-service men take away

* Poland.

the clothing to the sorting place. Women and children also have to undress completely. Then comes the last act of the Treblinka tragedy. The terrorized mass of men, women, and children starts on its road to death. At the head, a group of women and children is driven, beaten by the accompanying Germans, whips in hands. Ever quicker the group is driven; ever heavier blows fall upon the heads of the women, mad with fear and suffering. The cries and laments of the women, together with the shouts and curses of the Germans, shatter the silence of the forest. The people finally realize that they are going to their death. At the entrance of Death House No. 1 the chief himself stands, a whip in his hand; in cold blood, beating them, he drives the women into the chambers. The floors of the chambers are slippery. The people slip and fall; they cannot get up any more for new groups of forcibly driven victims fall upon them. The chief throws small children into the chambers over the heads of the women. When the execution chambers are filled to the brim, the doors are sealed and the slow strangulation of live persons by the steam issuing from the numerous vents in the pipes begins. In the beginning, stifled cries penetrate to the outside. Gradually they quiet down, and fifteen minutes later the execution is complete.

Now comes the gravediggers' turn. Shouting and cursing, the German overseers drive the diggers to work, which consists of getting the bodies out of the execution chambers. The gravediggers stand at the troughs near the valves. The valves open, but not a body falls out. Due to the steam all the bodies have been fused into a homogeneous mass cemented together with the perspiration of the victims. In their death agonies, arms, legs, trunks interwine into a large, macabre entanglement. To make it possible for the gravediggers to get out individual bodies, cold water from the nearby well is poured over that mass. Then one body separates from another and may be taken out. As a rule, the surfaces of the bodies are not deformed; only the faces and buttocks are purple. The gravediggers, constantly beaten and driven by the Germans, place the corpses in the troughs until the chambers are empty. The bodies lie piled up like slaughtered cattle; now the burying takes place. Formerly (during the first half of August), the grave-diggers had hand-carts to convey the bodies to the ditches, which had to be done at top speed. Lately, however, the chief disposed of that facility. *Ein Mann — zwei Leichen* (one man — two corpses), meaning that each gravedigger has to bury two corpses. He ties legs or arms of the body with the belt from his trousers and, running, pulls the body from the trough to the ditches, throws it in and, again running, has to return for the next load. Formerly, the graves were right at the death house, so that the burying of corpses could take place quickly. As new victims were added, the grave-line moved ever further to the east and pulling the corpses to their place of eternal rest now takes longer. After a ditch is filled, the grave-diggers quickly cover the bodies with earth and the digging machine nearby is already preparing the next ditch for the dead.

The execution of the men is identical. They also are driven through the road in the woods to their death. People react differently while being driven in the direction of the death house; some repeat loudly psalms of penitence, confess their sins; other imprecate God; but a sudden shout of the Germans and the blows falling upon their backs immediately bring silence upon the whole crowd. Sometimes all the victims cannot get into the overcrowded chambers; then the Germans keep the rest in the woods near the slaughterhouse. These people see and hear everything, but there is no attempt at self-preservation.

I have heard every item of horror in this report first-hand from various men and women in Palestine. I confess that when I first read the pages quoted I did not quite believe each detail. It was too insane. Now, after countless conversations with survivors, I can stop at every sentence and recall the faces, the voices, of the men and women who independently related all or part of this story. Now the account has for me the literary virtue of being succinct, comprehensive and restrained, instead of mad and exaggerated. That is why I use it in preference to writing an "atrocity story" of my own. And the ingenuity of the Germans in getting their victims to strip of their own accord — to facilitate the action of the gas and to preserve all articles of clothing unspoiled for the Nazis — becomes impressively clear.

Under such circumstances one can see how difficult was the struggle which the Jewish underground groups had to wage to win over the masses of the population to the realization that armed and unarmed resistance was essential. A long educational campaign had to precede the actual preparations for the uprisings in the camps and ghettos. When I spoke to the ghetto fighters in Daphne — leading figures all of them in the final resistance — each told me an anecdote from his personal experience which illustrated the psychology that had to be combated. When, at the Cracow station, one of the comrades made it his business to circulate among a transport that was being sent to Warsaw and whispered to a woman: "You are being sent to your death," the woman whom he sought to warn turned on him furiously with the rejoinder: "I don't believe you. The Germans are giving food to us now. You are just troublemakers." And she spat on him.

Even in the death trains the same psychosis prevailed. If a person sought to jump from the train, others held him, not to save his life, but because the Germans used collective punishment as an added check on the actions of an individual. The man who jumped knew that the entire train would be punished for his venture. He, therefore, had to be absolutely certain that there was no prospect of escape for those whom he was endangering by his act. The practice of collective punishment developed a sense of collective responsibility which enormously complicated the entire question of resistance.

It is necessary to understand the types of psychological as well as physical attack to which Jews were subjected in order to realize how difficult it was to weld these sick, bewildered, tortured human beings into a group capable of united action no matter what the cost. The systematic effort to demoralize these shattered beings, to play off one against the other, was an essential part of the Nazi campaign.

Nazi agents would plant rumors among Czech Jews that only Rumanians would be deported for extermination. Rumanian Jews were assured that they were safe and that only Hungarian Jews would be seized, and so on. This again served to maintain hope among various sectors of the Jewish population that the sentence was not final and absolute.

In addition to those clinging desperately to any shred of illusion which could protect them from the truth, were those too exhausted physically and nervously for further struggle. The psychic resources of human beings are not infinite. After a certain point, starvation and prolonged persecution rob the individual of the ability to plan or the stamina to fight back. Some had been reduced to the level of automatons who obeyed passively whatever directive was given, having the strength neither to kill themselves nor to battle the storm-troopers who drove them along the road to death.

It would be false, however, to leave the impression that passivity and a tragic readiness to be duped were the sole moods of the Jews in or outside the ghettos. These were an inevitable part of the picture, but side by side with these states of mind other forces made themselves felt. Just as it would be untrue to picture European Jewry as a consecrated band of heroes and heroines with no human timidity, or to emphasize that simple longing for life which makes men cling to existence despite every imaginable horror, so it would be equally untrue to fail to stress other factors. That the Jews of Europe were physically helpless in the face of the terror unleashed upon them is clear. That this sense of impotence inevitably invaded every aspect of their life is clear too. This was to be expected. More remarkable is the fact that, in the midst of the paralysis engendered by the sense that they were at the mercy of every outrage and that there was no place of appeal, a will to fight nevertheless arose. I am now not referring to the last battles waged. I speak of a struggle which began on the first day of the persecutions — a conscious effort to surmount the calculated degradations of the Germans. This was, in its way, as brave a fight as the subsequent attempt to attack the huge German military machine with frail bodies and a few rounds of ammunition.

3
The Struggle of the Spirit:
"To Live With Honor"

I HAVE before me the map of the Warsaw ghetto as it was first established. The names of some of the districts are familiar: *Nalewki, Twarda, Gliniya,* and others. As teeming centers of East European Jewish life, they have entered into folklore and literature. We have read about them; we have fed on them. From these streets have come illumination as well as squalor, wisdom as well as poverty. But on October 16, 1940, brick walls and barbed-wire fences shut off the zone of Jewish residence from the rest of the world.

As one reads the elaborate set of regulations and decrees drawn up by the Nazis for the conduct of life in the ghetto, one wonders why they bothered issuing ordinance after ordinance to give a pseudo-legal aspect to their spoliations and killings. The predetermined Nazi program of mass murder was to begin in less than two years; in the light of that knowledge the stubborn effort of the 500,000 Jews penned within the ghetto to maintain some human standard of existence assumes an even more heroic and tragic character.

October, 1940, to May, 1943 — that was to be the life span of the Warsaw ghetto. We are amply informed as to the physical conditions of life there. We know of the systematic starvation, of the epidemics of typhus without medication, of the unheated hovels in which the population froze and perished, of the incredible misery to which the community had been reduced. We know less of the extraordinary struggle waged in that wretchedness to preserve the integrity and dignity of the human spirit.

In the *Gazeta Żydowska*, the official paper published in Polish three times weekly, we can read many German ordinances, like the one which specified that each one-window room must accomodate no less than three and a half persons. That was the minimum — enormously exceeded by the constant influx of new arrivals into the ghetto. Less familiar is the information that, outside these one-window rooms, the inhabitants strove to plant window-boxes so that some green blade might spring for the people to see, or perhaps a tomato or radish for some child to eat. As late as 1942, hundreds of Jewish boys and girls studied agriculture in classes organized by the *Toporol* (Society for the Promotion of Agriculture among Jews). The sole places where this knowledge could be employed were apartment-house courtyards or balconies. The truck-farming diligently taught and studied had no place to flourish save some dingy corner of the narrow ghetto streets, yet who will doubt that every leaf that managed to grow on such a plot was a banner of defiance?

The titles of the various courses organized in the

ghetto make strange and bitter reading now. There were classes in engraving and watchmaking, leather work and architectural drawing. There was even a class in "cosmetics" — perhaps the most sadly ironic course of all. What dreams of liberation must have sustained the students, what expectations of new worlds where these laboriously acquired skills could be tried out! All this went on in the midst of a perpetually shifting population to which fresh thousands of Jews from all parts of Europe were constantly being added to replace those who were perishing each hour of disease, starvation and violence.

At the same time, the effort to distribute whatever food and medical care were available continued. Soup kitchens, nurseries and clinics were established. 120,000 persons received a plate of soup every day. That was their principal meal. The mortality rate kept soaring, of course, according to the Nazi plan. The medical knowledge of the great Jewish physicians working in the "clinics" could be of little use in the presence of famine without relief and epidemic disease without medicines. Nevertheless, be it remembered, there were three Yiddish theaters in the ghetto and one Polish theater. Occasionally there were even symphonic concerts in which world-famous musicians incarcerated in the ghetto practised their art to solace themselves and their auditors. And in the midst of the horror, a Jewish scholar wrote learned articles on the roots of Jewish optimism, while little Jewish children composed poems of faith in the essential goodness of man. The articles and poems can be read in the bleak pages of the *Gazeta Zydowska*. I shall refer to them again below.

Dr. Emanuel Ringelblum, the Jewish historian, who

was among the last to be murdered by the Germans, wrote a report on the underground cultural activities in the ghetto shortly before his death. The report, written in code, was forwarded to London in May, 1944, and deciphered. The document is addressed to the Yiddish Scientific Institute and is a compact, unadorned record of the types of educational work carried on clandestinely. It is a historian's, not a litterateur's, account. There is neither time nor space to expatiate; only the bare outline of the facts can be given by him; yet in its simplicity and brevity it is one of the most revealing and moving memorials to Polish Jewry.

The writer knows that he will not survive. He is not inditing an appeal; he is writing solely for the record:

We write to you [he begins] at a time when 95% of the Polish Jews have already died in the throes of horrible tortures in the gas chambers of annihilation centers in Treblinka, Sobibor, Chelmna, Oswiecim, or were slaughtered during the numberless liquidation campaigns in the ghettos and camps. The fate of the small number of Jews who still vegetate and suffer in the few concentration camps has also already been determined. Perhaps there will still survive a small group of Jews who are hidden in the "Aryan district" in the constant fear of death or who wander through the woods like hunted animals. That any of us, the community workers who carry on under conditions of two-fold savagery, will outlive the war, we greatly doubt. We, therefore, want to take this means to tell you in brief about those activities which link us most closely to you.

I venture to say that few more eloquent sentences have ever been composed than the dry words of the concluding sentence of this paragraph: "We, therefore, want to take this means to tell you in brief about those activities which link us most closely to you." About to die, what are the "activities" which the Jewish historian salutes and which link him most closely to his people? Ringelblum tells us in detail.

The intellectual life of the ghetto was largely clandestine. The Germans had permitted the establishment of some vocational classes, but wider educational opportunities, from the elementary school to the adult level, were greatly restricted. In addition to German prohibitions and the risk involved in violating them, the chief foe to any genuine intellectual activity lay in the increasing weariness of a population too exhausted nervously and physically for the constant effort to rise above the zoological world created by the Germans. The community leaders were aware of this danger. A clandestine cultural organization was formed under the name of Jewish Cultural Organization (*Yikor*). It organized lectures, commemorated literary figures, such as Perez, Sholem Aleichem and Bialik, and arranged literary and dramatic programs.

The enumeration of each of the many activities of *Yikor* always ends on the same note — the murder of the leaders of the work. The following matter-of-fact sentence is typical: "The spirit of *Yikor* was the young scholar Menahem Linder, an economist, murdered by the Germans as early as April, 1942."

A net of underground schools and a children's library were formed. Hundreds of children's programs, in which the children themselves participated, were secretly presented in dormitories and homes. The programs were continued as long as any children were left alive in the ghetto.

An underground press representing all ideological trends in the ghetto — Zionist, anti-Zionist, communist, labor, right-wing — continued to flourish in the very shadow of death. The zeal to make converts, to define truth, burned undiminished till the end. These journals were smuggled out for distribution in the smaller ghettos of Poland.

A secret Jewish archive was formed by a group of qualified scholars headed by Dr. Ringelblum. Masquerading under the name of a Society for the Pleasures of the Sabbath, the staff amassed a huge amount of material relating to the martyrdom of the Jews in Poland. These memoirs and first-hand documents were collected and placed in hiding for some future historian. Those who compiled the archives knew that they would not live to tell the story, but they made certain that someday the indictment would be made.

New talents appeared in the ghetto. Ringelblum enumerates some of them:

A symphony orchestra under the able leadership of Szymon Pullman was active in the ghetto. Whenever the occasion presented itself, concerts of beautiful orchestral and chamber music provided moments of rest and escape. Pullman and almost all the members of the orchestra, including the violinist Ludwig Holanan, were killed in Treblinka. The young concertmaster, Marion Neuteich, was murdered in the Travniki camp. The phenomenal young singer, Marysia Aisensztadt, the nightingale of the ghetto, daughter of a choir director of the Warsaw synagogue, shone like a meteor. She was murdered by the S. S. during the liquidation campaign. Of special high quality was the children's chorus under the direction of J. Faywicyz. He was killed in the Poniatow camp.

Other choir-leaders, like W. Gladstein, Zaks and others, were murdered in Treblinka. The Jewish artists and sculptors living in extreme poverty occasionally prepared exhibitions. Particularly active in this field was Felix Frydman. All Jewish artists were put to death in Treblinka.

These names mean nothing to most of us. The individuals mentioned were not famous and they had no chance to become so, but we know from this small paragraph that eager and gifted human beings sang and composed music and painted pictures — till Treblinka. The slogan of this conscious, organized group in the ghetto was: "To live with honor and die with honor." Each lecture attended, each concert heard, each picture seen, was a fulfillment of the first part of this creed.

The effort to preserve human values went on even in the concentration camps. Ringelblum writes:

Know then that the last surviving educational workers remained true to the ideals of our culture. Until their death, they held aloft the banner of culture in the struggle against barbarism.

And he concludes his account with the characteristic words:

We doubt whether we shall ever see you again. Give our warmest greetings to all leaders of Jewish culture, writers, journalists, musicians, artists, all builders of modern Jewish culture and fighters for the salvation of the Jews and all humanity.

We are familiar with the story-book figure of the Englishman who dresses for dinner in some God-forsaken outpost of his Empire, or of the prisoner who forces himself to trudge up and down in his cell to prevent the disintegration resulting from prolonged solitary confinement. These are the classic examples of stamina. What words can we find to describe the quality of spirit displayed by Ringelblum and his associates?

One gets a notion of what these activities meant to the youth and children from the statements of some of the survivors Mary Berg, who was imprisoned in the ghetto from the age of 16 to 19, and who finally escaped because she was the daughter of an American citizen, touches on the role of the school in her diary of the Warsaw ghetto. * In 1941 the Germans permitted the opening of a school of graphic arts. The typhus epidemic was at its height. Deportations to ' slave labor camps" had already begun. Shootings and manhunts were the order of the day. In her entry for September 23, 1941, Mary Berg describes a pogrom in the ghetto streets; but only five days later, under the entry of September 28, we read a description of an exhibition held by her school. Of all the drawings, the most popular were "still lifes." Realistic pictures of fruit and flowers were pleasanter to see than the grim drawings of emaciated beggars and cadavers that many of the young students had made. The beggars and corpses were a routine spectacle on which few wished to dwell, but the painted forms of apples, carrots or roses belonged to another world.

More striking was the subject matter of the graphic designs — the primary purpose of the school. One could see designs for powder compacts, book-covers,

*Warsaw Ghetto, by Mary Berg, edited by S. L. Shneiderman. New York, L. B. Fischer Co., 1945.

posters for theaters, cafés, stores. One young illustrator, Manfred Rubin, was selected for special praise. "The teachers predict that a great future is in store for him." There were beautiful and original textile designs. A young girl, whose dress models attracted considerable attention, would surely be a great fashion designer, "if she survives."

A special hall was devoted to architectural designs — modern homes with many windows and surrounded by gardens. Much glass and much greenery — of these the ghetto architect dreamt. "The visitors at the exhibition look with pride at these housing projects for the Jewish population of the free Poland of the future, which will abolish the crowded houses of Krochmalna and Smocza Street, where the darkest cellars of the ghetto are situated. But when will this come about, and which of us will live to see it?"

A daring young artist had made a stylized Hebrew poster in which the letter *lamed* was drawn to suggest hands raised in prayer. The text quoted was from Obadiah: "For thy violence against thy brother Jacob, shame shall cover thee ..." Those who knew Hebrew stood before the poster reading and re-reading the text, marvelling at the courage of the artist and drawing strength from the prophet's imprecation. Fortunately, the Nazis did not understand Hebrew.

Mary Berg comments on the pride the spectators took in the exhibition. Those who came were witnessing more than the display of individual talent, and those who exhibited were not merely showing aptitude. The exhibition was essentially one of fortitude. To use the words of the girl who was herself one of the exhibitors: "Our youth has given tangible proof of its spiritual strength, power of resistance, courage and faith in a newer and juster world."

Children of seven and over were receiving instruction in Yiddish schools conducted by the community. The school program included "supervised play" for the children. The young people of the art school decided to help provide a more attractive environment for the play hour.

Yesterday Professor Greifenberg took all the students in his class at our school to the little park opposite the community building. This park is on the site of a bombed house, where the *Toporal* gardeners have planted grass and flowers. Today it is green there. Jewish workmen have constructed swings, benches, etc. The pupils of our school went to paint a fresco of animal cartoons on one of the walls of the ruined house. All this is done to give the ghetto children a feeling of freedom.

The date of this entry is May 6, 1942 — a little more than two months before the mass liquidation of the ghetto was to begin. It is the month of May and all is "green," thanks to the *Toporal* gardeners. The "park" was formally opened by president of the ghetto, Cerniakow. The children were given some molasses candy manufactured in the ghetto. There was community singing, and the bit of grass sprouting on a bombed site — the only spot where a little free space could be available in the ghetto congestion — became a park, consecrated to childhood and its delights.

How did the children fare? I do not mean physically. There are no mystical substitutes for food and warm clothing and sunshine. The child mortality of the ghetto (not including children killed outright in the Nazi massacres) was almost as high as the Germans could wish. I speak of something else. What happened to the minds and spirits of children brought up in the abysmal wretchedness of the ghetto. In this scramble for existence, in which every non-Jew was a potential murderer, in which destitution and death were the normal scheme of living, how could even a "park" flowering on a ruin, or a few hours of clandestine schooling, safeguard against brutalization?

It would be ridiculous to speak of "juvenile delinquency" in this connection. One could not use the term in reference to human beings subjected constantly to torture at the hands of history's most inventive thugs, even if there were evidence to indicate that by ordinary standards the term were justified. Strangely enough, there is no such evidence. On the contrary, the battle waged by the adults for the souls of their children was in a large measure victorious.

By this I do not mean that children emerged spiritually unscathed and went to the slaughterhouses with no scars on their minds and hearts. It would be nonsense to pretend that such a situation could obtain. Nor do I refer to the fact that though famished and freezing and hurt they maintained the routine of studying lessons, particularly Hebrew — for the dream of Palestine sustained the ghetto. These were manifestations of will-power, of a disciplined desire to oppose with every moral resource the invading sense of futility and despair. The presence of such a will is, under the circumstances, remarkable enough. But something even more remarkable took place. The children not only showed a zeal to learn and to progress toward some kinder future. In addition, they were conscious of nobler qualities and traits in man's nature than they had been enabled to witness: they understood that these qualities, as well as their bodies, were being assailed by the Nazis.

Occasionally, the children wrote poems which were published in the *Gazeta Zydowska*. The prose translations of a few of these indicate the qualities I mean.

MOTELE

From tomorrow on, I shall be sad —
From tomorrow on!
Today I will be gay.

What is the use of sadness — tell me that? —
Because these evil winds begin to blow?
Why should I grieve for tomorrow — today?
Tomorrow may be so good, so sunny,
Tomorrow the sun may shine for us again;
We shall no longer need to be sad.

From tomorrow on, I shall be sad —
From tomorrow on!
Not today; no! today I will be glad.
And every day, no matter how bitter it be,
I will say:
From tomorrow on, I shall be sad,
Not today!

MARTHA

I must be saving these days
(I have no money to save),
I must save health and strength,
Enough to last me for a long while.
I must save my nerves,
And my thoughts, and my mind
And the fire of my spirit;
I must be saving of tears that flow —
I shall need them for a long, long while.
I must save endurance these stormy days.

There is so much I need in my life:
Warmth of feeling and a kind heart —
These things I lack; of these I must be saving!
All these, the gifts of God,
I wish to keep.
How sad I should be
If I lost them quickly.

Those two children, Martha and Motele, should not
be etherealized into symbols. They were very real, and
they loved life. The German youth also loved life.
Nathan Ek recounts an episode (*The Day*, July 4, 1945)
which is a companion-piece to Martha's prayer.

In September, 1942, after the deportation from the
Warsaw ghetto had begun, he had managed to reach
the ghetto of Czenstochowa. The 40,000 Jews of Czenstochowa were in a state of great depression. For some
weeks they had been receiving reports of the liquidation
of other ghettos in Poland and, at first, they comforted
themselves with the usual argument: since the Jews of
the ghetto slaved all day for German industry, why
should the Germans of their own accord destroy

such a valuable source of labor? The Nazis were too practical.

This phase of uneasy hope and doubt lasted for a brief period. It was then followed by a general conviction that in any case deportation might mean resettlement in the wastes of Russia. The warnings of individuals who harbored no illusions were disregarded in Czenstochowa as in the other ghettos.

The deportations to Treblinka began on September 23, the day after Yom Kippur. As usual, the Nazis displayed their historic sense by making the various points of their extermination program coincide with a solemn holy day of their victims. The liquidation of the Warsaw ghetto began the day after Tisha be-Av, the black day which commemorates the destruction of the Temple of Jerusalem.

The inhabitants of the Czenstochowa ghetto had been filled with foreboding for several days previously. They knew that deportations would begin at any time. There were signs. "Ukrainians" had been seen at the railroad station, and "Ukrainians" were known to be the assistants of the Gestapo in the mass round-ups of Jews. Furthermore, the Germans had demanded that all "taxes" be paid up by September 21.

Toward evening men and women would gather in small groups on the square and stand silently, as though waiting. This was the period when about a hundred girls belonging to the Hitler Youth chose to make a demonstration. At twilight they marched into the ghetto and circled about singing, paying no apparent attention to the unhappy human beings whom they passed. Heads held high, they marched and sang. The words of the song were hard to follow, but the sense was clear. It was a chant to the sun, to nature, to the beauty of life. With lusty voices and lusty bodies, the *Hitler-Mädel* tramped through the ghetto singing a paean to life and its excellence. It was a conscious demonstration directed at those who, they had been taught, were unfit to live. Perhaps a Martha stood among those who listened helplessly to the heathen tramp of the marchers in the ghetto twilight. And perhaps it was after such a scene that Martha prayed that she might be able to keep "kindness" and "thoughts."

We use the phrase, "cultural activities in the Warsaw ghetto," and it sounds like something taken from an evening-school catalogue. Its overtones are drab and a little pretentious. There is even a suspicion of artifice. Do human beings really want "culture" in the hour of death? But Martha explains. Through her we understand not only the purpose of the "activities," but the culture of the people whose child she was. Just as we understand the meaning of *Kultur*, not only from the Nazi slaughterhouses, but from the chant of these girls who chose to exercise their husky limbs and exult in the joy of "sheer living" amid the ghetto gloom, before the eyes of those whose fate they knew.

The child Martha, however, is not the whole of the Jewish youth in the ghettos. There were those who understood early that, in addition to creating and maintaining a cultural and social life within the ghetto, it was necessary to learn to think in terms of physical as well as psychic resistance. Such understanding was less natural to the Jewish spirit than the traditional reliance on spiritual resources. Consequently this realization developed slowly and involved comparatively small numbers. But from the outset there existed an active minority who were aware of all the implications of the struggle which lay ahead. This minority became the Jewish underground whose nucleus was provided by the Zionist "pioneer" youth groups.

4

The Youth Groups Prepare:
"To Die With Honor"

THE leading role played by the "pioneer" Zionist youth is readily understandable. As Zionists they had a sense of national responsibility. This sense could only be strengthened by the persecutions their people were enduring. Furthermore, as members of labor groups preparing for a pioneering existence in Palestine, they had received training which stressed the disregard of personal ease or safety for the sake of the group. In addition, the mere fact that they were enrolled members of *halutz* (pioneer) groups indicated that they were above the average in courage and initiative. They had been preparing for emigration to Palestine at the time when the calamity struck. Their lives were dedicated to the creation of a Jewish homeland, and they conceived this dedication in the most arduous personal terms. It was therefore natural that, being young, idealistic, and consumed with a sense of responsibility for the fate of their people, they were in the forefront of those who strove to organize the Jewish communities for psychic and physical resistance.

I do not wish to be understood as claiming that they were the only factor in the Jewish underground. As time went on, every political grouping in Jewish life joined in the organization of resistance. But just as the Jewish community of Palestine, despite its numerical smallness, played a disproportionately large part in all efforts to rescue the Jews of Europe, so the representatives of this movement in the Diaspora showed the same readiness for imaginative action. Within the countries under Nazi domination those accustomed to meeting Jewish problems in Jewish terms were least paralyzed by the blow. In the general impotence they still had nerves that could react and muscles that could move. Above all, they expected no saviour from the outside. They knew that there was no time to wait either for the brotherly cooperation of the Polish underground, the arrival of the Red Army, or the coming of the Messiah. All these would help eventually, though incidentally, for their own purposes. The major impetus had to spring from Jews themselves — if they were to live with honor as long as possible, and to die with honor when that became inevitable.

All political parties among the Jews came to share this conviction. The work of the Jewish underground resolved itself essentially into two phases: to maintain morale and dignity in the ghettos as long as that could be done, and to prepare for the final struggle.

A dubious kind of organization had existed in the ghettos from the outset. The Nazis had ordered the constitution of a Jewish council (*Judenrat*) whose function was to act as official representative of the Jewish community and to be responsible for the execution of all Nazi decrees. The council was assisted by the Jewish police, consisting of Jews selected by the council. This Jewish police had to maintain order in the ghetto and aid the council in securing the compliance of the community with the edicts issued by the Germans. Under these circumstances it was probably unavoidable that both council and police came to be viewed as the henchmen of the Nazis and detested as such.

But one must distinguish between the part played by the councils and that by Jewish police. I have heard many bitter attacks on the councils, or on particular individuals who served in them, on the ground that they toadied to the Germans or that the members strove to save their own skins at the expense of the community as a whole. In view of the function of the council such charges were bound to be made. Any body which had as its task the wretched business of enforcing Nazi orders could not escape accusations, in many instances justified. But it would be grossly unfair not to point out that a large proportion of the council members assumed their unwelcome positions in the hope of improving the lot of the community they represented.

The story of Adam Czerniakow, head of the council of the Warsaw ghetto, is familiar and in a sense symbolic of the moral *impasse* in which the councils found themselves. Czerniakow committed suicide rather than provide lists of Jews for deportation when he realized the true purpose of the transports. His suicide aroused the sympathy and admiration of the whole world. Yet, I have heard the most scathing criticism of Czerniakow from ghetto survivors. He had understood too late, they claimed. There should have been no negotiations with the Germans at any time. Nevertheless, it is obvious from the record that Czerniakow had been impelled by honorable motives throughout his dealings with the Nazi authorities, even though he has been strictured as shortsighted and timid. Like many of his fellows, he believed that he was tempering the fury of Nazi persecution by his parleys and compromises. When he understood the vanity of these hopes, he killed himself.

The condemnation of the Jewish police is more universal. Those who served on this force had to round up Jews for deportation if the required number failed to appear at the transfer point. In the beginning there were apparently many instances when the Jewish police strove to shield the community, but they finally degenerated into out-and-out Nazi assistants. When the Jewish police were informed by the Germans that, if they failed to deliver the required quota of victims, they and their families would be used as substitutes, many of them broke. Furthermore, the police were fed on the illusion that they would be permitted to survive in recompense for faithful service. As might have been expected, when their aid ceased to be of value, they shared the fate of the rest.

It would be pointless to adopt a holier-than-thou attitude and envelop the Jewish police in a blanket condemnation. One can understand the anger and contempt they aroused among the inhabitants of the ghetto, but those who were never subjected to a similar test should be wary of passing moral judgments. Certainly, men who sought to buy their lives by becoming agents of the Germans have small call on our sympathy. In justice to them, however, we must bear in mind that those who became members of the Jewish police knew that, if no Jews willing to maintain "order" in the ghetto were found, the task would be assigned to Ukrainians, Poles, Lithuanians, or S.S. men. In this sense they were helping the ghetto to avoid a worse alternative.

The breed of martyrs has never excelled by its size. We need not, therefore, be vicariously shame-stricken at admitting the existence of Jews who in the Nazi torture chamber showed themselves to be neither brave nor idealistic.

It is pleasanter to speak of the heroes. I met some of them face-to-face in Daphne, and in other parts of Palestine. Those who had died, or were still in Poland, were described to me by close comrades. It is hard to choose particular individuals and say this boy or that girl was the chief figure in the struggle. In every account the same names recurred: Zivia, Tosia, Hanka, Yitzhak Zukerman, Mordecai Anilewitz and others. But over and over again, some one would add: "Yes, these were brave; but the bravest of all was —" and I would hear a fresh and unfamiliar name. If I explained that I had never heard of the new figure mentioned, my informant would exclaim moodily: "That is reputation. It becomes a style, a fad. X was just as great as those who have gotten the glory. Maybe greater. It's not fair." And then I would be told the biography of some other boy or girl — for they were almost always young — and I would be urged to make certain that justice be done to the neglected memory. In regard to the accredited heroes I would often hear the complaint that the worship was exaggerated, the legend without adequate basis, the aureole spurious.

One element, however, remained constant — the heroism was always the same — so that one came to believe that essentially all the stories were true. Though only a small sector of the whole population took any part at all in the resistance, within that group the proportion of active figures was extraordinarily high. As a result, the historian, if he were to perform his office justly, might have to record a hundred or more names of leaders. But I make no pretense to a record whose accuracy is determined by its completeness. The truth can also be served by a symbol — by the one who stands for the many and who reveals the many more vividly perhaps than a conscientious compilation of names. For I do not wish to obscure the many by the many, and justice here is perhaps more to the deed than to the doer.

Of many young women who took leading parts in the resistance I heard it said: "She was called the 'mother'." Every ghetto apparently had its "mother," and sometimes more than one girl in the same ghetto was so addressed. This does not invalidate the authenticity of the title. In the desolation of the ghettos the young girls who voluntarily assumed the task of sustaining morale, of acting as links between ghetto and ghetto, of teaching the children and, finally, of inspiriting resistance, played a deeply maternal part. Because they were all in their teens or early twenties and without children of their own, the paradox of their roles of solace and authority impressed itself on the popular imagination. Nothing reveals the bereavement and helplessness of the ghetto more poignantly than these "mothers," to whom not only the young, but the old and middle-aged turned for comfort and assurance. It does not matter which one of the several young women so called merited the description most. The important thing to perceive is

191

the vision of a girl who flitted from dungeon to dungeon, from ghetto to ghetto, smuggling food, information or arms, as the case might be, and always strengthening the capacity to endure and struggle. Surely blessed among women — this girl whose maternity was not biological, but who, fructified by love for her people, became the image of motherhood for those orphaned through suffering!

The most famous figure of all is Zivia Lubetkin. Of Zivia, too, I heard it said that her halo had been fashioned by the popular need to create a legendary figure — a kind of composite of all who had fought and led. But one gets a notion of how central was Zivia Lubetkin's role from the fact that, in the entire underground correspondence of the period, Zivia's name was used as the code word for "Poland." "Hershel has gone to see Zivia," or "Zivia is very sick," gave required information in regard to conditions in Poland. That Zivia's name was chosen for this purpose was not arbitrary or a matter of chance. Another name would not have done as well. The word had to be self-explanatory to the recipients of the letters in the same way as the Hebrew words, used as proper nouns in the manner already described, required no previous information. It is, therefore, a great and spontaneous tribute to the extent and nature of Zivia's activity that her name came to be identified with the life of the Jews of Poland.

I have seen many pictures of Zivia. The first one was shown to me in Daphne by Renya and other friends who had finally reached Palestine in 1944. Zivia had stayed behind in Poland, insisting on remaining, even after the peace, to work among the shattered remnant of Polish Jewry. (She did not leave for Palestine till the summer of 1946.) The photographs cover some ten years, the age between the late teens and the late twenties. All the pictures show a serious, sensitive face — not pretty, but grave and intelligent. It is a typically "Jewish" face. Zivia's appearance was markedly "Semitic" her friends told me, and consequently she could not easily do conspiratorial work outside the ghetto. She worked within the walls.

It is hard to tear oneself away from Zivia's photographs. The deep brooding eyes, the thin oval face — it is a not uncommon type among Jews. "A Jewish intellectual — the kind who hungrily fills the concert halls, the lecture forums, and probably belongs to some movement to better the world" — one would say in ordinary times. Zivia's sensitive Jewish face, with the grave tragic eyes which make her look older than a girl in her twenties, on the last photograph taken after the ghetto slaughter and the ghetto battle, fits the part she played. The lovely, blond girls whom I had met were harder to visualize in the roles which they filled so gallantly. No picture of Hanna Senesch suggests her quality. But Zivia — stern, serious and sad — that was how she *had* to be, this "mother" of the ghetto.

Mashka, who had been in Birkenau and Maidanek and who had herself taken part in the uprising of the Warsaw ghetto, told me: "The thought of Zivia and Yitzhak (Zivia's husband) gave one the strength to live." And another girl told me that the last word on the lips of dying comrades had been: "Zivia."

It is impossible to dismiss such avowals as "legends" or blind hero worship — particularly as the worshippers were themselves of no mean stature. This slight girl will remain in Jewish history, as well as in the code of the underground, as the symbol of resistance in the Warsaw ghetto.

What did she do? Essentially her biography recapitulates that of many of the members of the Jewish underground. Before the war, as a girl in her teens, she had been an active member of *Hechalutz*. In 1939, she and a number of her comrades attended the Zionist congress in Geneva, which met during the last days of August just as war broke out. I was present at that congress also, but I have no recollection of the young girl who was to play such a tremendous part in the coming years. The delegates to the congress were too busy listening to the addresses of celebrities to pay much attention to the boys and girls who were representing the youth groups of the various countries. Though the expectation of war was general, no one could anticipate the scope of the calamity that was to engulf us, or foretell how glorious a role the blue-shirted, unpretentious boys and girls in our midst were to play. Only in the dawn of the last day of the congress, when I attended the session of the groups who were discussing plans for maintaining contact with Palestine during the impending war years, did I get a faint notion of the significance of these youth groups. The boys and girls were returning at once to their threatened countries. Zivia was getting ready to rush back as soon as possible to Poland, shortly to be invaded. They were preparing for the trial, though no one knew how sorely they were to be tried.

It is a poignant scene to remember — these hurried hours of an August dawn of 1939. The words which were spoken there — "We must fight the enemy; we must maintain contact with each other; we must help our people under the Nazi heel" — who could dream of the meaning with which each phrase was to become imbued, or with what fierce strictness every promise given would have to be kept? We at the congress had no prophetic insight; otherwise we would have gathered around Zivia and her comrades and looked long and hard at their young faces.

They scattered all over Europe, returning to their homes. The opportunity to fight the enemy on the battlefield was brief. Poland fell so quickly that its three and a half million Jewish citizens found themselves either in the hands of the Nazis or in the Russian-occupied zone almost immediately after the outbreak of the war. Many strove to escape from Nazi held territories, but comparatively few succeeded.

A curious phenomenon now appeared. Against the current of those seeking to escape from the German sphere, a countercurrent set in: some young Jews were consciously trying to fight their way back to German-held territory. As one reads the record of the time or listens to the stories of survivors, one is impressed by the steadfast refusal of the youth to take opportunities to escape — for if any were in a position to flee it was these vigorous, adventurous spirits who had the strength and adroitness for conspiratorial work. But, unlike many of their elders, they forbore to exploit their natural advantages. Instead, one sees a pure insistence on returning into the center of the peril. The Warsaw ghetto became the lodestar for the youth of *Hechalutz* which found itself outside the ghettos due to the fortunes of war. Zivia had been safe in Russian-occupied territory; but by 1940 she was already back in Warsaw teaching and organizing in the ghetto. Whether it be Renya or Frumka, Hershel or Yitzhak or another, they go from

Bendin to Bialystock, or Vilna, or Lemberg, or Warsaw; wherever the oppression is bitterest, the danger greatest, they appear.

The job is not easy. The youth cell in Lemberg, as yet not under Nazi domination, decides to send one of the group to the Warsaw ghetto. Hanka, a young girl with an excellent record as a worker, is chosen. She has to swim across an icy lake at night in order to smuggle herself across the border. When she steps into the freezing water, she loses her nerve and returns to Lemberg during the night. Her comrades are kind. They try to make her feel that no disgrace attaches to this moment of weakness. There is plenty of work for her to do in Lemberg. But Hanka cannot forget. Two days later she vanishes. When heard from again, she is in Warsaw. This time she has not failed. Nor does she ever fail again. She comes back for a while after her mission has been accomplished. But she goes to Warsaw once more — in March, 1943. She is in the ghetto at the time of the last stand and is among those slain in the resistance.

A routine story of the time! Yet how else were the severed communities to take warning from each other's fate, and the outside world — the office at Istanbul, the center at Geneva — to get word by code, or personal courier, of what was happening?

At first the emphasis of the youth groups was on maintaining morale and securing information. The Jews of the ghettos had to be kept alive spiritually by a hope transcending themselves. That hope was Palestine. Secret Zionist meetings were held, Hebrew taught and song recitals given, so that the children might learn and the adults not forget. The chain with the comrades in Palestine had to be forged. Finally the moment came when, to the letters from Istanbul spreading over the Balkans and seeping into Poland, Zivia could send back the postal card I saw in the archives of the Jewish Agency in Jerusalem; the awe of that moment in Istanbul, when a first faint knock was heard in answer to the desperate probings of those seeking to establish contact with the entombed, could still be sensed in the voice of the young Palestinian who showed me the files. A postal card from Zivia! At last the channel for sending money, help, directives had been dug. But for Palestine to get a reply, via Istanbul, a group prepared to answer and to act had to exist at the other end of the corridor.

Later, with the realization that to "live with honor" was an impossibility, the second half of the creed — "to die with honor" — became the chief objective of the youth. They had the task of persuading the community that deportation was synonymous with death and that resistance, though it could not save life, could at least save human dignity.

I have already mentioned the powerful psychological factors which complicated the efforts of those striving to bring the truth home to the ghetto. In addition to those obstacles, there was frequently the active opposition of the Jewish councils and of the Jewish police. All too often the councils opposed the notion of armed resistance on the familiar grounds that so desperate a step would only cause the immediate destruction of the ghetto, and that temporizing and yielding piecemeal to the demands of the Germans for more and more trainloads of deportees might save some lives. The appeals of the underground were characterized as the irresponsible propaganda of young hotheads who were prepared to bring catastrophe down upon all. Again, it should be remembered that this point of view was advanced by people who held it in good faith and who honestly believed that their strategy was most likely to ensure Jewish survival. Not all the councils of the ghettos, nor all the members, saw eye to eye on the subject of armed resistance — but the general trend was toward timidity and compromise.

Fewer excuses can be found for the Jewish police. Their opposition to the activity of the underground sprang from the fact that they had to deliver a prescribed number of victims for deportation daily, and any group which strove to prevent Jews from reporting to the transfer point was, from their point of view, a hostile element.

In addition to educational work to combat those forces in the ghetto which sought to bolster up the natural reluctance to believe in the reality of the German murder program, preparations for the moment of resistance had to be made. In every ghetto, bunkers were built where Jews could hide from the searches of the Germans. The bunker was not limited to the ghettos. Throughout Nazi-occupied Europe these secret shelters were constructed in a wall, in a cellar, under the earth — whatever human ingenuity could devise to foil the Germans. Some of these bunkers were elaborately fitted out with electricity and stocked with provisions and arms.

Machinery had to be set up for the publication of an underground press and for the forging of "Aryan" documents. Sometimes it was possible to purchase "Aryan" documents through bribery; in other cases, it was necessary to print false papers for those who were to be helped to escape or whose work lay outside the ghetto. A distinction has to be made between those who fled outside the ghetto and lived in the "Aryan" section by virtue of false documents, and the members of the resistance groups who went outside the ghettos in order to secure arms and to act as couriers between one place and another.

"How did you get arms?" I asked Renya and Mashka. Renya, because of her typically Polish appearance, was particularly useful for the job of smuggling arms. With a kerchief over her head and a basket on her arm, she was a pretty peasant girl going to market, and no S. S. man who tried to flirt with the attractive blond girl was likely to dream that she was a Jewess carrying a pistol concealed somewhere on her person or under the vegetables in the basket. The methods of concealment were of the crudest. Even a single weapon would have been too bulky to escape notice were a search instituted. The important thing was to avoid being searched. That was why the first requisite for smuggling arms was a disarming presence. This set a premium on young girls of "Aryan" appearance. German soldiers and guards, imbued with the notion that a Jew was someone who resembled a Streicher caricature, found it hard to believe that a girl who looked so much like the "Gretchen" of his dreams could belong to the proscribed race. Even in the case of a sudden street search, it would generally be a cursory affair if the girl's false papers seemed to be in order and her manner confident.

Renya told me of an incident which occurred on one of her trips between Bendin and Warsaw, after the first battle in the Warsaw ghetto. She was in the non-Jewish section of the city trying to discover whether any of the comrades who had led the uprising were alive.

The streets were tense: the Germans were searching intently for Jews who might have escaped from the flames of the burning ghetto. A Polish woman, who had known Renya, recognized her and started shouting: "Jew, Jew." A crowd gathered. Renya, with the assurance engendered by her "Aryan" appearance, approached the Polish woman and threatened: "If you call me Jew, I'll have you punished." Gestapo men came up to discover the cause of the fracas. Renya at once went up to them and complained about the Polish woman. The Gestapo men looked at her papers and laughed at the notion that she could have been accused of being a Jewess. She walked away safe, accompanied by Polish children who kept running after her shouting: "You should have given it to her for calling you a Jew."

Not a pretty story. Even the most passionately Jewish figures of the resistance — those who, like Renya, were risking their lives daily in order to serve the Jewish cause — had to exploit their "Aryan" appearance to the most ignominious and bitter degree in order to be able to function.

Arms had to be purchased or stolen — mostly purchased. There were Poles, and sometimes Germans, willing to be bribed. Sometimes a blessed opportunity presented itself: a comrade might be working in a place where it was possible to secure either a weapon or the raw materials for manufacturing a hand grenade or a bomb. Any smuggling done by a man was a much more risky affair, for, in the case of a search, even if his appearance would pass muster as "Aryan," there was always the telltale physical examination in case of doubt. Circumcision could not be argued away, unless proof of Mohammedan origin could be adduced. In the

5

e Last Stand: The Jewish Fighting Organization

◉

ediate impulse towards active preparations
was given by a report which was received
tions in Vilna. In October, 1941, a mes-
ent by *Hechalutz* to discover conditions in
d in Vilna, Lithuania. He brought back
on that the Germans had embarked on the
of the Jews in Vilna.

aw, Vilna, too, had been a great Jewish
r with a rich library and an intellectual
And, as in Warsaw, the establishment of
alculated degradation of the Jewish com-
e final destruction followed approximately
tern. There were the usual ingenious
trived according to the fantasy of the
inistration. In Vilna, the Germans hit
confusing the population by the issuance
of paper. At first the Labor Office in
ite slips to their Jewish slave laborers,

rough-and-ready decision of the usual search and arrest
there was no appeal from the sign of the covenant. This
made the use of girls as couriers and smugglers of arms
more desirable. However, men also took part in this
phase of the work despite the greater danger to which
they were exposed.

When it was necessary for someone of distinctly non-
"Aryan" appearance to use the trains, in order to travel
to another ghetto where his particular ability was required, the risk was taken as unavoidable. Here, too,
courage and presence of mind could save the day.
Mordecai, later a leader in the Bialystok uprising, had
been assigned the mission of reaching the Bialystok
ghetto from the Vilna ghetto. He had competently
forged papers. His appearance, however, was bound to
attract notice. On the train he sedulously kept reading
the *Voelkischer Beobachter*. This did not prevent some
Poles near him from starting to whisper that a Jew was
in their midst. He kept on reading pretending not to
notice. Through sheer chance or by virtue of his nerve,
he reached his destination without being subjected to
the dreaded physical examination.

The same comrade registered later for work outside
the ghetto, claiming to be a Tartar. He had the appropriate documents, all well forged. When he was asked:
"Can you prove that you are of Tartar and not of
Russian origin?" he answered with admirable aplomb:
"Certainly. If I were not a Moslem, I should not be
circumcised." He received the necessary work certificate
which enabled him to circulate outside the ghetto and
serve as a contact man for the underground.

Naturally, most interrogations could not be foiled
by audacity. Such exceptional incidents merely help

to explain how a small, valiant band managed occasionally to circumvent the Nazis.

Attempts were made to secure arms from the Polish underground. According to most reports, the cooperation which the Jewish fighters received from the Poles was, to put it mildly, luke-warm. Not until the very end did the Polish underground make any attempt to help, and even then in very limited measure. Polish cooperation was largely confined to giving information to the world, through London, about the massacre of Polish Jewry. For a long time, Polish leaders answered all pleas for arms with the statement that they were themselves short of ammunition. Only late in the day did they consent to sell some desperately needed weapons to the Jewish fighters.

One of the chief sources of supply came through Christians who worked in armament plants and trafficked in stolen arms with smugglers who had contacts with the ghetto. The great problem was to get money.

At first, the members of the movement sold everything they owned in order to get funds. Obviously, whatever they could raise in this way, no matter how great their personal readiness for sacrifice, was not enough to secure an appreciable sum. A system of community taxation was introduced. Perhaps "taxation" is too polite a term; "tribute" would be more correct. Some Jews were known to have hidden funds from the Nazis. The German robbers, despite their genius for plunder, had not always been able to discover the total possessions of those whom they sought to despoil. When the need for arms became acute, such individuals would be requested to contribute a given sum to the underground. Usually the requests were

honored. In the case of the re
and women of the undergrou
the necessity for compliance
generally saw the light. T
sporadic and inadequate sour

After the contact with Pale
been established, a steadier
period, the Joint Distributio
in Geneva were able to help
of the precise purpose of th
there were tragically few a
thousand times more pis
were ever available, they
quate defense against th
finally used to demolish
were rich only in darin
lives dearly. Thus ever
symbol of power. It
Renya's experience re
bit of ammunition w
Warsaw and Bendin
in the bosom of her
be nerve-racking be
searches and the co
the conviction that
If the pistol were fo
return it on her ne
by carrying arms o
poor to be able to
Besides, the peas
weapon at an ex
his customers de
might seek to ur

THE imm
for defense
about condi
senger was
Bialystok an
the informati
mass murder

Like Wars
cultural cente
life of its own.
a ghetto, the
munity, and th
the same pat
variations con
local Nazi adr
on the device o
of colored slips
Vilna issued w

with an expiration date which indicated that the bearer could not be shot till after the date stamped. Those without the lucky slip could be killed. Later the color was changed. One had to have a yellow slip to escape slaughter. The yellow slip even protected the owner's family. Afterwards the yellow slip had to be supplemented by a pink slip; the yellow slip alone was not valid. Finally, blue and green slips were added to the collection, and nobody could be sure which combination of colors would prevent shipment to the death camp of Ponary on the outskirts of Vilna.

For the Nazis who knew that no Jew would escape, no matter how the slips were shuffled and presented, this was an amusing game. For a mother who thought that her child might be spared if she could secure the right color, it was another way of going mad. "You are as dear to me as my yellow slip," became an expression of the period.

The mass slaughter of those without yellow slips began in October, 1941. Such was the information which the messenger sent by the Warsaw underground brought back. *Hechalutz* understood the full significance of the news: what had happened in Vilna was not a local phenomenon; it would be repeated throughout Poland. It was essential that resistance be organized at once in every ghetto, and particularly in Warsaw.

But the familiar argument — "It can't happen here, in the heart of Europe" — made itself heard. The efforts of the underground were opposed by those who argued that Vilna had suffered such a fate because it had been Russian-occupied territory. The slaughter should be interpreted as an anti-communist rather than as an anti-Jewish act. There was no need to add to the misery of the ghetto by arousing such extreme apprehensions, and so on.

Despite the lack of general response, the youth groups persisted and began the organization of actual fighting units who drilled secretly and developed a plan of action for the moment of attack. In the meantime, news kept filtering in which indicated that the time for total annihilation was drawing near.

In January, 1942, Frumka managed to make her way into Wolyn. She learned that the mass extermination of Jews was in progress there also. Similar reports were brought by refugees who escaped to Warsaw from Lodz: Jews were being loaded into trucks and murdered in the nearby forests.

Even this information was not enough to arouse a general realization of what was to come. Again the rationalizers found an explanation: the Germans were murdering Jews in the provinces incorporated into the Greater Reich. They were doing this in pursuance of their desire to transform these territories into purely German districts and consequently they were liquidating non-German elements. In the General Government of Poland, the same policy would not be followed. This reasoning found an echo even in the affected provinces. Warsaw, as the chief city of the General Government, became a place of refuge. Those who succeeded in escaping the Nazis in Lodz fled to the traps in Warsaw.

The underground was not deceived by the apparent respite. They knew that the Jews of the General Government would share the fate of the Jews of the other provinces. Therefore, in March, 1942, *Hechalutz* called a conference of all political parties and proposed the following:

1. To organize a general Jewish Fighting Organization.

2. To create a committee which should represent all Jewish parties and youth organizations and serve as a Jewish delegation with the Polish underground.

3. To set up an organization which would secure arms in the "Aryan" sections of the cities and establish workshops for the manufacture of arms within the ghettos.

Sadly enough, unity was not reached at this stage. Jewish socialists, who were not nationalists, refused to merge their groups with those of the socialist-Zionists. The realization that the situation was too desperate for political disputes or ideological differences had not yet struck home. It was to come a few months later, amid the smoke and flame of the ghetto's last stand.

The extermination of Jews in the General Government began during Passover, 1942. Lublin was the first city struck. The Jews of Lublin were deported to Belzec and murdered in gas chambers. The Jewish underground press published a full account of these occurrences of which they were informed by the messengers who arrived to warn Warsaw. Though now it was no longer Vilna, in former Soviet territory, but the region of the General Government itself that was affected, the Jews of Warsaw continued to be incredulous. Rumors were spread by assiduous Gestapo agents that the Jews of Lublin were being deported to Russia to become agricultural workers; the Nazis were eager to convert the Jewish middle class into "productive workers." This illusion was fed by the constant arrival of letters from Bessarabia, Smolensk and Minsk describing the happy life of the deportees. The letters, of course, had been written at the order of the Germans before the authors were put to death.

Not that there was a lack of fear or foreboding in the ghetto. The omens were too numerous to be ignored; the reports too circumstantial. But the Pearl Harbor psychology on which the Axis capitalized so aptly before every *coup* — this paradox of intellectual awareness and emotional unpreparedness — so that the world was always being surprised by Hitler, despite the reams of expert advance information being issued by every public agency and forum — was bound to prevail in accentuated measure in the helpless ghetto.

In the last weeks before the "action" began, a growing nervousness could be sensed. People began to be afraid to go out in the ghetto streets for fear that one of the frequent "shooting raids" would start. At the same time, while killings increased, the Jewish council was permitted to form some new elementary grade classes and kindergartens for children, though the effect of the new schoolrooms was marred by the knowledge that sixty empty cattle-cars had been assembled at the transfer point. The psychological confusion reached its height.

The liquidation of the Warsaw ghetto began officially on July 22, 1942. On that day the ghetto was completely surrounded by Germans and their Ukrainian, Lithuanian and Latvian assistants. The ghetto was beleaguered and every exit was blocked. To maintain the pretense that the purpose of the deportations was "re-settlement," the Germans issued the following order to the Jewish council:

1. All Jewish inhabitants of Warsaw, irrespective of age, will be resettled in the East.

2. The following categories are exempt from resettlement:

   a. All Jews employed by German authorities or enterprises and who are able to submit proof of it;

   b. All Jews who are members or employees of the Jewish council the day of publishing this order;

   c. All Jews employed by firms belonging to the German Reich, who are able to submit proof of it;

   d. All Jews fit for work but not yet covered by the employment procedure; these are to be isolated in the Jewish quarter;

   e. All Jews enrolled in the Jewish Guard;

   f. All Jews belonging to the personnel of Jewish hospitals as well as those enrolled in Jewish sanitary columns;

   g. All Jews, members of immediate families of persons enumerated under a to f; only wives and children are considered members of families;

   h. All Jews who on the first day of resettlement find themselves in one of the Jewish hospitals and are not fit to be released; the unfitness for release must be stated by a physician designated by the Jewish council.

3. Every Jewish deportee is permitted to take along 15 kilograms (33.3 lbs.) of his property as traveling luggage. Luggage above that weight will be confiscated. All precious objects, such as money, jewels, gold, etc., may be taken along. Food for 3 days is to be taken.

4. Beginning of resettlement, July 22, 1942, 11 A.M.

Point 3 in the program is noteworthy. The permission to take "precious objects" facilitated the Nazis' robberies, and the suggestion that food be taken lulled suspicions.

The Jewish council was ordered to supply 3,000 "deportees" daily; the number was increased to 10,000 daily as the tempo of assassination was speeded up. If the full complement did not appear voluntarily at the transfer point, bands of S. S. men and their henchmen would come roaring into the ghetto, surround a street and seize all the inmates cowering in their homes.

Complete chaos descended on the ghetto. Many thousands reported voluntarily for the reasons already outlined. Other thousands strove frantically to hide from the killers. On July 23, 1942, Adam Czerniakow, president of the Jewish council, committed suicide rather than provide the lists of "deportees" he had been commanded to prepare. But even his example failed to drive home the realization that there was nothing to wait for except death.

There was no lack of discussion. As soon as the liquidation of the ghetto began, a council of all groups in the community was held. A minority, including *Hechalutz*, demanded active resistance at once. The majority, however, favored a policy of waiting to discover how the situation would develop. Again rumors arose to comfort and betray. This time the notion was encouraged that not more than 70,000 Jews would be deported from Warsaw. The rest would be permitted to remain.

The liquidation of the ghetto continued with undiminished ferocity. Therefore, on July 27, 1942, the "pioneer" youth groups (*Hechalutz*) formed the Jewish Fighting Organization. The total arms at the disposal of the Jewish Fighting Organization at that time consisted of *one* revolver. Delegates were sent to the "Aryan" section to contact the Polish underground and secure arms.

While waiting for ammunition, the following steps were taken:

1. A call was issued to the Jewish population informing them that deportation was equivalent to Treblinka, and Treblinka was synonymous with death. All were warned to hide women and children and resist the Germans by all means at their disposal.

2. "Domicile permits," without which Jews were excluded from workshops, were forged.

3. It was decided to oppose the Jewish council and the Jewish Polish *Ordnungsdienst* which carried out the German orders. The commander of the Jewish police was sentenced to death. (He was later wounded.)

Despite all these efforts, the Jews of Warsaw still refused to face the truth. The underground was accused of manufacturing "atrocity stories" for partisan ends. Fake mail kept flooding the ghetto post office. Furthermore, the Germans were doling out the fatal bait of three kilos of bread and one kilo of marmalade to those who volunteered for deportation. Hunger, hopelessness and hope drove thousands to volunteer.

By September 12, when the deportation campaign was officially concluded, only 50,000 Jews were left in the Warsaw ghetto.

The Jewish Fighting Organization knew that a final liquidation would follow and decided to use the interval to secure sufficient arms. Up to date they had received five revolvers and eight grenades from their "Aryan" friends.

Delegates were sent to all large cities to organize defense movements in the remaining ghettos. Mordecai, of the wily ways, was sent to Bialystok; Frumka to Bendin; still others were sent to Cracow and Czenstochowa. Abba Kovner, of whom we will hear later as a partisan commander, was sent to Vilna.

By this time, the situation was viewed as sufficiently critical for all groups to join in the Jewish Fighting Organization. Even the most inveterate doctrinaires decided to merge their intellectual differences as to the nature of the true solution of the Jewish problem — should the emphasis be on the class struggle, or on Zionism, or on a combination of both — in the hour of death. At last unity was achieved; orthodox and atheist, communist, nationalist, assimilationist — representatives of all the various political trends which continued to flourish vigorously on the brink of the abyss — joined in the final conflict. Under the leadership of Mordecai Anilewitz, commander, and Yitzhak Zukerman, assistant commander, the Jewish Fighting Organization began the struggle.

In January, 1943, the Germans decided to complete the liquidation of the ghetto. They knew of the preparations for defense and that their game would no longer net volunteers. The ghetto was surrounded and detachments of storm troopers entered the ghetto to seize the remaining Jews by force.

During the three months that had elapsed since the conclusion of the last "action," many bunkers and fortified areas had been constructed. A greater store of arms had been acquired. Though the fighting groups did not expect an attack at the time chosen by the Germans, they met the German troops with armed resistance. A battle ensued in the course of which the Germans retreated. The losses of the Jewish Fighting Organization had been heavy. Many of its best men were killed, but they died knowing that Germans had fallen also.

The withdrawal of the Germans is a phenomenon worthy of comment. The S. S. men and storm-troopers who made up the "extermination squads" were so irritated by the notion of meeting armed resistance in the ghetto, and so unwilling to take the slightest personal risk, that they fled from their unequal opponents rather than endanger their own lives. The later German "victory" was accomplished with tanks and bombers.

The guerrilla fight was carried on in individual houses and streets. The dispatches from the Jewish underground tell of a battle at 56 Zamenhoff Street or at 63 Mila Street. We read:

> Israel Kawal and his small group fought with exceptional valor in the workshops. As a result of this fight we captured twenty guns and revolvers and killed and wounded fifty Germans.

Twenty guns and revolvers were a sizable addition to the arsenal of the Jewish fighters and the unknown "Israel Kawal and his small group" were one of many such units who defended a bunker or a rooftop.

After the flight of the Germans, the Jewish Fighting Organization knew that only a respite had been won. The Germans would return to raze the ghetto as soon as they decided to use heavy ammunition openly and drop the pretense of "deportation." While the Jews waited for the next assault, the respite was employed in strengthening the underground fortifications and in digging tunnels reaching to the ghetto walls. Even more important, the fighting will of the remaining 50,000 Jews in the ghetto had to be assured. Morale had improved enormously since the first open clashes with the Germans in January. The retreat of the Nazis before the ghetto fighters had made an enormous impression on the population.

As an added precaution, the Jewish Fighting Organization carried on a relentless campaign against any group guilty of collaborating with the Germans. Traitors were executed. The remaining Jews in the ghetto had no illusions as to the prospect of victory, but neither did they place any further credence in the assurances of the Germans. The Nazis were still unwilling to relinquish the notion that they could murder all the Jews at no cost to themselves. From the propaganda they let loose in the ghetto just before the last battles, one gathers how deeply they resented being obliged to expend men and arms on Jews whom they had been slaughtering so cheaply till now. All their blandishments were brought into play to secure the "peaceful" liquidation of the last 50,000.

Tebens, the German manufacturer in whose factories the Jewish workers slaved, and who was presumably interested in protecting the lives of his forced laborers, joined with his partner in contriving snares for his employees. Perhaps the Jews would believe the civilian "employer" even after they had lost faith in the promises of the Nazis. Tebens' "appeal" to his Jewish workers is probably one of the basest documents on record.

The fashion in which the "respectable" Germans co-operated with the Nazis in the execution of their murder schemes is pointedly exemplified in Tebens' call for more dupes:

To the Jewish War-Workers of the Jewish Quarters!

I wish to reply to the call issued by the Jewish Fighting Organization on the night of March 14–15. I want to state categorically that: 1. The deportation campaign will definitely not take place; 2. Neither I nor Herr Shulz have been ordered at the point of a gun to conduct such a campaign; 3. I give assurance that the last transport of deportees has not gone astray. It is a shame that the war-workers of the Tebens Plant did not take my advice. I regret, too, that I had to move one of my factories in order to take advantage of existing transportation opportunities. Furthermore, an order was given that the names of the workers who have already arrived in Trawnika be immediately ascertained and that their baggage be delivered to them there. The statement that the guard which accompanied the second transport of workers from Prosta Street to Poniatow does not know the fate of these workers is a criminal provocation and a base lie designed to influence the war-workers.

The escorts dispatched the trucks but did not accompany them. They only returned in freight trucks together with some workers from Poniatow in order to fetch the workers' belongings. The baggage was not taken away from Prosta Street, but remained there in the charge of a Jew, Lifszyc, who is an engineer, and from whom information regarding the whereabouts of the baggage can be obtained at any time. Every worker in Trawnika and Poniatow has now received his complete baggage.

Jewish war-workers! Do not believe those who want

to mislead you. They only wish to provoke you in order to bring about results that will be disastrous to you. Life in the underground fortifications is very uncertain, as uncertain as the life of a Jew in the "Aryan" quarters of the city. This insecurity only breaks the morale of the war-workers who are accustomed to work. Let me ask you, why do rich Jews who live in the "Aryan" quarters come to me for jobs? They certainly have enough money to live on, but what they can't stand is inactivity.

It is with the fullest conviction that I urge you to do the following: Go to Trawnika, go to Poniatow, because there you will have an opportunity to live and be able to witness the end of the war. The leaders of the Jewish Fighting Organization cannot help you. They only feed you with false promises. They sell you places in their secret underground fortifications for large sums of money. Later they will again drive you out into the streets and abandon you once more to your fate. Certainly you have experienced enough of their deceptions and tricks. Trust only the German managers of the factories, who will, with your help, produce war-materials in Poniatow and Trawnika. Take your women and children with you, because their welfare concerns us too."

WALTER Z. TEBENS

Director of Transportation of Factories
from the Jewish Quarter of Warsaw.

This time, however, the combined ruses of the German industrialists and of the Gestapo failed of their purpose. Even the beguiling conclusion of the Tebens manifesto, "Take your women and children with you, because their welfare concerns us too," no longer found any gullible readers.

The Tebens call was issued on March 20. By April 18 the Germans decided that, despite the loss of men, and even greater loss of prestige involved in making a full-scale armed attack on the ghetto, the "action" would have to start. Thousands of heavily armed storm-troopers with machine guns, tanks and trucks of ammunition marched into the center of the ghetto. The unequal, desperate battle was to begin.

The ghetto fighters understood from the outset that the battle would end with their deaths and with the destruction of the ghetto. But they were determined that this time Germans should also die. From their positions in fortified houses they threw homemade hand grenades at the Germans and shot at them with the precious rounds of fast-declining ammunition. While those too old, too young, or too weak to fight, sought shelter in the underground bunkers, the young men and women, many of them boys and girls in their teens, shot at the enemy, from rooftops, from balconies, from windows.

April 19 was a beautiful spring day, we are told by one of the fighters, and the youths standing at their posts wryly "lamented the joke that nature had played on them." It would have been fitter to go down amid the peal of thunder beneath a lightning-riven sky. But the air was balmy and the sun was bright even in the ghetto. The young people going proudly to their doom were not professional soldiers. They were intellectuals, artists, visionaries. Their knowledge of arms, of the tactics of struggle, even of such guerrilla warfare as they could wage, had been acquired in the past year at secret meetings and was still largely theoretical.

The bare factual reports of the survivors present an overwhelming picture. The groups at each fortified point fought as if each attack on a German patrol represented a major engagement. The Germans had to wrest control of the ghetto house by house, street by street. In the intervals of quiet, Moshe, we are told, would play the melodies of Beethoven and Schubert on a harmonica. One cannot help wondering whether the strains reached the representatives of German *Kultur* who were setting fire to the ghetto.

The headquarters of the Jewish Fighting Organization was in a bunker at 18 Mila Street. A radio and wireless apparatus had been installed there. Over the radio, accounts of the Warsaw ghetto's battle would sometimes reach the fighters gathered in the cellar. The voice broadcasting a last appeal for help gave those hearing it an illusion of contact with the outside world. Perhaps ammunition would come by parachute; perhaps Allied bombers would appear . . . But these were dreams, indulged in only for a moment.

The fighting dragged on till the middle of May. It took so long not only because of the reckless heroism of the ghetto fighters, but because of the German aversion to meeting armed Jews in hand-to-hand encounters. Fewer and fewer Germans entered the ghetto. Instead, the Nazis placed reliance on incendiary bombs and demolition by tanks. The attack on the ghetto became a siege rather than a face-to-face battle.

The resistance put up by the ghetto fighters in the flaming ruins embarrassed the Germans. To explain the tenacity and valor of the ghetto the Germans even resorted to the sorry expedient of claiming that the defense was being led by deserters from the German army. This rumor may have arisen because sometimes ghetto fighters, wearing uniforms stripped from the corpses of German soldiers, would pounce on detachments of Germans. This was one way of securing the hand-to-hand fighting Jews wanted.

For approximately three weeks, as long as a shot of ammunition remained, the fighters continued to try to repulse the Germans. But the tanks rolling into the smoldering embers of the ghetto, and the gas bombs thrown into the bunkers, could not be withstood. The formal end of the fighting may be said to have taken place on May 8, when the fortified headquarters of the Jewish Fighting Organization on Mila Street was surrounded by the Germans who hurled gas bombs into the entrances. The leaders of the Jewish Fighting Organization, among them Mordecai Anilewitz, kept their last shots for themselves rather than fall into the hands of the Germans. So perished the youth of the ghetto.

A few escaped through the sewers to the "Aryan" part of the city. Wading up to their shoulders in sewage, members of the Jewish Fighting Organization, who had been stationed outside the ghetto to secure whatever help and arms the Polish underground might give, returned into the burning ghetto to assist in the rescue of survivors.

Escape through the sewers was possible only for the strongest. Autos were waiting to take those who emerged into the woods. These preparations had been made by "Andek" (Yitzhak Zukerman) and those who were working with him in the "Aryan" section.

When the ghost-like, bedraggled beings emerged from one of the exits, one who surveyed the scene exclaimed: "Cats are coming out." Some of these survivors managed to reach the woods to join partisan regiments. Others were caught almost immediately.

The influence of the Jewish Fighting Organization was felt not only in the Warsaw uprising. As soon as the liquidation of other ghettos began, the resistance cells went into action. Throughout the zone of Nazi occupation a new phenomenon appeared: Germans had to fight in order to carry out their mass murders.

In the large ghetto of Bialystok, in the east of Poland, a pitched battle lasting eight days took place. The liquidation of the Bialystok ghetto started on August 17, 1943, just four months after the destruction of the Warsaw ghetto. A trainload of children had been rounded up by the Germans. It was rumored that before being killed, the children were to furnish blood for wounded German soldiers. When this train was about to start, the ghetto began to fight. Here, as in Warsaw, the Jews were not only hopelessly outnumbered, but their weapons were scanty and inadequate. To the armored tanks and field artillery of the Germans they opposed hand grenades and a few machine guns. But the Germans were forced to follow the same course as in Warsaw. They set the ghetto afire to stamp out the stubborn resistance they encountered. The report of a survivor reads: "Several hundred Germans and Ukrainians fell or were wounded during the battle." Not an impressive number certainly, but enormous when measured against the resources of the ghetto and the might of the Germans.

The Germans showed no inclination to minimize the importance of these uprisings. The mere fact that practically nameless, "cowardly" Jews were able to offer any kind of opposition to the Nazi military machine was in itself humiliating. Besides, the ghetto revolts were among the first mass uprisings against Nazi rule among the civilian populations of the occupied countries. They were a dangerous example to the "Aryan" quarters of the regions in which they were placed. Therefore the ghettos had to be razed to the ground by fire and bomb. The Nazis, the most economical and systematic plunderers in the world, must have been deeply vexed at the necessity of destroying houses and furnishings no matter how poor. If the ghettos had not fought, more housing and more loot would have been available. In addition, the fighters who perished in the bunkers or who leapt from flaming rooftop to rooftop deprived the Germans of another source of revenue. The Nazis were ghouls of genius. We know how carefully they removed gold fillings from the teeth of their victims, how they cut off the long hair of women and made blankets and mattresses of them, how they used human fat for soap. All these ingenious and profitable devices for increasing the wellbeing of the Reich were foiled by the fighters.

In Bendin, in Tarnow, in Vilna, in Czenstochowa — wherever the delegates of the Jewish Fighting Organization penetrated with their great gift of courage and their small gift of arms — the Germans were met with organized resistance. And in these final battles, one by one, the leaders of the Jewish Fighting Organization perished.

Even the death camps became centers of active resistance. In Treblinka itself, at the gate of the death chamber, the victims finally roused themselves and fell upon their German and Ukrainian guards. After disarming and killing them, they set fire to the gas chambers and crematoriums and escaped to the neighboring forests. The guards were so completely unprepared for this desperate move on the part of their usually helpless victims that the attack was successful.

The death camp of Sobibor, in the Lublin district, was the scene of another furious effort to resist. On October 14, 1943, at a given signal, the six hundred Jews still remaining in the camp threw themselves upon the Germans. Again, because of the element of surprise, they succeeded in killing many. They wrecked the murder chamber, ripped the barbed wire surrounding the camp and fled to the woods. About half their number were caught by the Germans who pursued them on the day following the attack, but several hundred escaped to participate in further resistance with the partisans.

6

The Indictment

❂

THE fighters were young; the messengers — the *shlichim* — were young too. The physical and nervous tension of underground activities required the dexterity as well as the intrepidity of youth. But it would be false to leave the impression that valor and a readiness for self-sacrifice were the monopoly of the young. I have already mentioned the scholars and intellectual leaders of the ghetto who continued to teach and record for the verdict of the future. The archives of the ghettos are literally being dug out of the ruins. Manuscripts are being unearthed which were hidden by their composers as luckier peoples hid weapons or treasures. These manuscripts contain the history and the indictment of the Nazi era framed by its chief victims.

As the hour of the gas chamber approached, Jewish poets and writers made it their task to leave a documentary record of their people's fate. The manuscripts were buried in the woods to await the hour of victory, or were smuggled out of concentration camps. They round out the picture, not only of the events themselves, but of the manner in which the sufferers reacted. The men who insisted on fashioning the record with their last ounce of energy were also sharers in the fight.

One of the most interesting of these documents is the long poem, *The Song of the Slaughtered Jewish People*, by Yitzhak Katzenelenson, a writer of reputation in Yiddish and Hebrew. Katzenelenson had been in the Warsaw ghetto together with his wife and three sons. His wife and two younger children were among the first to be deported for extermination. Katzenelenson and his oldest son were kept at forced labor and then sent to the internment camp of Vitel in France, from where they too were later deported — "destination unknown." While in Vitel, Katzenelenson wrote his poem in Yiddish, making two copies, each of which was buried in a different place. I saw the copy which reached Palestine.

It is difficult to evaluate this work which consists of a number of related poems. *The Song of the Slaughtered Jewish People* is certainly a great human utterance. By virtue of its simplicity and sincerity, it has the total effect of poetry, though many individual stanzas are prosaic and flat. However one may choose to evaluate it as literature, it is the most powerful Jewish *J'Accuse* so far written.

The poem recapitulates the various stages of the ghetto agony. In one respect, Katzenelenson differs from other narrators. He claims that the Jews instinctively sensed their doom from the beginning. He writes (the original Yiddish is rhymed, I am merely reproducing the content, not the form):

Alas, I knew it and my neighbors too.
All of us, big and small, we knew the truth;
But not a word was said . . . hush, not a word,
Before each other nor in our inmost thoughts;
We kept the secret buried in our breasts.

Before they penned us within ghetto walls,
Before Chmelno or Belsitz, long before Ponary,
If we met any friend upon the street,
We'd quickly look away and only press
Each other tightly, tightly by the hand.

Not lips, not eyes, not words . . . we even feared
To look directly in each other's faces,
For glances may reveal what the heart dreads,
But our hands spoke; our silent hands spoke loud;

Tekel, Tekel, they said — like words unseen,
The handwriting inscribed upon the wall!
Not only we, the walls of every house,
The stone of every street knew of our fate.

The birds and fishes knew, all of us knew,
The Gentiles all around us — they knew too:
We would be murdered; each of us was doomed;
No reason given; nothing to be done.
The order had been issued stark and plain:
Slaughter the Jewish people, child and man!

There is no attempt at literary artifice in the poem.
The images are commonplace, but one is caught in the
mounting horror. Katzenelenson describes in hackneyed
similes the trains which keep coming to the transfer
point for more victims, and yet the Yiddish original has
the raw intensity of immediate experience:

Fear seizes me, great fear falls on my heart;
The trains are back again. Just yesterday
They started out, and now I see them stand
Once more upon the transfer point. Their mouths
Gape wide. What do they want?
They are not sated; they want more and more;
They want more Jews to fill their hungry maws . . . .

The most moving sections of the poem are those in
which he addressed his dead wife, Hannah, and the two
children who were killed — Benjamin and Benzion. In
Vitel, he keeps remembering and reliving episodes of
the past:

I like to say your name, to utter it,
To turn to you since you were snatched from me
Together with my people. In my grief
You answer me with eyes of light and love;
Your wistful smile shines on me as of old.
I like to call you in my loneliness,
And ask you, Hannah, do you still remember?

Do you remember, Hannah? Come to me.
Sit close beside me; put your glorious head,
Your long black hair with only one white strand,
Upon my shoulder. Put your arms around me.
Quicken me. I called you from your peace;
Oh do not rest, my Hannah! let the eternal wound
Not be forgotten in oblivion . . . .

Sit down beside me, for I love you so . . .
Hear what I say.
You hear! You hear! In my great misery
You comfort me, my wife.
I fill you with my anguish as with seed;
Bear my accusing words as once my sons,
Bear them, and carry them from world to world.

He begins his accusation with a description of an orphan home on Tworda Street. He asks his wife if she remembers the fifty laughing little boys for whom he had once written a play: *Mich Zieht in Gass* (I want to go outside.) The children had produced the comedy, and the writer had become friendly with them in the course of the rehearsals. In those hours, the children were merry even in the ghetto. But what Katzenelenson remembers most clearly is the day on which the children were led away to extermination.

There are many descriptions of these processions of children going hand-in-hand through the ghetto streets to their deaths. Sometimes they walked as far as the cemetery outside the ghetto limits, where they were shot in a mass execution; at other times they went directly into the fatal trains. Occasionally, the children thought they were going for an outing and were gay; often they suspected something of the truth and were afraid. But always they went, and their teachers with them. Since adults capable of work could be "liquidated" later, the teachers were generally assured by the Germans that the children could be "deported" without them. But the teachers rarely left their charges. The children had the comfort of a trusted presence as long as comfort was possible.

Katzenelenson names the teachers who were his friends, just as every account of the ghettos speaks of the men and women who were last seen deliberately climbing into the trucks into which their pupils were herded, or walking at their side to the transfer point. Again, one asks why did the ghetto dwellers let the children be led unresistingly to their doom. Again, one hears the same answers: they did not know, they did not want to know, they believed the Germans until it was too late. The few who understood were afraid that they would precipitate the immediate murder of the children by interference.

The instruction of the Jewish Fighting Organization was: "Hide your children." This could be done by individuals, but the inmates of children's institutions such as orphan homes and schools were the most difficult to conceal. The homes could only be defended through such armed uprisings as were to come later.

Besides, the Nazi bag of tricks was inexhaustible. A physician of Vilna, who later worked with the partisans, told me of one of the last schemes used by the Nazis to secure the cooperation of parents in the round-up of children. One day an order was issued that all children were to be brought to a central office for a medical examination. Supplementary food rations were to be issued to those requiring them. The youth groups warned, "Don't send the children," and in some cases their wiser counsel prevailed; but many mothers and fathers dressed up their children as best they could — so that they should look neat and attractive and move the Nazi examiners' hearts — and brought them as commanded. That saved the Germans a deal of trouble. There were fewer children to hunt for in bunkers or among "Aryan" families.

This particular group of children was not exterminated immediately. First, the skin of the children was removed for grafting operations upon German soldiers who had suffered bad burns on the German front. Yes, I know, this sounds like an atrocity story. Yet flaying Jewish children, like draining them of blood, to assist in the recovery of injured specimens of the master-race was a perfectly logical extension of Nazi theory and practice. It was certainly no worse than the extermination centers whose existence no one any longer presumes to doubt. However, just as it was logical for Nazis to act as they did, it was equally logical for Jewish parents not to be able to credit the Germans with such bestiality. That was why they sent their children neatly washed and combed for the "examination."

It is such scenes that Katzenelenson describes. The poem is not a threnody. A tone of lamentation is inevitably present, but the dominant moods are fury and astonishment. Probably the first reaction of any normal human being to the revelation of the Nazi murder factories is incomprehension. A baffled amazement precedes indignation. Bitterness and the demand for retribution come only after the knowledge has been assimilated in some fashion. In Katzenelenson's narrative one returns to the initial uncomprehending "why," more damning than any judgment.

Hannah, the wise and tender wife, and the two sons — bright, earnest little boys — become the symbols of all the mothers and wives, of all the eager children, killed by the Germans. And as one reads the poem, the "six million," the unhuman, meaningless figure, resolve themselves into individuals, each one dear.

Zivia mentions Katzenelenson in a letter written May 24, 1944, a year after the Warsaw uprising. She speaks of the heroes of that battle, and of the other battles which flamed up in the ghettos and concentration camps of Poland once the signal had been given. Unaware as yet of the poem Katzenelenson had left behind or of his fate, she writes:

"We ask you to remember our poet, I. Katzenelenson. During the second attempt to liquidate the ghetto, when the first armed struggle with the *Haganah* took place, in January, 1943, he refused to hide. Together with his oldest son (he had lost his wife and younger sons in the first action), he took part in the resistance to fight for our people. He was sent to Vitel and we have no news of him."

Zivia's letter concludes with a paragraph which has a specially poignant ring to-day:

These days, when our national tragedy is without parallel, and when our prospects for the future are perhaps equally grim, we — the remaining members of the underground who are far from our homeland — are sustained by one hope. We trust that, when this slaughter is over, our efforts will not have been made uselessly and our blood not have been spilled in vain. In the name of the few of us who are still alive, we send greetings to the *Yishuv* and to our comrades.

We know how the hope which sustained the fighters was answered in the first year of liberation. Another ghetto fighter, describing the fate of Jewish survivors in the closing months of 1945, wrote a year after Zivia's letter: "Were a dog to lick my heart, he would be poisoned." These words are in their way as fierce an indictment of the world as the *Song of the Slaughtered Jewish People.*

7

"Understand It Humanly"

O NE wants to sum it up — this epoch on which is the sign of Maidanek and Oswiecim. Editorial adjectives occur readily enough: the most "tragic" period in Jewish history, the most "evil" in that of mankind. The banal summation is the truest, and one cannot get much beyond its far-reaching inclusiveness. But in addition to the primary indictment, there are subsidiary questions to which we seek the answers.

"It was terrible," say the survivors, and by "terrible" they mean not only the crematoriums and the pathological bestiality of those by whom they were beset. This comes first to their minds and tongues, but then follow other memories of the "terrible": the mother who choked her child in a bunker lest its cries reveal the hide-out; the Jews who collaborated with the Germans to save their own skins; the brutality and indifference of some of the sufferers themselves in the anguished scramble to live. Each survivor adds to the mass picture of a savage world, the peculiarly terrible (to him) detail of a corrupt, obsequious, or rapacious Jewish figure who became the creature of the Germans.

"Should one tell this too?" I asked of several ghetto fighters. "Tell the whole truth," they answered. "It is all part of the crime against us. One has to understand."

"How can one understand the mothers who choked their children? Did they do it to survive themselves or because of those in the bunker with them?"

The young blond girl with the wise, unyoung eyes answered: "One must understand it humanly. She did it for both reasons — to save herself and the others with her. The instinct of self-preservation . . ."

"But where was the maternal instinct — the strongest of all?"

The girl with the cool, all-comprehending eyes, answered with a smile which had neither malice nor mirth:

"You see, you don't understand. Of course, the normal mothers died. You ask me of exceptions. You want me to tell you there was none. There were. There were the weak, the bad, the crazy. What did you expect?"

And then she added, as did so many of the survivors: "We belong to two different worlds; we cannot understand each other. You who were not there will never understand."

"But all in all, despite everything, was it an heroic epoch?" I insisted.

"Yes," she said, and for the first time her eyes softened. "The best perished; you will never know how wonderful they were. This, too, you will never understand."

"The best perished!" It is perhaps enough to say: "Six million perished," and among them how much wisdom, goodness and beauty! The Nazis had dreamt of despoiling a whole people of its characteristic virtues:

an inquiring mind; a zeal for truth; and a passionate
faith in man, the brother. They succeeded only in despoiling the world. This one may say even after hearing
the "whole" truth. One dares to say it even after hearing reports of ˙demoralization and despair among the
survivors in the camps of "displaced persons" in Europe.

Etiquette does not demand that those, whose nails
were ripped off, display a fresh manicure, nor that those,
whose skins were flayed, follow the correct rules of make-
up. First they must be healed. Perhaps some of the
flayed and tortured Jewish survivors are not attractive
beings — less attractive than their flaxen-haired, pink-
cheeked torturers. But the process of regeneration which
must take place in the murderers and their abettors is
more fundamental than that needed to restore their
victims. The wonder is that so many of those who
emerged from the ultimate indecency of the ghetto and
crematorium still have the energy and the will for a
decent life.

The survivors can judge best. Chaya Grossman, a
heroine of the Bialystok uprising and of the Jewish
partisans — another one of those young blond girls
with the unyoung eyes — has characterized the period
and those who remain alive:

> My comrades have asked me where we got our
> calm, our patience. I will answer: we were always
> calm; we were always patient. It was the calmness
> which our comrades felt before and during battle.
> The battle was our watchword; this was the minute
> for which we waited and hoped.
>
> It is much easier for us to bury time-bombs than
> to deliver speeches; what we can tell you is this —
> we are alive. We exist; our movement was large and

strong and it was beautiful, even in its defeat. To live is not a difficult task. You must know how to live, and more than that, how to die. We knew that by our death everything would not have ended, that our death would become a symbol upon which a generation would be educated. These thoughts were ours in the ghettos, and this was our Torah; we studied and memorized it, each moment, calmly, deliberately, patiently.

And I want to tell you this, although it is difficult to bring such words to my lips: the heroes of the people are not necessarily its recognized political leaders. The true heroes of a nation are small people, silent, unknown.

I desire to recall a heroic chapter in the history of our struggle. With trembling lips I recall the memory of the daughters of Israel who fell heroically on the battlefield—Lonka, Tosya, Frumka, and many others like them—who will forevermore hold a glorious place in the annals of our movement.

Silence was their most characteristic beauty. The daughters of Israel who fell in battle excelled in that. They were the nerve-centers of the movement. Tosya and Lonka for the first time brought us tidings of Warsaw and Vilna and news from our movement here, and you will never be able to understand what this meant to us. We will never forget them and their images shall be before our eyes as an eternal example for future generations.

We didn't come here to ask for pity nor to glory in our plight. We came only to bridge the gap between us and Israel and to tell you that we are alive, that we shall go up to the Land, and that we are with you.

V. Jewish Partisans in Eastern Europe

1

The Woodmen

"THE Woodmen" — that is the name I heard given to the men and boys who had existed for months in the forests of Poland, of Galicia, of White Russia and Lithuania, and who emerged, finally, savage and alive. I use "savage" advisedly, for they are not a gentle breed, these men who dwelt in the woods hunting and being hunted. One had to be strong for life in the forests — without shelter in the freezing winters of Eastern Europe and without the support of a friendly population ready to give food and secret aid. "They are wild:" that was a complaint I heard often in Palestine from those whose task it was to reintegrate the partisans into the pursuits of civil life and into an appreciation of civilian niceties.

"We are wild," a young partisan said to me when he told me of his two years in the woods of Stasher in Southeastern Poland. After the fierce, tense life of the woods, it was hard — as well as pleasant — to sleep in soft beds, to shave daily, to follow an orderly routine of work.

The boy who spoke to me was aware of the psychological problem that he and many of his fellows presented.

He was a husky lad, but I could feel his restlessness and inner tension. The sense of exclusion from the world which had begun in the ghetto and which had reached its climax in the two years of solitary struggle in the woods, the constant impulse to spring at the throat of the enemy, were factors which obstructed the return to what we call normal life. But the boy to whom I spoke in the *kvutzah* of Negba, on the southern rim of the desert in Palestine, was making a conscious effort to leave the forest. He had chosen a new settlement deliberately, not out of the national idealism which prompted the ghetto fighters whom I met in Daphne, but as a voluntary form of self-discipline. In reclaiming the soil of Palestine, he would be reclaiming himself. Breaking a furrow through the hot sandy earth of Negba was far from crouching in a snow-covered bunker of twigs and leaves in the forests of Stasher, but it was also a fight.

"You know," he said to me just before I left, "had I known that I would remain alive, I probably would never have taken so many risks. I never expected to remain alive."

This boy was not a hero, and it would be pointless to seek to transform him and others like him into heroic figures. The partisans had their heroes, just as the ghettos did — and of them I shall speak later — but many a man who took to the woods did so largely because he had the physical stamina and the resourcefulness for such a life. To exist, he was constantly obliged to display exceptional courage and endurance; but he was not necessarily dedicated to a cause transcending himself, as were the parachutists or the ghetto fighters.

A distinction has to be made also between those who

went into the woods primarily to escape, and those who joined organized fighting units. The former are the "woodmen"; eventually they generally entered the organized groups but, until they did so, they could not, properly speaking, be called partisans. That name must be reserved for the guerrilla fighters who escaped to the woods for the express purpose of harrying the enemy and of rescuing Jewish survivors from the ruined ghettos and the still functioning concentration camps.

Before one presumes to discuss the activities of the Jewish partisans, one must understand that their lot differed radically from that of other partisan units — whether Russian, Polish or Yugoslav. The Jewish partisans were, in a sense, as isolated in their forests as the ghetto fighters behind their ghetto walls. It was a lonely struggle in which frequently he who should have been a comrade was as hostile as the German enemy. Polish, Lithuanian or Ukrainian guerrilla bands were as likely to turn on the Jewish partisans as to cooperate with them. This charge has been made so consistently that its truth must be accepted, nor is it surprising in view of the anti-Semitism known to be rampant in those localities.

The hazards under which Jewish partisans had to operate were aggravated not only by the constant danger of attack from other partisan units roving the woods, but by additional serious factors. The success of a partisan movement is in large measure dependent on the cooperation of the native civilian population. The Russian partisans enjoyed the active support of the Russian towns and villages under Nazi occupation. In the Russian peasant they found a brave and trustworthy ally in the fight against the Germans. He could be counted on for food, for the smuggling of arms and for sabotage. Above all, he could be trusted not to betray.

The situation of the Jewish partisans was far more difficult. The Polish or Lithuanian peasants were, for the most part, enemies. There were exceptions, of course, but by and large the Polish peasant's native anti-Semitism, stimulated by Nazi propaganda and the object lessons of Nazi practice, was stronger than his hatred of the German conqueror. Consequently, the Jewish partisan units entrenched in the woods near Vilna or Warsaw could expect little help from the local population. Worse, they had to be constantly on their guard against betrayal and attack. Everyone, not only the Germans, was a potential enemy. This not only increased the danger to the individuals in the units. It immensely complicated every operation in which even a minimal measure of local assistance had to be relied on. The experiences of Jewish partisans were such as to intensify their sense of isolation from the world — particularly as many had entered the forests with the obstinate and naive faith that in their fellow-fighters they might find brothers.

Some Jewish partisans joined existing partisan units of other nationalities; others formed autonomous Jewish units. Many Jews who escaped from the ghettos became members of a Russian partisan corps, since Russians were those most likely to welcome Jewish recruits to their ranks. In those instances where conditions were favorable, they joined bands of Polish and Lithuanian guerrilla fighters. Independent Jewish partisan movements developed comparatively late — after the liquidation of the ghettos. One may well ask why the Jewish youth waited for the final act of the catastrophe before venturing into the woods. I asked this question of Rushka and of Abba Kovner, leaders of the Vilna partisans, whom I met in Palestine; I asked it of a physician who had spent a winter with a Lithuanian Jewish partisan corps; and I asked it of the rank and file — men who were neither military nor political leaders.

One towering six-foot-three partisan answered me with a contemptuous: "They were afraid; they would rather choke in the ghetto than go out into the cold forests."

Looking at his huge hands, his powerful frame, it was easy for me to understand the origin of his disdain for "cowards and softies." He could "take it." But his answer was far from the whole truth. The leaders of the Vilna partisans gave a clearer picture of what had prompted the delay.

2
In Vilna: The United Partisans

❀

IT WOULD have been comparatively easy for the more vigorous and alert youth of the ghettos to escape and join partisan groups as soon as such began to be formed — shortly after the attack on Russia. It would even have been possible for thousands to escape before the liquidation of the ghettos and form autonomous Jewish units. The advisability of such action was debated in Vilna. There the United Partisans Organization, under the leadership of Abba Kovner, began to function at the end of 1941. Yet the Vilna partisans did not go into the woods till September, 1943, immediately after the ghetto had been destroyed. What was the reason for this delay of nearly two years? Since the United Partisans Organization of Vilna was one of the best organized and most active of the Jewish partisan units, its history will illustrate most plainly the problems that had to be met.

The young men and women who formed the U. P. O. (United Partisans Organization) had no illusions about the ability of the majority of the ghetto dwellers to exist in the woods. They knew that old men and women, children, the sick and the feeble, would perish at once in the rigors of an East European winter, without heat or shelter of even the most primitive kind. Furthermore, a mass exodus involving several hundred thousand people was obviously impossible. Only the youngest and strongest could save themselves by this means. That, however, would have meant a desertion of the ghetto, a course which the Vilna youth declined to take. Like the youth of Warsaw, Bialystok, Lodz, or Bendin, they remained to share in the ghetto's fate.

The work of the U. P. O. fell into two phases. The first lasted from December, 1941, till September, 1943, and consisted of preparations for resistance in the ghetto itself. The second comprised guerrilla warfare in the forests, and lasted from 1943 till 1944 — when Vilna was liberated.

The task of the resistance leaders in Vilna was the same as that of the youth of Warsaw. The Jews of Vilna had to be persuaded as to the true nature of the deportations. They had to understand that the way from Vilna led to the death camp of Ponari, just as the way from Warsaw led to Treblinka. The U. P. O. began to warn and organize the population for the final struggle. Bunkers had to be built; a secret radio and a secret printing-press were installed to issue proclamations; and an educational program was conducted among the children, just as in the other ghettos.

In Vilna, as in Warsaw, Jewish scholars and scientists fought barbarism. Alfred Rosenberg, the Nazi theoretician, had demanded that the scholars of the famous Yiddish Scientific Institute of Vilna classify the great library of the institute for inclusion in Rosenberg's collection. To bury or conceal important books meant death; but the scholars working on the catalogue were determined to preserve the heritage of the Jewish spirit. They secretly buried the treasures of Jewish wisdom and scholarship, though aware that few of them would live till the day when the books would be dug up again. In Vilna, as in Warsaw, literature, history and scientific research were pursued till the end.

How consciously this insistence on intellectual activity was viewed as a form of resistance can be gathered from the words of A. Sutzkever, one of Vilna's foremost writers, who is among the few survivors:

> The Jews of Vilna knew that with schools they could defy Hitler. The writers were partisans, with words as their weapons. The musicians were partisans armed with music. Zlakindson, the son of the eminent Vilna physician, wrote a great work on astronomy. Vilna did not surrender to the executioner's sword. It kept its glorious tradition alive.

From Vilna, as from Warsaw, Bialystok and Bendin, the *shlichim*, the messengers, went on their rounds from ghetto to ghetto. Word was sent to Warsaw of the exterminations at Ponari, in the hope that Warsaw would be able to resist in time. Names of the boys and girls who gave their lives in these missions illumine the records of Vilna as of other ghettos. The password of the U. P. O. was "Liza calls," in commemoration of a young girl, Liza, who had left the ghetto to organize resistance in a nearby town and had been caught and killed.

Till the liquidation of the Vilna ghetto, the U. P. O. smuggled weapons into the ghetto and drilled its members in the use of arms. And daily and persistently it rallied the population. The text of one of the proclamations of the Partisans read as follows:

Call of the Jewish Partisans in the Vilna Ghetto:

Do not believe the tricky promises of the murderers. Do not believe the assurances of traitors. There is only one path for those who leave the ghetto: to Ponari. And Ponari means death.

Jews, we have nothing to lose. Death will come anyhow. Who believes that he will still remain alive when the murderer is exterminating all systematically?

Jews, rise in armed resistance. The German and Lithuanian executioners have come to the ghetto door. They are going to slaughter us. They will soon lead us in files from the gates.

So they led hundreds on *Yom Kippur*.

So they led those with the "white," the "yellow," and the "pink" badges.

So they led our brothers and sisters, fathers, mothers and children.

Don't let yourselves be led like cattle to the slaughter.

Out into the streets!

Whoever has no weapon, should seize an ax.

Whoever has no ax, should seize a bar of iron, a stick.

For our murdered children!

For our parents!

For Ponari!

Attack the murderers. On every street, in every room, in every yard, in the ghetto and outside the ghetto.

Beat the dogs!

Long live freedom and armed resistance! Death to the murderers!

While still in the ghetto, members of the U. P. O. carried out acts of sabotage against the Germans. They would steal out to dynamite railroad tracks and to participate in night raids on German munition factories; but their chief activity consisted in fortifying the ghetto and digging the underground passages which made contact with the outside world possible.

In September, 1943, the Germans surrounded the ghetto. For a week the U. P. O. gave battle to the Nazis, using the tactics of house-to-house defense. The struggle ended with the razing of the ghetto and the extermination of most of its inhabitants. Only then did the surviving partisans decide to escape to the woods through the subterranean passages they had dug.

When the U. P. O. emerged from the passages and took stock of the human resources available, they found that only about eighty members of the organization had managed to survive the last stand in the Vilna ghetto. These trained fighters had brought along several hundred untrained survivors, among them a large proportion of women, many no longer young. Further hundreds were brought from other liquidated ghettos in the vicinity. All told, about one thousand Jews were collected and brought to the forests by the U. P. O. Of this amorphous, untrained mass, only four hundred could be used as fighters.

Four units, of a hundred men and women each, were formed. They were considered part of the Lithuanian Partisan Brigade which was connected with Moscow and the Red Army; but, despite this affiliation, they functioned as an all-Jewish group. Though they were subject to instructions from Russian headquarters, the Vilna partisans carried out all actions independently and led an autonomous existence. The Lithuanian partisan units, who were in the same forests, helped them neither with arms nor provisions. The best the

Jewish units could hope for in the way of assistance was to be permitted to operate without hostile interference from the Lithuanians.

Life in the forest was described to me by Rushka, one of the chief Vilna partisans — a dark, stockily built girl of twenty, with a frank, wholesome face.

"How did you stand the cold?" I wanted to know. The question bothered me because I remembered from recent experience how wretchedly uncomfortable even a modern New York apartment could become. The heating system had gone out of commission for several days. During that period an air of calamity pervaded the house. Tenants with babies fled to their mothers; those without such refuge sat huddled in thick coats drinking hot beverages. Husbands stayed as late as possible in their offices. Despite all these mitigating circumstances, only a few stalwart souls had been able to think of anything except of how to combat the cold.

In the woods, sub-zero temperatures were frequent. I knew that partisans dug caves in the earth, which they covered with sod and grass. When it was safe to come out, they could make open bonfires. That still did not explain the ability of hungry, ill-clad people to endure the rain, snow and blizzards of the long and bitter winter months.

"Cold! of course it was cold," Rushka told me. But it had been cold in the ghetto; and in the extermination centers only the crematoriums were warm. Rushka did not quote the melancholy Jacques, but she made it clear that, if there had been no enemy "but winter and rough weather," the lot of the partisan could have been borne by the young and strong. With the passage of time, ways of making the caves livable were devised.

This task was entrusted to the older women who remained at the base. Their job was to cook and nurse. The younger girls were among the combatants.

The chief problem was the lack of weapons. Every point of the partisan program — from the securing of food to attacks on the Germans — depended on the possession of arms. When the U. P. O. left the ghetto, they brought along the few rifles they had with them, but most of their ammunition had been exhausted in the ghetto. So poor were they in arms of any kind, that they were obliged at first to use wooden guns, pretending that these were the genuine article, in order to secure either food or ammunition from the local peasants.

The guerrilla fighter, perforce, had to live by a code of his own. The necessary means for carrying on the struggle with the enemy had to be requisitioned from the peasantry. To avoid betrayal the partisans were careful not to antagonize the village closest to the forest, and only distant points would be entered to induce the peasants to contribute according to their means.

Rushka assured me that the poorest peasants were never touched. Nor were the last heads of cattle of even a prosperous peasant taken. A certain morality was observed in the manner of levying tribute, but one cannot pretend that these seizures made for good will, particularly in the case of the Jewish partisans. The Lithuanian partisans could be sure of a warmer welcome, though even in their case the peasant's cupidity might exceed his patriotism.

The peasants were warned against betraying the partisans, and they knew that swift punishment would follow upon any reports to the Nazis; but, despite all precautions, seizures of food were always fraught with danger. On the way back there was the ever-present likelihood of ambush and many a time potatoes had to be paid for in blood.

The U. P. O. called their unit, *Nekomah*, the Hebrew word meaning vengeance. The woods afforded opportunities not available in the ghetto. There was scope for greater initiative, particularly because it was no longer necessary to take into account such considerations as those of collective responsibility and, consequently, collective penalty. Each partisan knew that his acts endangered only himself. While still in the ghetto, when German rule was at full might, the U. P. O had sent a squad to derail a troop train. Such operations had been undertaken in the heavy consciousness that discovery of the participants would involve the entire ghetto in acts of reprisal of the bloodiest kind. The train had been derailed at a point so distant from the ghetto that suspicion did not fall upon those responsible. However, as long as the U. P. O. operated from the ghetto it was constrained to consider the possible repercussions of any act, and to weigh the risk against the gain. In the forests, there was freedom. Everyone in the partisan units, whether originally a fighter or not, knew himself to be a member of a militant group whose purpose, as its name indicated, was vengeance. Fear for the fate of the old, the feeble, or the very young, no longer had to serve as a check on the character or range of the partisan exploits.

Obviously, the Jewish partisans were too few for open attacks on the Germans. But they developed great resourcefulness and efficiency in other forms of guerrilla warfare. First of all, they attacked communications. They destroyed telegraph wires and dynamited railroad tracks. This last was dignified in a special manner by the Russians. They called it *relsovaya voina*, "track war." The concerted dynamiting of railroad tracks at several points could be more efficiently carried out by guerrillas than by planes and bombs.

On one occasion the staff of the Lithuanian Partisan Brigade was ordered by Moscow to cut off Vilna from all train communication for several days. The various partisan units in the forest, including the Jewish one, were each assigned a special section of the track to dynamite in the course of the night. Rushka told me with what a glow of power and joy the Vilna partisans dynamited their sector and listened to the answering detonations in the distance.

"It was a wonderful feeling," Rushka said, and I knew she was thinking not only of the destruction of the enemy which the successful dynamiting of the track implied, but of the all too rare sense of fighting together in comradeship with the other partisans, instead of alone.

The partisans succeeded in dynamiting railroad trains so often that, towards the end of the war, the Germans stopped sending troop trains at night. Wreckage was too frequent.

Another important job of the partisans was known as *Rasviedka*; that is to say, the discovery of essential information through contacts with the peasants or through independent explorations. After it had been determined how many German trucks and autos had been seen in a vicinity, how they were armed and in which direction they were headed, it was possible to place an ambush. The attacks from ambush involved fairly large numbers, but the original investigations on which the ambush was based could be made by comparatively few. Women were particularly valuable in this activity, though they participated in all forms of fighting.

The girls among the partisans proved to be strong and brave. Rushka told me that each of them felt a special responsibility, because their behaviour would determine whether the corps as a whole would consider women trustworthy and competent guerrilla fighters. The girls would often outmarch the men because they were more afraid of admitting fatigue. On one occasion Rushka, whose mission was to dynamite a track, fell into a pond on the way. It was midwinter and her clothes froze. One of her companions on that expedition told me how they urged her to go back and thaw out, but she insisted on continuing; she went through with her job though incrusted in ice. And Rushka was not unique. Rushka herself described her companions in an address to the working women of Tel Aviv which merits quotation:

When I review the course of our work from beginning to end, I think constantly of young girls, close friends many of them, with some of whom I grew up and with some of whom I shared the days of danger. It was they who maintained the contact between the ghetto and the city; it was they who traveled from one city to another with false papers, though the penalty was instant death; it was they who brought the idea of resistance from city to city. It was they who carried on the technical work in the ghetto, and it was they who later took their place among the partisans. I can think of no part of the work with which the name of some girl comrade is not associated.

I want to tell you something about them. And I want to say one thing: they were not extraordinary women. They were not women with special training or qualifications. They were young girls who had grown up in the work and had risen to its demands.

And they were not exceptions. All were like that. We saw how human beings rose to the needed height in the daily execution of their tasks. And that was the hardest, the fact that the work had to be done every day, from day to day. That requires greater courage than a heroic exploit which lasts a few minutes. Those girls had to have a daily heroism — and they had it . . . .

From a fellow partisan this is high praise. Rushka told me something of these girls. During engagements with Nazi detachments in the forest they used a rifle or a hand grenade as skillfully as the men. But Rushka stressed particularly their readiness to return into the zone of danger. This was perhaps more valuable than any other quality. One girl made the journey from the woods into Vilna seventeen times. Her task was to find groups of Jews who might still be hiding in the ruins of the ghetto or in the "Aryan" part of the city, and to lead them into the woods. The nervous endurance and physical courage required in these expeditions was enormous, and a much smaller number of trips would have won her the right to a respite; but she went back and forth seventeen times, each time bringing with her people, information and medicines.

The work of *Nekomah* justified its name. The group was fortunate in its leadership. Abba Kovner, whom I met in Palestine, bears small outward resemblance to the conventional figure of a partisan. A slight young man, with the sensitive face of an artist, it was hard to visualize him as a guerrilla leader in the woods. But one had only to hear him speak to understand the motive power which had transformed this young man of the delicate hands, the large melancholy eyes, into a guerrilla leader.

The same transformation had taken place in more than one young Jewish intellectual.

Abba Kovner, and those associated with him, obviously had little innate predisposition for a life of grenade throwing, dynamiting and incessant military drill. I heard people say of him in astonishment after they met him for the first time: "He looks more like a *Yeshiva-bocher* (Talmud student) than a partisan." Or else they said: "He looks like one of those long-haired artists." This characterization had an element of truth, for Abba, in the days before the Vilna ghetto, had been a sculptor.

The Abba Kovners of the Jewish people, with their frail bodies and taut, hypersensitive faces, derived their stamina from sources other than those provided by well-exercised muscles and plenty of red corpuscles. It was not only the passion for vengeance which transformed these young men and women, apparently completely unfit by instinct and tradition for the lives they were leading, into people for whom a hand grenade and a bomb became as natural as a pen or a book. Not only hate of the Germans motivated them. A more creative force impelled them also — a passion for Jewish resurgence — and their dream, still obstinately held, of a just human society.

The correspondence and speeches of the ghetto fighters and partisans make curious reading. Their "orders" are probably unique among military documents in their peculiar fusion of ideological and tactical considerations. Every act, even if it involved only a few bunkers in a doomed ghetto, would be placed within the larger strategy of a world vision. Perhaps this sprang partly from the knowledge that for the Jewish fighter there could in any case be no successful military strategy. But fundamentally it came from the nature of the fighters themselves, from the stubborn idealism which had made them the champions of a cause since earliest youth, and still impelled them to unfurl its banner — in the literal sense — in the meanest and most brutal of circumstances.

3

"Jerusalem" in White Russia

❀

Some Jewish partisans were of a rougher cast — lusty fellows whose physical strength and sound constitutions, as well as shrewd intelligence, gave them the assurance to command men and wage guerrilla warfare. These were inclined to belittle the "bookmen," who could make fine speeches and issue fine proclamations. "Where were they when we were in the woods? Why did they become heroes so late?"

I have already given the answer. The organized Jewish youth remained in and returned to the ghettos out of choice and conviction, so as to be at the side of the hundreds of thousands who could not escape. But there were those who considered it wiser, and bolder, to take to the forests at the first opportunity and to organize a fighting unit. One of the best known of such guerrilla leaders was Anatol Belsky, commander of a partisan corps of 1,200 men in White Russia.

Belsky is a huge fellow. A more complete antithesis to the delicate, slightly-made Abba Kovner could hardly be contrived. And the difference is not only physical.

One could be reasonably certain that no theoretical discussions of right and wrong, of this or that social philosophy, had preceded his departure for the woods. Belsky had the ability and the will to fight, and he was going to kill Germans rather than be killed by them. The story of his unit casts a light on the activities of other Jewish groups of this kind who fought in the forests.

Belsky came from the Baranowicz region in western White Russia. In December, 1941, the Nazis murdered thousands of Jews in this section, among them Belsky's parents and his two brothers. They killed seven thousand people in two days. Belsky fled to the neighboring woods with his two younger brothers. Though he was acting as an individual, having no connection with any organization, he was not content merely to be a "woodman," a person who ekes out an existence in the woods by virtue of his wits and his superior vigor. He determined to organize a guerrilla band which would rescue Jews from the ghetto of Novogrudek and which would fight the Germans.

Through a Christian friend, who had been brought up in the same village, Belsky sent a message to a cousin in the ghetto. He quoted it to me verbatim four years later in Tel Aviv. He had written: "Organize as many friends and acquaintances as possible. Come to me in the woods. I wait for you. You must know the slaughter is not the first nor the last. The German has decided to destroy the Jews and he will do it. So come to the woods. I wait."

It is interesting to observe that the appeal is not to "comrades," to fellow believers in some idea, but to "friends and acquaintances." And there is a minimum of literary adornment.

Eight young men came in answer. In the course of some weeks, a few other recruits dribbled in, among them some women and children. By August, 1941, there were thirty people in the group, of whom only eleven were fighters. A meeting was held at which Belsky was elected "commander."

People continued to come in twos and threes. The "division" grew slowly. The winter months passed in acquiring arms and training. No acts of any kind were undertaken because the men were too few and ill-equipped. By spring, however, Belsky had a hundred men under him. Within two years his corps numbered 1,200 people, of whom 600 were fighters and 600 were women, children and men unable to fight, who worked at the base.

While his division was gradually growing in size, Belsky had to come to terms with the local peasants and with the Russian partisans who were also in these woods. He had gotten arms in the usual ways. No military headquarters was sending him supplies by airplane or parachute. He had to rely first on gifts smuggled out of the ghetto, and then on tribute. Food was an equally urgent problem. Nothing could be grown in the forests in the winter months, and there was no money with which to pay for all that was needed. What could not be purchased had to be requisitioned.

The villagers accused Belsky's unit of pillaging and complained to the Russian partisans whose needs they supplied as a matter of course. The Russians passed a sentence of death on Belsky's men.

The situation became untenable. It was impossible to have mortal foes in the town and the forests in addition to fighting the Germans. Belsky managed to meet the commander of the Russian partisans and appealed to his Bolshevik conscience.

"We are both fighting the Germans," he said. "We must explain to the people what a partisan is. You are not a true Bolshevik if you think of me as a Jew. We both come from Russia. Let us work together and fight together."

The White Russians, like the Poles and Ukrainians, had been heavily infected with anti-Semitic propaganda, but Belsky's appeal apparently had an effect. The Russian partisan and the Jewish one agreed to hold weekly meetings to coordinate activities. They also agreed to send stray Jews in the forest to Belsky, whereas Russians would be directed to the Russian.

To obtain greater cooperation from the peasants they went together to the local villages and made speeches clarifying the situation. Belsky would assure the peasants that, though the Germans were near Moscow, they would eventually be destroyed "like Napoleon." And he would conclude his exhortation with the warning: "Therefore, peasants, don't betray us to the police. Remember, peasants, all people who fight the Germans with guns are partisans."

To what extent these orations were instrumental in securing the friendship of the peasants is uncertain. What was probably equally effective were the stories of Belsky's prowess which began to circulate. The fate of notorious traitors, who were punished by Belsky's squads, was widely bruited about and acted as a deterrent of further betrayals.

Belsky told me of an episode which was characteristic of many. One peasant in the nearby town of Belkiewicz had the reputation of betraying partisans, particularly

Jewish ones. Belsky made short work of him. With fifteen well-armed partisans, he surrounded the peasant's farm. When they entered, the peasant failed to recognize them as Jews and, in giving an account of his activities, boasted that he had helped rid the land of many Jews: *Zhivem, zhidov boyem* (We live and beat Jews).

To ingratiate himself he gave a graphic description of how he had caught a Jewish woman and her two children and had handed them over to the Germans.

Belsky demanded: "Have you no heart?"

The peasant shrugged his shoulders: "What do you want, *pan*? Hitler said we must kill them."

At this point, the partisans made themselves known and shot not only the peasant but his sons who had been his assistants. On the bodies they deposited notes declaring: "All dogs who serve the Germans will get such a death."

Not a pretty story, but the effect was salutary. The sport of trapping Jews and betraying them became less popular among the peasants. And it must be admitted that Belsky showed no hesitation in refreshing the peasants' memories whenever new evidence of treason was discovered. Neither Belsky nor his men were squeamish about the nature of the penalties they inflicted.

Accident also helped to increase the prestige of Belsky's unit. In the fall of 1942, the Germans seized the local harvest. They made preparations to thresh the wheat and send bread to the front. Before this could be carried out, Belsky's men set fire to the fields. At midnight flames broke out illuminating the entire landscape. It happened that Russian airplanes, flying on a mission East, saw the burning fields and decided to assist the good work. They dropped a few bombs. This coincidence created a tremendous impression. The peasants and the local authorities began to believe that Belsky had contacts with the Eastern front. Rumors arose that he had a large army secreted somewhere in the woods. A reward of 10,000 marks was set on his head.

As Belsky's reputation grew, his numbers were swelled by stray groups of escaped Jews who, without organization and authority, were running the danger of degenerating into marauding bands, interested merely in saving their own lives without taking part in fighting the Nazis. Hiding in bunkers in the forest, from which they issued only to seize food, these men were becoming a demoralized and demoralizing element. Whenever Belsky would learn of such groups, either from the complaints of Russian partisans or from the reports of his own men, he would make it his business to persuade them to join his corps.

Belsky's independent career lasted till March, 1943. Up to this time, his partisans destroyed telephone connections, dynamited railroads and, upon their own initiative, laid ambushes for the Germans. In the spring of 1943, the Russian command sent a general to unite the partisan movement in western White Russia. The various divisions were made units of regional brigades which operated under the command of the Soviets. The first task of the new brigades was to cooperate in building aerodromes which Russian planes could use for the purpose of bringing arms and of removing the wounded.

By the fall of 1943, Belsky's division numbered over a thousand men, women and children. Life in the woods without adequate shelter was becoming more and more difficult as the size of the groups increased. Nor could such numbers continue to live by foraging. It was decided to form an organized community in the woods. A census of the division was taken, with the skills and previous training of each member noted. Lists of specialists were drawn up — so many carpenters, shoemakers, tailors, doctors, nurses, etc. A camp was built consisting of many barracks. Work was allotted. A school was established for the children. An infirmary was equipped with the modest means available. Those who were not active fighters ran various enterprises to make the division less dependent on the outside. The camp had its own bakery and manufactured its own soap. So complete was this "town" in the woods that the Russian partisans, half-mockingly and half-admiringly, named it "Jerusalem." The children would occasionally give plays to which all the partisans of the region would be invited. Seeing a play in "Jerusalem," became one of the forest pastimes.

I saw the maps of the "town" in Tel Aviv. With obvious and forgivable pride, Belsky showed me the barracks where the school had been housed, the "factories," and the "hospital." To this shelter, refugees from more distant ghettos began to filter. Jews from Novogrudek sent a message to Belsky begging to be taken out. He answered that this was impossible. They had to escape by their own means. A group of over a hundred dug a tunnel and got out. Forty were killed in the course of the escape, but the rest joined Belsky. He had built a "Jerusalem" in the forests of White Russia in a truer sense than those who had given the nickname had realized.

The community existed in the woods for an additional

year. When the Russian armies began driving the Germans back, the partisans would catch groups of Germans fleeing through the forests. Belsky's men were no tenderer with them than with treacherous peasants. There was one particularly happy moment in the history of the corps, when they gave battle to a group of retreating Germans and the Germans surrendered to the Jewish partisans.

When the Soviet tanks rolled into White Russia, the partisans joined the Red Army. Guerrilla warfare was over. It had been a good fight, in which Belsky's men had shot over a thousand Germans and had carried out countless acts of sabotage. And, as Jews, they had had the special satisfaction of killing the enemy instead of being helplessly murdered.

There were still other Jewish partisan groups in the forests of Eastern Europe. One guerrilla band, calling itself *Bar Kochba*, after the leader of the Jewish rebellion against the Romans, operated for months near Hrubiecer, Poland. Another group was active in the Lublin district. So numerous were these bands, harrying the rear of the German armies in occupied Poland and pursuing them in retreat, that the *Westphälische Zeitung* was forced to admit that the Jewish guerrilla bands were becoming a "danger to the security of the Nazis" because of the serious damage they succeeded in inflicting.

It must be stressed again that, in addition to forming independent Jewish units, many Jews joined the Russian and Polish partisans. When the liquidation of the Kovno ghetto started, united youth groups representing all political parties marched out of the ghetto to join the Russians in the woods. On their way, they were attacked by the Lithuanian police and the majority were captured. A small number, however, managed to contact Soviet guerrillas between Vilna and Minsk. Russian correspondents writing in *Izvestia* and other Russian journals have testified to the fierce zeal of the Jewish partisans who joined Soviet units. But an account of their activities does not belong in a discussion of independent Jewish resistance movements any more than would a report of the exploits of Jews in the Allied armies.

The Jewish partisans who fought under their own flag and with their own insignia, whether they called themselves *Nekomah*, or *Bar Kochba*, or *Machnoth Ghetto*, were like no other fighters the modern world had seen. If they wanted their women and children to live, they had to take them with them into the open forests. They had to start their battle not after a flight from a conquered but friendly town, but after having been immured in a ghetto which could offer nothing but a dungeon shelter while waiting for the summons to the slaughter-house. Even in the wild retreat of the woods, beside a camp-fire or on a forest path, they had to worry about such importations from civilization as anti-Semitism — the anti-Semitism of Poles, Lithuanians, Ukrainians and White Russians. But they did not lose heart. Many a partisan and ghetto fighter has told me that he knew no real discouragement till after the peace. The tension of danger, the will to avenge, the even more stubborn will to believe in a decent future, had sustained hope. Something, some one, would survive, and the "something" was more important than the "some one."

The Vilna partisans had a song which like most songs of this kind has little intrinsic merit as poetry, but illuminates the state of mind from which it sprang. It begins, *Sag nit az du gehst dem letzen weg* ("Do not say that this road is your last"), and each stanza concludes with the assurance:

> The longed-for hour will come —
> Oh, never fear;
> Our tread drums forth the tidings:
> We are here!

The song concludes:

> We wrote this song in blood for all to sing;
> It's not a gay bird's carol on the wing.
> But amid crashing walls and fiercely flaming
>   brands
> We sang it, holding grenades in our hands.

The triumphant "We are here!" of the refrain is a new note in the martyrology of the past decade. When Rushka sang the song for me in Tel Aviv, the imagery did not seem trite nor the lines lumbering — though both criticisms could with justice be made. And I know that no words could have seemed truer or more powerful to Rushka, for she herself had hummed the melody with "grenades in her hand," and she and her comrades had themselves experienced the great exultation of being able to march bearing the tidings: "We are here!"

The ghetto fighters and the partisans were really one. The surviving fighters became the guerrillas. The bunker under the ghetto house became the dug-out in the woods. Those who mounted the last barricades and those who lived to believe that their road was not the "last" were of the same family. Both answered "present" when the call came, and both could say with stern conviction: "We are here."

There was one thing more that the Jewish partisans told me. In the woods, the Poles, the Russians and the Lithuanians dreamt of the village to which they would return. They had a home, a ruined home perhaps, but nevertheless a friendly hearth where a fire could be relit among the ashes. The Jewish partisans knew, while roaming the forests, that the only ashes that awaited them were those of the crematoriums. And if they had any illusions as to the welcome they would receive in Lydda, or Novogrudek, or Vilna, or Warsaw, they quickly learned the truth. That is why I found them in Palestine, saying again, "We are here!" with the same resolution but in a different sense.

VI. In Western Europe

1

In Holland It Was Different

◎

"IT is the same story," one is tempted to say of Jewish resistance in Western Europe. Again the endless struggle against multiplying odds, and perhaps a handful saved when the last count is made. This time the borders to be crossed lead to Spain, Portugal or Switzerland instead of to the shores of the Black Sea or the Mediterranean. Here the man and woman who plot salvation sit in Geneva and Lisbon, rather than in Istanbul, though steady contact between the several rescue centers is maintained, no matter how tenuously.

In Western Europe, Jewish agencies — the officials of the Joint Distribution Committee, the *shlichim* from Palestine — paralleled the rescue activities radiating into Eastern Europe from the secret office in Turkey. Proceeding from the opposite direction, Geneva sent couriers to and received couriers from Poland, Slovakia and Croatia. Information reaching Switzerland could then be transmitted through secret channels in France to neutral Lisbon. If luck had been with the messengers and they had managed to escape the traps of the Gestapo and of Vichy, reports could then reach the Western World from Portugal. The processes were reciprocal and repetitive; the underground channels crossed and crisscrossed each other. But each center of rescue and resistance had its specific as well as parallel function. Lisbon was an outpost on the Atlantic. Geneva was an asylum of refuge in the heart of Hitler Europe. Istanbul was a lighthouse on the Bosphorus directing escape from Eastern Europe and guiding men and ships to Palestine.

The same story, and yet not the same — for in Western Europe it is a shade less somber. Not that appreciably more were saved. The percentage of destruction reaches the same astronomic figures, but a human note sounds occasionally in the cacophony of evil. The accent of Christian compassion is heard. In the Scandinavian countries, in France, in Belgium, in Holland, the Jewish underground received help from non-Jews. In Eastern Europe, too, there had been individuals who had risked danger and death for the sake of bringing aid to the martyred Jews in their midst, but these had been isolated instances whose exceptional nature only served to underscore the indifference or enmity of the majority.

In Holland in particular, Jews found fellow fighters among their Christian neighbors. The Dutch underground took an active part in protecting the Jews of Holland. Some of its leading figures sacrificed themselves to save Jewish lives and human honor. The veteran Dutch socialist leader, Professor Sam de Wolff, the old friend of Karl Kautsky and Rosa Luxemburg, told me in Jerusalem how the longshoremen of Amsterdam rushed to the defense of the Jewish quarter when the Nazis began their attacks. The young members of *Hechalutz Holland*, whom I met at Dahlia and Chubeza spoke of their Christian comrades, who had fought with them in Holland and who had helped them to reach Palestine, with a love and abiding gratitude which I heard lavished on no other European country.

It was therefore no accident that the Christian representatives of the anti-fascist underground in Europe whom I met in Palestine should have been two Dutch women, one Catholic and the other Protestant. Throughout the Nazi occupation they had devoted themselves to rescuing Jewish children by hiding them with Christian families. Two sweet-faced, middle-aged women, staid of manner and appearance, they looked like school-marms rather than revolutionaries. But this deceptively mild-looking pair had been among the bravest fighters of the Dutch underground. As devout Christians, impelled by a deep religious conviction, they had felt called to save Jewish children. Frau Molen and Frau Nolte had been imprisoned by the Nazis and released. They spoke of that jail sentence, which could so easily have ended in front of a firing squad, with obvious relish. But the words, "When I was in jail," sounded so strange on their lips, that even the Nazis must have been inclined to give them the benefit of the doubt. At any rate, they had been released for lack of evidence. After the war, they went to Palestine to see for themselves how some of the children whose lives they had saved were faring there.

In Denmark, too, the population had rallied in defense of its Jewish citizens. But of all the countries mercilessly oppressed by the German conqueror, it was apparently Holland whose record of courage and humanity was brightest.

Because of the smallness of the country, and the completeness and swiftness of the Nazi occupation, conspiratorial work in Holland encountered obstacles of a special kind. The neatness of the Dutch, the care with which records had been kept, the trim little houses, all of them in apple-pie order, the flat landscape, were unfavorable factors for the underground. The more disorganized the terrain, the greater the opportunities for confusing the enemy. The accuracy of Dutch records made the issuance of false papers, the forging of documents, more difficult than in countries where government bureaus had functioned less punctiliously. The check-up on suspects was simpler. Since conspiracy involves concealment, change of identity and the possession of documents which cannot stand too close scrutiny, one can see how, paradoxically, Dutch virtues complicated the task of the underground.

Other Dutch virtues, however, were all to the credit side of the fight. A passion for independence, a spirit of compassion, a love of freedom — these were of even greater worth than a slipshod bureau of vital statistics and readily accessible hiding-places. Small, friendly cottages, with their well-kept, blooming plots of flowers, were not the best places for bunkers or tunnels. That increased the value of Dutch cooperation.

The lack of mountains and thick forests further diminished the possibilities of resistance and escape. These physical features must be borne in mind because they served to determine the forms which Jewish resistance could take. Partisan activities require wooded or mountain country, as the experience of Poland, Yugoslavia, Russia and the French Maquis, who were most active in mountain passes, indicates. The types of resistance adapted to a trim little land like Holland, which lay

the Jews' luggage . . . . On the tunnel wall was a large sign: "Till we meet again." And we even saw a Christian teacher weeping like a child.

As Nazi repressive measures increased, the Christian Church, Protestant and Catholic alike, continued its exhortations to its flocks and urged resistance to the anti-Jewish decrees. A pastoral letter read:

> We know what conflicts of conscience result for those concerned. In order, therefore, to eliminate all doubts and uncertainties that you may have in this respect, we hereby declare most explicitly that no compromise in this domain of conscience is allowed; and, should refusal of collaboration cause sacrifices to you, then remain steadfast in the certainty that you are fulfilling your duty towards God and man.

The Dutch took the injunctions of the clergy seriously. These were not merely Sunday pronouncements, to be heard respectfully in church and then forgotten in the work-a-day week. They knew that each clergyman who spoke boldly from his pulpit did so at deadly risk to himself. The truly Christian sentiments they heard were not being delivered at a discreet distance from the Nazis. The sinner, as well as the sin, was being challenged. And the congregation proved worthy of the teachers. Some 20,000 Dutch Christians were deported to concentration camps because of their opposition to the Nazi racial decrees. The two Dutch women whom I met in Palestine were examples of the spirit which such a Church could arouse in its disciples.

Religious and secular forces met in the Dutch resistance. How much weight the organized movement attached to the rescue of Nazi victims may be judged from the fact that the first point of the program of the Dutch underground read:

> It is the duty of each Dutchman morally and materially to help his compatriots — old or young, male or female, Jew or non-Jew — who are suffering as a result of German persecution.

The staunch fiber of the Dutch can be measured by this insistence.

2

Rescue Is Resistance

❀

THE Dutch had understood that a genuine resistance to the Germans demanded, first of all, defiance of the Nazis' most characteristic decrees. "Aryans" who wore the badge with the Star of David were not only expressing sympathy with the persecuted but expressing their opposition to the whole Nazi regime. Through every act of rescue, they were fighting the enemy as well as helping the victim.

Jewish resistance, too, with the exception of such open conflict as took place in Amsterdam, and which was swiftly and inevitably quelled despite the help of the Dutch workers and the general strike, had to concentrate chiefly on rescue. This meant, not only defying the Nazis, but combatting the influence of the Jewish council which in Amsterdam played the same unenviable role that it had played in Poland. The Jewish council urged Jews to report meekly for deportation to supposed "work centers" in the east. The Jewish underground had the counter-task of explaining the true meaning of the deportations and of exhorting the population to disobey the German orders. Such urging, however, would have been useless if there had not existed an organized effort to provide means of escape from the Germans.

The difficulties of concealment in Holland proper have already been pointed out. Some children of "Aryan" appearance could be hidden with Christians who accepted them as their own. This was not only extremely dangerous, involving the child and the family in the daily risk of discovery, but insufficient. Means of rescuing adults and children who had not been sheltered by Dutch families had to be found.

There were some attempts to lead a "bunker" existance even in Holland. A vivid description of one of these attempts was written by a member of *Hechalutz* who managed to reach Palestine:

> The expanses of the Netherlands are endless. The monotony of the landscape depresses the stranger and makes him feel lonely. It is difficult to find shelter in a country with no hills or deep forests. To hide here one must indeed be inventive, but necessity is the mother of invention.
>
> Our *schuilplaats* (hiding place) lay deep under the surface of the earth. It was an underground passage so cunningly concealed that no one could find it, though it was in the immediate neighborhood of human dwellings. It was twenty meters long, one and a half meters wide, and one meter high. At its end there was a sort of "landing" of the same width, three meters long and one and a half meters high. Though there, too, one was not able to stand up straight, one could at least remain seated on a box without having to stoop. That "landing" was to become our "living-room," while the rest of the passage was an ideal place for bedrooms.

When the Nazis started deporting Jews to Poland, we decided to try to save ourselves, come what might. All of us tried to find some hiding-place. The situation was desperate. We realized full well that deportation to Poland meant death. A few of us were offered this particular underground passage. We were told that, though it was not ideal, it was safe from detection. When we first entered it, it was with heavy hearts. We did not delude ourselves. We realized that the war would last at least two more years and that, if we wanted to survive, we would have to spend all that time here, underground, in this dark and dirty cave. We decided that it was worth it. It would be better than Poland. Having made the decision, we stuck to it for two whole years before our escape. There are two things which enable a man to hold out in any condition — dire necessity and a firm will. In our situation both were present.

Knowing that we were due for a long stay, we lost no time in cleaning the place up. We worked at night, creeping along on hands and knees, scooping up the dirt by the light of a stinking kerosene lamp. Here and there the walls needed reinforcing, so on moonless nights we used to bring stones from outside, carrying them to the entrace of the cave, where we lowered them into the passage and put them into position. All this had to be done noiselessly. The slightest sound was dangerous. Our next big job was to bring in an electric cable from the main nearby. It was a great moment for us when light dispersed our darkness. Then, bit by bit, we started furnishing our cave with straw mattresses, blankets and crockery, mats and books. We installed a stove for the winter and brought in a rather big store of food. Our cave had become quite habitable, and we started taking pride in what had been achieved.

Thus we entered upon our life in our voluntary prison — a prison locked from inside. For two whole years it meant being cut off from life, from sunlight, from physical exercise. But the atmosphere outside was becoming increasingly tense, and our underground passage, despite all its deficiencies, held out hopes of eventual freedom. The shelter was deep beneath the surface of the earth, but it could not be deep enough. All the sounds of the outer world were deadened by walls five meters thick. During the first few days I slept like a log, exhaused by the tension of the days prior to my arrival. Then the need arose to fix some kind of timetable. In the morning we got up and prepared coffee for breakfast on the electric heater. After breakfast the study of languages began — Hebrew, French, English.

At noon sharp, the event of the day came when three knocks were heard. The trap door opened and daylight fell into the entrance of the cave. Our protector was bringing us lunch and food for the rest of the day. We then held a short conversation, the only conversation in twenty-four hours:

"What is the news?"

"How do you feel down there?"

"Cheerio!"

Then the door was closed again. In the afternoon the study of languages was resumed, and later there was reading time. We did a lot of reading in those days. I had the opportunity to make up for what I had missed during the previous years. I made a thorough study of classic German literature and philosophy, reading Goethe, Schiller and Lessing. Sometimes, when it seemed safe enough, I ventured to leave my hiding-place and take an hour's walk around our shelter to get a breath of fresh air. It was a very risky thing to do.

Our protector! That is a story which cannot yet be told. It is too early and too dangerous. He offered us safety in the offhand way which was characteristic of him. "I have known you long enough, and I do not want to let you go," he said simply, though he realized perfectly well that concentration camp, torture and death would be his fate if he were found out. Yet he refused to consider the risk or accept our gratitude. "It's my duty," he said, and there the matter ended. There were thousands of people like him in the Netherlands. They risked their lives and helped us as much as they could. Intellectuals and students, workers and peasants — you can find them in all classes. I do not want to eulogize them, for they do not like high-sounding words. We are unable to convey our gratitude to them, for they do not want it. What they have done cannot be rewarded with mere thanks. We honor them as they deserve, and we honor the nation to which they belong.

One evening, at an unusual hour, there came a knock at the door. A comrade of *Hechalutz* had arrived with an important message.

"What news do you bring me?" I asked.

"I bring you liberty," he said.

The Jewish underground had to find such *Verschwindungsplätzer* (places for disappearance) and then to maintain the contact between those who lived "legally" in the open and those who were in concealment. Food had to be brought; documents had to be prepared for the moment when it might be possible to escape from the hiding place and to attempt crossing the frontier. The *Verschwindungsplatz* was one of the ways of foiling the *Vernichtungslager* (extermination camp) of the Germans. Endless ingenuity and courage were required to make it possible for those who had "disappeared" to exist.

A consecrated band of young people devoted themselves to the task of defeating the Germans of their prime purpose. The chief figures among these were the Jew Shushu and the Christian Joop.

In Palestine, whenever I met the handsome, sturdy

281

young Jews from Holland, the talk would eventually turn to Shushu and Joop. Whether on a haywagon driven by a Dutch boy who looked as if he had stepped out of an advertisement featuring Dutch windmills, or sitting in a field in Chubeza, I would hear of the Jewish and the Christian hero of the Jewish underground.

Shushu, whose real name was Joachim Simon, had fled to Holland from Germany in 1938. Despite his youth — he was still in his teens — he soon became a leader of *Hechalutz* in Amsterdam. At the same time he was closely affiliated with the Dutch labor movement.

Professor de Wolff remembered his first meeting with him. The old Dutch socialist leader had been enormously impressed by the boy's brilliance and scholarship and the variety of his interests, which ranged from an intensive study of Hebrew, history and economics to such remoter subjects as higher mathematics and music. But most of all he had been moved by the force of the young man's personality.

The road for Shushu was set. As soon as the Nazis occupied Holland, he joined the Dutch underground through his ties with socialist circles. But as the full Nazi anti-Jewish program went into effect, he determined that his special task should be to organize Jewish resistance. Under his leadership the work of the Jewish underground developed — always with the cooperation of the Dutch labor movement.

The boys and girls who had been Shushu's intimate associates and who had accepted his authority even though he was no older than they, tried to describe the young man who had been their leader. Like Professor de Wolff, they spoke of his extraordinary intellectual gifts, but most of all they dwelt on other qualities:

despite the fact that he suffered from asthma, he had great physical energy; he was religiously devoted to the work he had chosen, and would go without food, sleep or rest for long periods of time. To save a few cents of the scant funds at the group's disposal, he would walk for miles rather than take a trolley in the cold Dutch winter. In his friends' recital, this disdained trolley became a curiously vivid symbol of Shushu's ascetic idealism.

At first the movement concentrated on finding hiding places, particularly for children. But as the situation deteriorated, it became clear that the creation of *Verschwindungsplätzer* would have to be supplemented by more radical measures. Ways of reaching France and Switzerland had already been established. Shushu and his wife, Adina, had been smuggling children into Switzerland for some time with the assistance of the rescue office in Geneva. Shushu's imagination, however, was fired by the notion of organizing escape to such neutral centers as Sweden and Spain, since these promised the possibility of final departure from Europe. The notion of Spain was particularly attractive because a neutral country on the Mediterranean offered hope of eventual emigration to Palestine.

Shushu was of marked Semitic appearance. The problem of posing as a non-Jew was complicated for him not only by the danger of the physical examination, which threatened every suspected Jewish male, but by coloring and features which might go unnoticed in France but would arouse doubts among Nazi police in Belgium or Holland. Nevertheless, he secured false "Aryan" papers and went to France to establish contact with the Jewish underground there. Finally, he evolved a plan for leading Jews from Holland to the Spanish border and crossing the Pyrenees. He went back and forth three times with a group that he personally led. On the homeward lap of the third expedition, as he attempted to cross the Belgian border back into Holland, he was caught by the Gestapo. While imprisoned by the Nazis, in January, 1943, he committed suicide by slashing his veins; he was afraid that he might weaken under torture and reveal the names of his associates.

In the meantime, Adina, the young bride from whom he had been separated most of the time because of his activities, had made her way into Switzerland with a group of children whom she was conducting. She wrote from Switzerland:

> We (Shushu and Adina) spent a few weeks together and now we are again separated. To my sorrow, nothing else is possible. Shushu travels a great deal, and I try to help him from here.

A few weeks later she received from Holland news of Shushu's death. A friend broke the news:

> I want to take your hand, because we must inform you of a great blow, the greatest blow that we could have received. Your comrade is no longer among the living.
>
> I can assure you that if he suffered, it was not for long. He chose death freely. We will soon let you know whatever we know about this. Adina, we all think of you now, but you must think of us also, what a misfortune this is for us. I would like to write a great deal, but each word obscures the reality. I am not yet strong enough to be able to see the misfortune as *he* would have seen it. Now I know only one thing: I have never met such a person . . . I know that nothing was taken from him; he could not be injured. . . he was the purest man that I have known. He wanted

to do this last deed. He would not return to Holland before the others had left. He had many opportunities, but for him such a course was out of the question. He did not want to run away from the last sacrifice. He could not do otherwise because he was forged of a single piece of steel — a single piece.

One gets a notion of the Spartan code of these young people, of the deliberate disdain of personal happiness, from the imperious request to the young wife that she think of her comrades in the midst of her own sorrow.

Shushu had been associated in his work with a Christian, Joop Westerwell, who assumed the leadership of the rescue action after the death of Shushu. Joop was a Christian anarchist and a pacifist. Though the son of a pastor, he had apparently embarked early on an unconventional career. In his youth he had gone as a teacher to the Netherlands East Indies, where he agitated against the exploitation of the natives. He urged the Chinese to rebel against colonial oppression. In addition he refused to serve in the army because he was an anti-militarist. It is therefore not surprising to learn that he was imprisoned several times.

After six years in the Indies he returned to Holland where he established a Montessori school. He was interested in modern pedagogy and conducted progressive educational experiments. Through one of the Jewish leaders in his school, he became acquainted with Shushu. By this time Joop was a man past forty with a family of four children, but neither age nor family obligations had dampened his crusading spirit. He made the cause of the Jews his own. A number of his teachers and followers became involved in the work of hiding Jewish children.

After Shushu's death, Joop undertook to organize the escape of Jews into Spain. A survivor of one of these journeys has given an account of the farewell words spoken by Joop at the foot of the Pyrenees:

> Cross this difficult road successfully and build your homeland, a homeland for the whole Jewish people. But do not forget that you are bound to all humanity, something which you perhaps learned in Holland. Do not forget us, your non-Jewish comrades.

On one of these expeditions, Joop Westerweel was caught by the Gestapo. A letter from his wife which reached Palestine in June, 1945, told of his end:

> How good to get your letter, to know that so many of you reached Palestine. Joop would have found it wonderful if he had known it. He was shot in August. He was the mainstay of the nine others who had worked with him. You did not know him so well, but you can imagine what his loss means to me ...
>
> On September 6, I was sent to Ravensbruck. I shall not write about the tortures. Of one transport of 750 women, only 250 survived. We were freed by the Red Cross and are now in Sweden.
>
> In September I shall be back in Holland; but what is my house to me? I have heard nothing of my children since August, 1944. Write me about Palestine; I am interested in your experiences.

Such is the letter of the Christian wife of the Christian Joop.

The young girl who spoke to me in Dahlia said to me of Joop and Shushu: "They gave us a sense of dignity so that now we can live." And she added: "*How* we live is more important than *that* we live."

The importance of the rescue action lay not only

in the actual salvation of thousands. It consisted also in the heightened morale of the individuals who had participated in it. They had not submitted passively to the decrees of the Nazis. They had not reported for "work" as the Jewish council had recommended. They had not fled when in a position to do so. On the contrary, from 1940, the date of the Nazi invasion, till the day of liberation they had fought the German assassins with every available means. Each Jewish child smuggled over the Alps into Switzerland, each adult led across the Pyrenees, each person hidden and helped at daily peril, represented a victory over the Germans in which the risks were as great as in open battle.

Often a child who had been hidden for a year or two would emerge to go into underground work. One beautiful, brown-eyed girl of twenty, who had been an active worker in the Jewish underground both in Holland and France, told me how Joop had placed her originally with a poor Dutch working-class family. She spent eight months hidden in the house without venturing out. When she walked past the window of the living-room, she would have to bend low for fear that some less sympathetic neighbor might see her. (There was, however, one serious drawback — the family kept trying to convert her to Christianity. Had Meta been younger, the attempt would probably have been successful. Many small Jewish children were converted by well-meaning Christian families who sheltered them, not only in Holland, but throughout Europe.) Meta was then sixteen years old; she had been a member of *Hechalutz*, and she felt that she could not remain in a *Verschwindungsplatz* indefinitely. Through her comrades, she received "Aryan" papers and went to France as a Dutch worker.

A number of young Dutch Jews managed to get into France by securing certificates as Dutch workers who were prepared to work for the German forces of occupation. By getting employment with the Wehrmacht and the Gestapo, they were enabled to be of great value in the French underground. Frenchmen would have been suspected, but these Dutch "Christians" were apparently trustworthy. Of course, fresh-cheeked young girls of what seemed to the Nazis to be unquestionable "Aryan" appearance were ideal candidates.

Meta worked as a typist with the Gestapo in Paris. In this capacity, she not only had occasional access to valuable information, but she could secure blank forms for documents that were needed by those who had to pose as "Aryans." Once the essential document, as well as the appropriate official stamps, had been secured, it was possible to make accurate imitations on the underground printing presses. Meta showed me some of the identification cards and travel and residence permits that had been successfully forged in Paris. She showed them proudly, as one shows trophies. These were her "souvenirs" — brought from her combat area.

It had been a dangerous service. Of *Hechalutz Holland*, working in Holland and France, only a few survived. One after another the young men and women were captured, as Shushu and Joop were. The final blow came in Paris, when the majority of the group were caught shortly before the liberation. Meta's eyes filled with tears as she spoke of them. She showed me also a letter from a Dutchman — the Christian friend of her young husband, who had been among those executed. The Dutch comrade had written to her in Palestine:

You know that I would like to devote most of my energy to working among the people of my best friends. You know that I would rather be a street-sweeper in the service of the good, than the most important personage in the service of the bad.

Such letters, like the letter of Joop's wife, explain why the only group of Jewish survivors who had no words save of gratitude for the non-Jews among whom they had lived, were those who had come from Holland. There was no trace of the intense bitterness, the fierce disillusionment of the Jews of Poland and the Balkans. Even the Jews of France had tasted the misery of persecution at the hands of the French collaborators. But Holland had been singularly pure.

One gets an idea of the love inspired by Holland from an appeal which was published in the *Davar*, the Labor daily of Palestine, shortly before the end of the war. This appeal, signed by a number of Dutch Jews who had escaped to Palestine, among them old Professor de Wolff, urged young Palestinians, who had received their agricultural training (*Hachsharah*) in Holland, to return to Holland to aid in the Dutch underground, now that large-scale resistance was becoming possible.

The victory came shortly after this call was published, so that it is impossible to state how it was answered. But the mere fact that such an appeal could have been made by the leading figures of Jewish resistance in Holland, is evidence enough of how the valiant little land of the tulip-beds and dykes was remembered by the Jews who had struggled there. The words of Joop at the foot of the Pyrenees — "remember us, your non-Jewish comrades" — would not be readily forgotten.

Such words had been all too rare in the experience of Jews during the Hitler decade.

The sense of isolation from the rest of mankind, which is perhaps the chief scar on the souls of the Jewish survivors, is not to be observed among the young people who came from Holland. I can think of no greater tribute to the Dutch people. The survivors from Holland are less tragic, because less lonely, figures than those who came out of Eastern Europe. Their physical sufferings were as great; their families and friends had also been murdered by the Germans; but they had been enabled to feel that their suffering had one source — the infamy of the Nazi. Holland was a Christian oasis in heathenized Europe, and from its spring of charity Jewish hearts drank deep.

3

France — Service des Jeunes

FRANCE, the classic land of freedom and enlightenment, held many unexpected shadows for its Jewish citizens. French collaborationism consisted of more than lip-service to the Nazi overlord. The failure of the great democratic tradition of France to stem the anti-Semitic tide set in motion by the Germans was a blow as sharp as grosser failures in Eastern Europe. Many sectors of the French population strove to protect the Jews in their midst, but enough French fascists united with the Nazis in hunting down "non-Aryans" to make the lights of *La Cité Lumière* seem extinct rather than extinguished.

As a French underground movement began to develop, however, Jewish as well as Christian morale improved. Opportunities for Jewish resistance began to present themselves. Jews joined French units of the Maquis and later formed autonomous Jewish units which were eventually recognized as part of the F. F. I. (Interior French Forces).

The formation of Jewish Maquis groups came after a preliminary stage which consisted chiefly of underground rescue. The earliest forms of resistance followed the pattern noted in other parts of Europe. The first and most immediate form of foiling the enemy was to prevent the seizure of the intended victims — particularly children. From the occupied zone to the unoccupied zone, the contraband crossing of borders into Spain, Italy and Switzerland, the flight either to the shores of the Mediterranean or to the sanctuary of neutral Switzerland — all this went on in France, as in Holland and in the Balkans.

When France collapsed, in June, 1940, there were close to 350,000 Jews within its borders, including about 80,000 refugees who had fled to France after the rise of Hitler. By 1945, it is estimated that some 180,000 Jews remained. To destroy nearly half the Jewish population of France, the Germans used their familiar techniques, including the sardonic attempt to secure the cooperation of the victims. Certain psychological factors, stronger in France than elsewhere in Europe, aided the Nazis. Native French Jews, imbued with French egalitarian traditions, proudly patriotic, refused to believe that any French government would ever adopt the Nuremberg laws. Even after the Vichy government introduced "anti-alien" legislation, clearly directed against Jews, French Jews persisted in believing that Marshal Pétain would not permit the complete anti-Jewish program to be enacted on the soil of France.

The open letter of protest sent by the Jewish General Boris, formerly Inspector General of the Artillery, to Marshal Pétain after the passage of the first discriminatory laws, indicates the spirit of French Jewry:

I am the highest-ranking Jewish officer in the French army, and, though I have not been authorized to do so by anyone, I take it upon myself to add my protest to those of all my comrades-in-arms who spilled their blood for the fatherland in 1914–18 and 1939–40. I believe it is my right and my obligation to raise this protest: my right, because I am a member of a family, a French family for many centuries, which gave France a number of honored and worthy army officers and civil servants; because I myself have served France honorably for forty-four years, as has been generally recognized; and, finally, because I refuse to recognize anyone's right to control my love of my fatherland, a love which is part of my heritage, of my heart, of my mind, a sanctum of personal refuge, barred before any outsider.

The conviction that French collaborators would not deport French Jews to extermination centers trapped many. By the time Pétain and Laval had demonstrated the falsity of these hopes, the nets were too tight for large-scale escape.

As the meaning of the anti-Jewish measures became clearer, the Germans sought to control the movements of the Jewish population through the Jewish welfare organizations which were attempting to mitigate the plight of thousands of Jews suddenly pauperized by the economic pogrom which marked the first stage of the German attack. *L'Union Générale des Israélites de France* (General Association of French Israelites), known as UGIF, was set up in Vichy France. This body, in which all Jewish organizations were represented, was expected to serve the same ignominious function as the Jewish councils in Poland. The Gestapo and Vichy anticipated that UGIF would become a handy instrument for bringing Jews who had failed to register out of hiding.

The thousands of destitute Jews who were bound to apply for relief would be conveniently listed for deportation when that phase of the Nazi program should be reached. The officials of the UGIF, however, systematically foiled these plans. While not openly defying the government, the various branches of these organizations cooperated in furnishing false addresses and in assisting those Jews who were in immediate danger to escape.

As early as 1941 the Germans realized that many Jews were successfully evading registration with the connivance of the body they had established for the express purpose of ferreting them out. UGIF staff workers were arrested and the offices searched. Many of the officials of UGIF in Paris, Lyons, Marseilles, Nice and other localities were seized and deported, first to Drancy and then to extermination centers.

All Jewish organizations took active part in the secret rescue of adults and children. In view of the unsavory role of Vichy in regard to its Jewish citizens, it is important to stress the aid Jewish bodies received from French Christians. Protestants and Catholics, ecclesiastics and laymen, all classes of the population, risked their lives to save Jewish children. One Protestant group belonging to CIMADE (*Comité d'Intermovement Auprès des Évacués*) devoted itself primarily to rescuing children entrusted to it by the head of the social service section of UGIF. When OSE (*Ouevre de Secours aux Enfants*), a Jewish organization which had maintained children's homes in France, was obliged to go underground after the German occupation, one of its most faithful workers in the rescue of children was a Catholic girl.

In 1941, *L'Amitié Chretienne* (Christian Friendship), an organization for the saving of Jews, was formed under the sponsorship of Cardinal Gerlier, Archbishop of Lyons. Protestants and Catholics headed this group which placed children in Christian institutions, promising at the same time that the children would not be converted. It was Cardinal Gerlier who challenged Vichy by refusing to surrender a group of Jewish children concealed in Catholic institutions whom the government had tracked down.

Witnesses have testified how deeply the French population was shocked by the seizures of Jews in Paris. On the terrible July 12, 1942, when the citizens of Paris first saw the mass round-ups of Jewish families, French passers-by ran after the trucks filled with men, women and children, begging the police to let them save a child. And despite the efforts of Doriot, Laval and Pétain, the German *Tagesanzeiger* (Nov. 5, 1942) was obliged to confess that "racial anti-Semitism of the Central or East-European design has not won the French people."

The main brunt of the rescue work, however, had to be borne by the Jewish youth of France. Their first efforts were directed to smuggling Jews from the occupied to the unoccupied zone. The *Eclaireurs Israélite de France* (Jewish Boy Scouts) and the *Mouvement de la Jeunesse Zionist* were among the chief groups engaged in this work, an important feature of which involved the provision of false identification papers — as otherwise the individual in question would be arrested in his new illegal home. An elaborate procedure for securing such papers was developed. One method was that called *doublages* or *synthesization*. The identity of a Frenchman known to be out of the country would be chosen. Through the reports of sympathetic acquaintances, enough of his history would be reconstructed so that his age and the town of his birth would be ascertained. Then a request for a copy of his birth-certificate would be sent to the town in question, presumably to replace a lost original. French officials generally issued such transcripts without too much fuss. Once armed with an authentic document, it would then be more readily possible to request further documents, such as cards of identity and ration cards.

Even school children collaborated in the securing of these precious initial papers. They would discover the birthplaces and dates of birth of schoolmates who had been born in other parts of France. Requests for copies of such birth certificates would be made, and when received forwarded to still another town, where they could be used as the first link in the chain of getting a set of official papers that would pass muster.

The mainstay of the system was the ability to produce one genuine document to start the series. This method, like the rest, naturally had its perils. In addition, it was slow. Long periods of time might elapse before the *département* or *mairie* would reply. And it would be unsafe to press the point. Consequently, "passport factories" were established by the underground. A whole set of documents, from beginning to end, would be forged. Here again, some authentic element had to be obtained if verisimilitude was to result. Sometimes French presses, which printed official papers for the Germans, cooperated in printing those of the French and Jewish underground. Then at least the form was correct. Sometimes blank forms would be secretly brought out of the offices of the Gestapo itself by young Jews planted there as "Aryans." Meta of Holland was one of these. After the proper official stamps had been secured, it became possible to copy them when the presses of the Maquis underground — French and Jewish — began to function. Eventually practically all official stamps could be duplicated with considerable skill and exactitude. Of course, the possession of even competently forged documents did not invariably throw the Nazis off the track. When they or their Vichy henchmen suspected *doublage*, terrific grilling would ensue. In the case of men, the *visite medicale* was introduced as a check on possible "doublers." Circumcision would generally make further attempts at simulation of "Aryan" identity impossible. But there were some hardy souls who insisted on their "Aryan" origin despite the tell-tale sign. Occasionally, they succeeded in persuading their torturers that in their cases there had been physical rather than theological reasons for the operation.

It does not sound like an attractive art to acquire — the forging of documents and the constant game of hide-and-seek with the police. No more incongruous conspirators than the doe-eyed Meta or the gentle, staid Frau Molen could be visualized. But this was part of the topsy-turvy moral order which the Nazis had created in Europe. Only collaborators and Nazi stooges could afford to be "law-abiding."

How much intelligence and grace of spirit had to be spent in concocting the papers which meant life for some fellow human being! Of all the curious veterans of this struggle whom I met, the strangest perhaps was Lia — who was all of nineteen when I saw her in Jeru-

salem. A real "French" beauty, vivacious, pert, co-
quettish — it was even harder to visualize her as a rebel
engaged in acts of mortal peril than the quiet golden-
haired girls who had fought in the ghettos of Poland.
But Lia had worked so competently and faithfully in
rescue work in Vichy France that an account of her
activities may be read in *Jeunes Filles de Grenoble* (Young
Girls of Grenoble), a bulletin issued by the Youth
Department of the World Zionist Organization in Jerusalem. The author, who saw Lia in the mountains of
Dauphiné near Grenoble, described her as she appeared
at the time of meeting: *Avec ses joues rouges, ses yeux
marrons (fort malicieux), ses cheveux noirs et toufous, Lia
ressemble à une poupée. Elle a dix-huit ans à peine et les plus
jolies mains du monde. Elle est gaie, rieuse, insouciante . . .
'Je ne suis jamais fatiguée,' me dit-elle un jour.* ("With her red
cheeks, her brown eyes (full of deviltry), her black curls,
Lia resembles a doll. She is hardly eighteen and has the
loveliest hands in the world. She is gay, laughing, happy-
go-lucky . . . 'I am never tired,' she told me one day.")

When I saw Lia she was still the beautiful, apple-
cheeked child described by the enraptured observer.
Not so gay perhaps, because the business of becoming a
part of a normal, work-a-day world was a soberer one
than the perpetual play with danger and death which
had marked her childhood, but her eyes sparkled when
she told me of the "escapades" through which she had
outwitted the Germans.

Because of her appearance, she was an ideal "messenger" — someone to bring directives or funds or documents to children and adults who were being concealed.
Sometimes weapons had to be transported. Lia told
me of a favorite trick of hers. She was an excellent

bicyclist; when she carried something particularly dangerous on her person, she would ride swiftly with deliberate *insouciance*. If she had to pass a policeman, she would let go the handlebars and skim by, smiling roguishly at the guardian of the law. It was a pretty stunt, and the policeman would generally smile back. The merry young girl didn't look like a character who required questioning.

Sometimes children would be placed with peasants who were told that the children were Christian orphans whose parents had been killed in bombardments or in the resistance of *France Libre*. The messengers had to bring the children to these points of security, keep them supplied with means of procuring food and other essentials, and be prepared to transfer them to more distant villages if the particular locality no longer seemed reasonably safe. The most dangerous phase of the work involved the smuggling of children across the borders into Switzerland and Spain. That claimed its martyrs, among them the twenty-year-old Marianne Cohn who was shot by the Gestapo when caught shepherding a group of forty children across the Alps.

Lia told me how *Gdud Grenoble*, her group, had smuggled children into Switzerland. When the Germans occupied all France, it became essential to remove children out of the zone of danger as quickly as possible. Many of the previously fairly safe retreats could no longer be relied on. Word would reach Grenoble that a group of children should be sent to Oncy where another branch of the Jewish resistance was working. Lia and her friends would go out on their bicycles and leave word that the children had to be ready by morning. The night would be spent in manufacturing the documents appropriate to the occasion. Then the children would be taken by train to Haute Savoie on the pretense that they were French children going on an outing. From that point on, with the assistance of professional guides who knew the mountain passes, the children would be smuggled across the border.

Sometimes the road to Switzerland led through a chain of Christian assistance. A child would be brought from convent to convent, hidden for a while in one place and then sent further on to religious institutions closer to the border. Christian boy scouts were also helpful. They would take Jewish children with them on hikes which led toward the Swiss border. Mingled in a group of French children, the Jewish boys could escape detection. There then remained the smuggling of the border proper, but the risk of discovery had been greatly reduced because of the escort of Christian children for the greater part of the way.

An extraordinary feature in all these accounts is the confidence which the rescue squads enjoyed among parents who, despite their dread and sorrow, entrusted small children to young people who seemed little more than children themselves. The same heart-rending confidence had been displayed in the ghettos of Poland where the legendary "mothers" were often in their teens.

"Young ones had to make the contacts," Lia said to me simply. She was among the lucky ones. In time, she herself made the secret journey across the Pyrenees and reached Palestine, but many a boy or girl of Toulouse or Grenoble was captured and killed by the Germans. A Lia who lived, a Marianne or Maurice who died! The names are put down almost at random. There were many to choose from.

Rescue activities in France were in large part dependent on the assistance of the Joint Distribution Committee located in Geneva. The messengers who led children across the Alps knew where provision for their maintenance would come from. The concentration of Jewish organizations in Geneva made Switzerland the nerve-center for rescue operations in Western Europe.

Switzerland, anxious to maintain her neutrality and fearful of being swamped by refugees, was in an unenviable position. The Swiss government objected to the open organization of rescue activities within its borders. The Geneva center therefore had to conduct its work most circumspectly. Swiss civilians and soldiers were often more generously disposed than were Swiss officials. Once the frontier had been crossed, however, the historic role of Switzerland as the asylum of political refugees was likely to be honored.

The Swiss newspaper, *Die Nation*, used to run a column headed: "What Pained Me Most This Week." Frequently the column featured protests by Swiss soldiers who complained that they had been ordered to send back refugees. This, they said, was contrary to the spirit of Rousseau and Pestalozzi.

All told, some 15,000 children were saved in France. The number is tragically small — as are all the numbers of the saved. But even this handful could only be wrested from the assassin through an immense expenditure of courage and selflessness. *Le Service des Jeunes* (Service of the Young) was the name given to this branch of the resistance movement — and the *jeunes* in this case were those who served, as well as those who were served.

4

The Jewish Maquis

THE development of a French resistance movement provided the impetus for the formation of secret Jewish military units. A great many native French Jews had joined the Maquis as soon as they began to operate; but others felt that since Jews had been singled out for specific attack, autonomous Jewish units should be formed within the F. F. I.

This feeling was particularly strong among refugee Jews who had escaped to France from Germany or other parts of Europe. At first the proposal to form special detachments of Jewish Maquis was opposed by the French on the ground that they objected to religious divisions. But the argument that people who had been attacked as Jews should be permitted to fight as Jews finally prevailed. Jewish units were recognized as part of the F. F. I. and assisted with arms and military directives. The Jewish partisans were organized into two divisions which cooperated closely: the *Combattants Zionistes* and the *Combattants Juifs* (non-Zionist). All ideological groupings participated in resistance as in rescue. Jewish communists had units of their own which made a notable contribution to the struggle.

The first secret military unit was formed in 1942 by a Zionist Youth group in Toulouse. That was the beginning of the *Armée Juive* (Jewish Army). It was joined almost immediately by the Jewish Boy Scouts. The original intention of the *Armée Juive* had been to train young Jews for service outside of France. Attempts were made to smuggle into Spain young Jews anxious to enlist in the British Army in Palestine or in the forces of General de Gaulle. As the scope of the general resistance movement increased, the *Armée Juive* changed its name to *Organisation Juive de Combat* and became a combat unit within France itself.

The O. J. C. organized Jewish Maquis in Toulouse, Lyons, Limoges and St. Étienne. Though the chief emphasis of the O. J. C. was on military drill, its formal program stressed all aspects of Jewish resistance: the rescue of children, the punishment of traitors, the organization of youth convoys to Palestine, the assistance of needy families in hiding, and — education.

Not only in Poland and the ancient centers of Jewish learning in Lithuania and Eastern Europe did the will to persist spiritually become a part of the general defense against the Nazi. The boys and girls who risked their lives daily in direct resistance were at the same time expected to study Hebrew, Jewish history and literature, and to sing the songs of Palestine. Accounts of the manufacture of arms and of documents are intertwined with memories of secret meetings in honor of Herzl or Bialik, and discussions of Isaiah or perhaps a more modern prophet of Israel. The secret printing-presses turned out Hebrew grammars as well as proclamations of more obvious urgency. Yet probably without the will to study, the whole struggle would have been impossible. An attempt was made to issue a journal, *Quand Même* ("despite everything.") The printer was arrested after two numbers and the experiment was not renewed, but the spirit of the title persisted — *quand même* there would be Isaiah, a story of Sholem Aleichem, a Palestinian *hora*, and the lights of Paris.

In 1944, all Jewish organizations, whatever their ideological bent, united in the *Conseil Representatif des Juifs de France* (Representative Council of French Jews). This united front of all groups greatly strengthened the resistance movement.

The Jewish Maquis made the following vow: *Je jure de lutter jusque'a l'écrasement totale de l'Allemagne Nazie, pour l'honneur, la liberté, et le droit à la vie du Judaisme.* ("I swear to fight till Nazi Germany is completely crushed, for honor, for liberty, and for the right of Judaism to live.") They kept this vow by participating in every phase of French resistance. The prestige of the Jewish Maquis increased enormously when it was learned that many of the most spectacular exploits against Nazi officials and the Vichy police had been their work.

In the mountains of Tarn the O. J. C. formed a Maquis group which became the Jewish squad of the Free Corps on the Black Mountain. Though their leader, Lt. Raymond Lévy, was caught and executed by the Germans when the squad was attacked by several German divisions, the group reformed and participated in the battles which occurred after Allied troops landed along the Mediterranean.

The Jewish Boy Scouts, part of the O. J. C., formed a

company of three sections under the command of Captain Robert Gamzon, head of the Jewish Boy Scouts of France. The company was named after Marc Haguenau, the secretary of the Jewish Boy Scouts, aged 38, who had been caught by the Germans in Grenoble while he was engaged in transporting false papers. He was tortured and killed. The Marc Haguenau Company joined forces with the First French Army and fought in the Belfort region.

The city of Castre, not far from Toulouse, was freed by French Maquis. The town, with a population of some 30,000, was the seat of a large German garrison. In 1944 the Germans in Castre were anxiously awaiting a train with fresh supplies of ammunition. The O. J. C. was ordered to intercept the train and a group of Jewish Maquis attacked it. The Germans, fearful of an explosion, and under the impression that they were being attacked by a superior force, surrendered. When the Jews took charge of the train, each one shouted at the Nazis: *Ich bin Jude*. The Jewish Maquis then brought the train to Castre and, with the assistance of French patriots, liberated the town.

Oblique evidence of the role of Jews in French resistance was provided by the Germans themselves. They were constantly trying to discredit the French resistance movement by pretending that it was "Jewish" and "foreign." This was as subtle as calling Roosevelt, "Rosenfeld." Occasionally, however, they would concoct a formidable indictment. On February 13, 1944, Radio Paris reproached the French Committee of Liberation in Brazzaville for acclaiming ten saboteurs in Paris as "liberators and true Frenchmen." Protested Radio Paris:

Is Grieswachs, the perpetrator of two outrages, a Frenchman? No, he is a Jew, a Polish Jew. Is Elek, who was responsible for eight derailments and the deaths of dozens of people, a Frenchman? No, he is a Hungarian Jew. Is Weissbrod, who derailed three trains, a Frenchman? No, he is a Polish Jew. The other terrorists are also Jews: Lifshitz, Fingerweiss, Stockwerk, and Reiman.

Free France was not shocked by these disclosures. And when General de Gaulle marched into Paris, the Jewish Maquis, marching in the procession with the blue and white of their epaulettes, knew that they too had won the right to be present on the day of liberation.

VII. Resistance in Palestine

1

Haganah: a People's Army

❀

Tʜɪs account began with the parachutists, and it is not literary artifice which makes me return to them in conclusion. For they came back. Within a year after the execution of those after whom the vessels were named, the *Hanna Senesch* and the *Enzo Sereni* came to the shores of Palestine carrying "illegal" passengers — Jews without certificates. The boats were caught along the coastline of Haifa, just as their namesakes had been captured in Budapest and in Italy. But the men and women the ships carried entered the land and in time were free. The original mission on which the poetic young Hungarian girl and the fiery Enzo had set out two years before was being partially fulfilled — not as they had planned, perhaps, but not too far from the fashion of their dream. For it was still the youth of Palestine which made its way into the European charnel-house and bore the survivors back to the air of life.

Any discussion of Jewish resistance must include the *Haganah*, the "illegal army" of Palestine, whose dissolution the British have demanded. For it is in the *Haganah* ("defense") that all the threads meet. The parachutists, the ghetto fighters, the conspirators who plotted salvation in Geneva and Istanbul and the partisans had been, or were to become, a part of this strange soldiery whose mission was the bringing of life and whose greeting was *Shalom* ("peace").

Soldiers — I might just as accurately call them sailors. For they manned and brought in the ships, just as they stood watch over the settlements where those they had saved were to be sheltered. But perhaps it is idle to try to find the exact English equivalents for the Hebrew words which describe the functions of the *Haganah*. Palestine has created new terms for which as yet we have no adequate English translation, because we have no corresponding concepts. We translate the Hebrew *ʿaliyah* as "immigration," but the Hebrew word means "ascent" — the newcomer to Palestine "ascends" to the land. In any other country, he may be merely an immigrant, a wanderer who comes in. But the act of entering Palestine has the quality of rising towards the fulfillment of an ideal. It is a pilgrimage up a holy mountain and is still "ascent" even when the settler goes down to the depths of the shores of the Dead Sea.

In English we call the Jews of Europe who seek asylum outside the quota "refugees" or "illegals." In Palestine, a Jew who tries to enter the country without the benefit of a certificate is called a *maʿapil*, a word meaning one who advances despite overpowering odds. A *maʿapil* is one who "assaults" hardships. A man striving to scale Mount Everest might be a *maʿapil*. And it is typical of the temper and intuitive grace of Palestine that the battered beings, whom its young men bring in literally on their backs, are called not "refugees" but "stormers" or "assaulters." In the very moment of their completest prostration, when they are carried ill-clad, wet and hungry to the shore, they are invested with the greatest dignity. They are the victorious heroes of a struggle, not the defeated who flee seeking mercy.

Similarly, the *Haganah* cannot be explained merely by its English equivalent "defense." Note that the concept precludes offense or attack, yet it is more than an organization for defense. Nor does the term "secret army" define it any more accurately, for an "army" implies purely military objectives, whereas the purpose of the *Haganah* embraces not only defense of the settlements against attack, but also defense of the right of Jews to enter the Jewish homeland. It involves the active rescue of those unable to reach Palestine because of barred doors on either side of the Mediterranean. A Polish girl's account, printed in *Time* (May 6, 1946), has described one of the "battles" of the *Haganah*:

> At 11 o'clock at night, our ship arrived. We could see a small light blinking from the Palestinian coast.
> Rowboats came to meet us ... One by one we climbed down to them. Everything happened very quickly then. In the boats were Palestinians. They shook hands with us and said *Shalom* — welcome home!
> When we came on shore there were more boys from the *Haganah*, and they were armed. We walked through the fields for a few miles ... I saw men and boys all along the road. Our guides told us that these people were all members of the *Haganah* standing guard for us ... There was a chain of them all the way to the shelter of a settlement inland. As we passed them, they smiled and quietly called to us, *Shalom, Shalom*!

311

I had occasion to see members of the *Haganah* celebrate a victory. And perhaps nothing could illuminate the special quality of this "army" more clearly than the nature of the gathering I witnessed. I had been visiting a *kvutzah* in the Emek, going through the usual tourist routine of admiring the advances in horticulture, bee-culture, and every other kind of culture that had taken place since my last visit. Then I was invited to a party. The young people, whom I saw seated around long tables, were very young indeed. The average age was probably not over nineteen. Modest refreshments were on the tables — some plain cookies, hard candy and tea. And, of course, there were flowers — grown in the settlement and decorating the simple tables. The party had a curious air of solemnity. No one had as yet touched the refreshments. The boys and girls were taking turns at reciting and singing poems and songs of modern Palestine. A passage of Scripture was read. I assumed that this was some kind of "literary" evening which I had chanced on by accident. Great decorum was maintained throughout. Each person who recited or read was listened to silently. There was no applause at the conclusion of the numbers. One understood that this was due to custom rather than to indifference. At the end of the program, when tea was served, the mood became gayer, and I heard the kind of chatter and banter that one might expect of boys and girls in their teens. But the essential mood was one of festive earnestness.

Later, the reason for the party I had been allowed to witness was explained to me. The boys and girls seated at the tables had been the ones who had participated in the freeing of "illegal" immigrants from the detention camp of Athlit several nights before. All

Palestine had rung with the exploit: a detachment of the *Haganah* had surrounded the camp, cut the wires and liberated those detained to prevent their threatened deportation. The operation had been carried out smoothly and successfully, with almost no casualties on either side. That too was cause for rejoicing. The gathering which I attended was the "triumph" of the victors. The "soldiers" were giving thanks because they had been able to bring freedom and the hope of life to several hundred survivors of Hitler's concentration camps.

Several weeks later I met a girl of eighteen who had not been seated at a table, although she had earned the right to be one of the celebrants. She too had been at Athlit, and had lost an eye during an explosion there. When I saw her, with a bandage over the empty socket, she was surrounded by her comrades; I had reason to believe that plans were being made to enable her to continue to work further for the salvation of Hitler's victims. Such are the soldiers of the *Haganah*.

The *Haganah* was formed at the end of World War I. Its original purpose was to protect the pioneer settlements against either Bedouin marauders or organized Arab attacks such as have taken place periodically since the start of Jewish colonization in Palestine. The *halutzim* early realized that, just as the soil they settled had to be reclaimed by their own labor, so its protection had to be their own responsibility. "Self-defense" became as much a national slogan as "self-labor." Both indicated the realization that a nation could be built only by men who were prepared to assume the primary obligations of nationhood. In addition, by making participation a form of voluntary national service, the democratic character of the *Haganah* was assured. It was to be a people's militia, not an independent force of professional soldiers.

Every able-bodied man and woman in Palestine can join the *Haganah*. The workers in the fields, the clerks in the cities, the students in the schools can all qualify for membership in the *Haganah* by taking periods of voluntary training which will prepare them to use arms in an emergency. From the *Haganah's* inception, the *Yishuv* has had more than one occasion to be grateful for its existence. During the Arab riots of 1920 and 1929, British authorities were of slight help in putting down the attacks on peaceful Jewish settlements. In the ancient orthodox communities of Hebron and Safed, where no units of the *Haganah* had been organized, several hundred Jews were ruthlessly massacred. In other places, the Arab attackers were swiftly repulsed. After the tragic experiences of 1929, the Jewish community understood the necessity for developing a self-defense force capable of guarding the *Yishuv* against Arab onslaughts.

Being a people's army, the *Haganah* reflects the moral tone of the community. During the savage Arab outbreaks of 1936–1939, when Arabs subsidized by Axis agents and incited by local demagogues of the stripe of the Grand Mufti, the notorious collaborator of Hitler, engaged in acts of wanton terrorism against the Jewish settlers, the *Haganah* accepted the precept of *Havlagah* — "self-restraint." That is to say, Arab terrorism was not to be met by counter-terrorism. There was no retaliation for pillage and murder by a resort to similar acts. The guilty were sought out for punishment; the settlements were bravely defended whenever attacked; but the code that only the actual criminal be punished, and that no spirit of indiscriminate vengefulness be unleashed, was rigidly honored.

The *Haganah* has never tolerated terrorism. There are small terrorist groups in Palestine who reject the discipline of the *Haganah* and the Jewish community, but the people's army has consistently adhered to the policy that no blood be wantonly shed. Force has only been resorted to for well-defined objectives: defense of those already in the land and defense of those who must enter the land. When the *Haganah* recently dynamited two coast guard stations between Tel-Aviv and Haifa whose function was to signal the approach of "illegal" boats, the British soldiers at the stations first received a warning to evacuate the installations. Such warnings certainly did nothing to simplify the operation, but the desire of the *Haganah* to avoid useless bloodshed is so deep-seated that the risk was taken. This policy is followed in all actions likely to involve the loss of life. Stupid and brutal murders of British soldiers, such as have sometimes occurred since 1945, have been the work of irresponsible, numerically small terrorist bands — the Stern gang or the *Irgun Zwai Leumi* — not of the *Haganah*.

In some periods the *Haganah* was accorded a semi-official status by the British. During the Arab riots of 1936–1939, the British deputized about 16,000 members of the *Haganah* as supernumerary police and even went so far as to provide them with weapons. In World War II, when Rommel's armies were beating at the gates of Alexandria, the British military authorities realized the value of the *Haganah* as a potential force of guerrilla fighters. Members of the *Haganah* were trained as guer-

315

rillas with the knowledge and cooperation of the British. And throughout the war, members of the *Haganah* consistently volunteered for the most dangerous missions against the Nazis. Almost as spectacular as the venture of the parachutists was the attempt of twenty-three chosen members of the *Haganah*, led by a British officer, to demolish the Tripoli Oil Refinery. All twenty-three lost their lives. And when England invaded Syria, it was members of the *Haganah*, familiar with the terrain and local conditions, who acted as scouts and reconnaissance patrols for the British troops.

The exact size of the *Haganah* is not known. It has been estimated at anywhere between 60,000 and 100,000 members. It can safely be said, however, that in addition to a compact trained nucleus, which is always ready to spring to arms in case of an emergency, most of able-bodied Palestinian Jewry can be counted on to join the ranks of the *Haganah* in a time of crisis. It is the rallying point for all elements, young and old, able to join the forces of defense and resistance.

Because it is a people's army, its directives are accepted and obeyed even by those who are not formally its members. I was in Palestine at the time of the British search for "illegal" entrants in the agricultural settlement of Giv'at Hayyim in the Valley of Sharon. When thousands of British troops with tear-gas and machine guns began to advance upon the settlement, word was sent at once to all the farms throughout the valley. Thousands of workers began to pour along the roads to the defense of the beleaguered settlement. Without weapons, they surrounded Giv'at Hayyim with a living wall to prevent the entrance of British troops. The British fired on the unarmed throng, killing seven men and women.

They forced their way into the farm and started a search, but they found no "illegals" because every member of the settlement refused to show his identification card. There was no means of distinguishing between those lawfully and "unlawfully" there. Mass arrests followed, in the course of which girls and boys insisted on climbing into the soldiers' trucks to swell the number of those taken into custody, thus indicating the scope of Jewish passive resistance to an unjust decree. The jails and detention pens were soon filled to overflowing — but the British did not discover who were those who had come without certificates.

Some weeks later, I had an opportunity to chat with a group of boys and girls who had been arrested in the course of the march on Giv'at Hayyim. They were young people who had themselves recently escaped from Nazi Europe. Now they knew from personal experience the meaning of the *Yishuv's* resistance slogan: "We will defend the right of every Jew to enter the Jewish homeland." They had heard the sound of British bullets whizzing over their heads, and they had tasted the pleasures of confinement in a British pen. They could have no romantic illusions as to the safety or comfort of the struggle of which they were a part. Yet when I asked them how they would answer a similar call, if the need again arose, they looked at me with bewilderment. One seventeen-year-old girl said to me without any pose or affectation: "We are here, but the others have to come. How can we leave them in Europe?"

Members of Yagur, a large collective settlement, freed nine illegal immigrants who had been captured by the British police. When the British threatened Yagur with mass arrest unless a check of the identity cards of all the inhabitants was permitted, Yagur refused to be cowed. As soon as news that Yagur might be searched by the British spread through Haifa, hundreds of schoolboys left their classes and flocked to Beth Oren and Yagur by bus and truck. Workers from various factories in Haifa and Haifa Bay, clerks and storekeepers left their places of employment and rushed to the threatened settlement to show their solidarity with the settlers who were protecting "illegals."

The British forces withdrew, but sent a demand that the "illegals" harbored by Yagur be turned over to them together with the persons responsible for their liberation. Yagur answered with a letter which has become famous throughout Palestine:

> "The settlement does not recognize the validity of this demand . . . . We will not hand over illegal immigrants to the police, but will always help them.

One can enumerate any number of such incidents. They serve to show how the active resistance of the *Haganah* is supported by the passive resistance of the population as a whole. The armed attack on the detention camp of Athlit and the unarmed barricade of flesh and blood thrown around Giv'at Hayyim were aspects of the same struggle.

2

The Poetry of Action

❀

THE workers who fell at Givʻat Hayyim were given a funeral — with honors. They were not military honors, though the dead were viewed as soldiers. The pioneer settlements have evolved a ceremonial of their own — solemn and stoical — whose curious poetry also helps to explain the complex phenomenon which we seek to describe as Jewish resistance.

The funeral parlor where the body lay was the workers' meeting hall. There were no flowers. The plain wooden coffin was draped in the blue-and-white flag of Zion and the red flag of socialism. Around the hall, the comrades of the dead youth stood watch. Dressed in the blue shirt of the *halutz*, they stood silently at attention. The young widow also stood in the circle. Silent as the others, she kept swaying back and forth. Outside, in the hot sun, hay-wagons filled with workers from the neighboring settlements waited to follow the body to the *kvutzah* where the burial would take place. Only one sound finally broke the immense quiet. When the body was carried out and the line of mourners formed, the old mother of the boy, unschooled in the stern discipline of pioneer Palestine, sobbed aloud. And the anguished sob, so familiar at Jewish funerals where the lamentations of the bereaved rend the air, came as a shock. It was out of character. The silence, the solemnity which sprang from no pomp of traditional vestments or liturgy, created an ascetic ritual of its own, with its own meaning and sanctity. The dedication was there. The heroic will of a people prepared to die for its cause echoed in the motionless quiet. It was another form of the determination to resist. Had the youth died of malaria or in an accident, he would have been buried without this stern watch, all the more impressive because its members had neither arms nor uniforms, but stood in the simple cotton shirts of farm-workers. The punctilio was of the spirit.

The autochthonous poetry that proceeds from Palestine is not the product of littérateurs. The constant creation of new ceremonies, as well as the investment of old forms with fresh and living content which is characteristic of the *Yishuv*, is nothing contrived. It has the imagination of action, not of fancy. Perhaps that is why it rises to dramatic heights which have never been reached before in modern Jewish history. The "passport" found on the "illegal" immigrants of the *Fede*, the old 750-ton wooden cargo boat which was caught at La Spezia just as it was about to set sail for Palestine, is an example. The passport, duly issued by those who had arranged the voyage, was carried as an official document by the *ma'apilim*. It read:

Mr. . . . . has been found qualified by the representatives of the *Yishuv* for repatriation to Palestine.

Authority:

A. "And they shall abide in the land that I have given unto Jacob My servant wherein your fathers abode, and they shall abide therein, even they, and their children, and their children's children forever."— Ezekiel, 37.

B. "With great mercies will I gather thee." — Isaiah, 54.

C. Lord Balfour's Declaration, November 2, 1917.

D. The Mandate for Palestine.

These august authorities were offered in lieu of the duly stamped visas of consular offices and the whole elaborate rigamarole of exit and entry permits.

It is essential to understand the frame of mind which in all seriousness offers the Bible and the Mandate as an adequate substitute for official seals. For unless one understands it, one cannot appreciate the special quality of Jewish resistance. Essentially it is an act of faith — faith in the covenant, be it with God, be it with the moral law which enjoins compassion, be it with international tribunals. And the religious intensity of this faith is so pure that it becomes a code for political action. This is not the first time that articles of faith have been taken with complete seriousness in the hills of Galilee or on the Judean plain. The prophets, who clamored with an exalted literalness that the word must become the deed, would recognize their descendants in the young men who gravely invoke ethical concepts as their safe-conduct — a procedure all the more remarkable since they are not cranks holding revival meetings, but youths skilfully organizing dangerous expeditions which require the maximum of adroitness, hardihood and cold common sense.

Palestine is capable of grandiose gestures because the mood of the people has grandeur. No Hollywood producer, in his most ingenious fancies, could have staged the supreme drama of the hunger-strike which took place in Jerusalem to secure the right of entry to Palestine for the "illegals" aboard the *Fede* at La Spezia. Consider the elements that went into the spectacle: the figures of the fasters, all leaders of the *Yishuv*; the pilgrims who trudged from every corner of the land to the courtyard of the Jewish Agency building, where the strike took place, to offer prayers for the success of the fast and the well-being of the fasters; finally, this being the season of Passover, the mystical *seder* in which the strikers took part. They broke their fast by eating a piece of matzoh the size of an olive as a symbol of their bond with their people on the great national holiday. One of the fasters, though weak with hunger, chanted the ritual from a Haggadah which had been printed before the expulsion of the Jews from Spain — the only one of its kind extant. Outside in the courtyard a great throng joined in singing the liturgical chants of the Passover, and no household that sat down to the traditional feast in Palestine was unaware of the ceremony being enacted in Jerusalem.

There have been memorable *seders* before in Jewish history, but perhaps none in modern times so charged with meaning. No other Jewry in the world could have presumed to partake of this fast-feast because, for any except the Jews of Palestine, it would have been a melodramatic and presumptuous affectation. The creativeness of the images Palestine instinctively employs flows from the moral force of its deeds. If the *Yishuv* is imaginative in expression, it is primarily because it has the imagination to act. Valor and resolution are not invariable guarantees of a commensurate poetry. Ethics and aesthetics, as we know, are not inevitable concomitants. But in Palestine the two are intertwined. It required an act of imagination to conceive of Zionism to begin with, and every subsequent act calculated to recreate a nation had to be daring in thought as well as execution.

New symbols are evolved in periods of fresh vitality when the spiritual energies of a people swell high. When the creative burst subsides, the exuberant new forms become stratified into established ritual. Palestine, at this stage, is an agent which ordains destiny; that is why it is constantly enriching and revivifying what has already been ordained.

Nor is this surge of fantasy to be observed only in moments of life and death. I was present at the opening of a new road in Elon, a *kvutzah* in the mountains of Upper Galilee. One must witness the fierce fusion of dream and reality which constitutes modern Palestine to understand the unflinching resolution of its people. A simple gravel road, leading up the hill to the settlement, had been completed. The road would have created no stir in any except a poor and small community. But it meant that trucks and wagons would be able to come up the hill in the heavy winter rains without sinking in mud, and that the settlers would be able to trudge up with greater ease in all weather. A simple accomplishment one would think, and hardly meriting much fuss. But the opening of this bit of road was an illuminating moment for the observer.

The settlers gathered at the foot of the hill and formed a procession. Little children carrying small flags of blue-and-white, and of red, went first. Big-bellied women, walking with the grave pride of pregnancy, followed them. Next in line were women who pushed baby-carriages bright with blue and red paper streamers. The future was advancing. The rest of the settlement marched behind.

The ascent up the new road began to the tune of a young partisan's playing. (He had recently escaped from Eastern Europe.) Across the gate leading to the settlement was strung a blue-and-white ribbon. When the procession reached the gate, all stopped. A boy who had survived Bergen-Belsen stepped forward. He raised his bare arm, on which could be seen the concentration-camp numbers tatooed on his skin, and cut the band. All looked up at the large placard over the archway bearing the inscription:

"May all the homeless walk up this road."

The young partisan began to play again. The children started once more. The road had been opened, and none but the smallest of the children could fail to understand that the road was more than a convenient path up a hard slope. It was a manifesto and a pledge. It too was a form of Jewish resistance, for the declaration that all the homeless would march up this road was being made at a time when British warships were patrolling the waters of the Mediterranean to intercept those who might seek to come, and British Tommies, from a neighboring soldiers' camp, were stolidly watching the ceremony.

Another indication of the wholehearted support given by the *Yishuv* to the resistance policy of the *Haganah* could be observed in the attention paid to *Kol Israel*, the secret radio station of the *Haganah*. In the first place, the failure of the British to catch the broadcasters was in itself evidence of the kind of cooperation the underground radio was receiving. Armed with radar equipment and with all conceivable technical facilities for detecting the location of the station, the British should have been able to discover the whereabouts of a station which had been broadcasting within a comparatively small area for some time. One can only assume that more than a few in the *Yishuv* were assisting the station in changing its location as need arose.

The authority enjoyed by the broadcasts of *Kol Israel* (The Voice of Israel) was a sign of its representative character. It was truly the people's voice. At 2 P. M. when the broadcast would be made, one could hear the electric words, "Listen to the Voice of Israel, the voice of Jewish resistance," booming from every open window. I have even seen a policeman in uniform get off his bicycle and stop beneath a window from which he could hear the radio explain the reasons for an attack on British installations and the nature of future policy.

If there was any doubt as to the origin of an incident, and the population was not certain as to whether it was the work of the *Haganah* or of one of the terrorist groups, the broadcast would provide the answer. If *Kol Israel* accepted the responsibility for the blowing up of a Jerusalem police station, then the people were prepared to subscribe to the wisdom of the act. If, as was more likely, the broadcaster would announce that the *Haganah* had had no part in the outrage, the denial was accepted as final. As a rule it was not difficult to differentiate between the activities of the *Haganah* and the *Irgun* and the Stern Gang. Anything likely to further immigration or colonization could *a priori* be ascribed to the *Haganah*. Wanton, purposeless terror could be chalked up to the "irresponsibles." The broadcast would usually merely serve to confirm what the population already surmised.

Sometimes, however, the demarkation line was not absolutely clear. Once, when railroad tracks had been dynamited, we were not certain as to the authors. There had been no loss of life, and the operation had been performed at many separate points with dispatch and efficiency. That pointed to the *Haganah*. On the other hand, why blow up railroad tracks? How did that serve Jewish immigration? *Kol Israel* accepted the responsibility. The purpose had been to interfere with British troop movements whose purpose, in turn, had been to crush "illegal" immigration.

The psychological stages by which the quixotically idealistic Jewish community of Palestine, which only a few years before had made a fetish of *havlagah* — nonretaliation even in the face of the most bestial Arab outrages — went to an acceptance of "activism"— the policy of active resistance — is an extraordinary chapter in Jewish history. I was in Palestine precisely during the period (September 1945—February 1946) when the crucial decisions were being made, and I was able to watch this psychic and intellectual evolution.

Undoubtedly, the fact that the final repudiation of British pledges was made by the Labor cabinet of Bevin and Attlee played a big part in the hardening of sentiment. A Labor movement which takes its convictions as seriously as that of Palestine could not make peace with the notion that a socialist government had been guilty of such gross betrayal. This phase of the disillusionment is likely to be underestimated among circles where faith in the reality of socialist ideas is less intense; but for the men and women of the Histadruth, for the youth of the collectives, it was a personal tragedy. It seemed to make further temporizing useless. There was nothing to hope for and no one to whom to turn, all appeals to international morality having failed. Palestine had to take its destiny into its own hands.

The resolve was not taken lightly, nor was there complete unanimity as to the forms that opposition to the British decree should take. I spoke to people of all parties and shades of opinion and know how much groping and heart-searching went into the final decisions. This must be stressed, because it would be wholly false to give the impression that Palestine leapt onto the barricades in a mood of bravado or irresponsibility. There was an agonizing desire to determine the right road, and those on whom the ultimate responsibility lay had no illusions as to the possible outcome.

When one speaks of hesitations and fears, one must always exclude the youth of the *Yishuv*. The young men and women, the boys and girls of Palestine, are held back neither by "minority" inhibitions nor the calculations of their elders. They feel themselves to be strong; they are brave and resolute; and they are not prepared to let injustice reign. It is centuries since the Jewish people has had such a youth — so gallant, so bold, and so simple.

Precisely this magnificent youth troubled those who decried a policy of active opposition to the British. To the argument, "We have nothing to lose," they replied indignantly that there was much to be lost: not only the comfortable homes of Tel Aviv, the beauty of the new and old Jerusalem, the flourishing settlements, but most of all this precious youth. Men and women kept saying: "Can we afford to squander this youth? How many more such boys and girls remain to the Jewish people?"

No more terrible question faces any people, even one large in numbers and powerful in resources. For a people which knows itself to be an 'am katan ("a small people") physically, the problem becomes overwhelming in its gravity.

Few of those who favored staking all in a last desperate gamble wanted another Masada — the symbol of Judea's futile though heroic rebellion against the Roman Empire. Even those who declared emphatically, "We have nothing to lose," did not anticipate a Masada to be the result of challenging the British Empire. On the contrary, they expected an improvement of the situation through a show of strength. They based their strategy on the notion that the Jews of Palestine, despite the smallness of their numbers, were a by-no-means-negligible factor because of their excellent organization and readiness for sacrifice. If Britain was prepared to sacrifice the Jews of Palestine in order to further her imperial interests in the Middle East, she had to be shown that peace in the Middle East was unobtainable unless the just demands of Jews, as well as the threats of Arabs, were considered.

It was not easy for a community which had made a religion of constructive work to reconcile itself to destructive acts. It was immensely difficult, psychologically and intellectually, to countenance violence in any form. It was therefore inevitable that, the more obvious the connection between any act and immigration or continued settlement, the more popular the support it evoked. More approval was expressed for the burning

328

of boats used to intercept "illegal" immigrants than for the mining of railroads. The question was not one of legality or violence. It was just as illegal and violent to cut the barbed wires around Athlit and to liberate immigrants as to blow up railroad tracks, but there was more enthusiasm for Athlit. The positive nature of the act was at once apparent. The same held true of the settling of new points in zones arbitrarily forbidden by the White Paper. The act, legal or not, was constructive in character.

The right to colonize, as well as to immigrate, is fiercely defended. The British White Paper has prohibited land purchase by Jews in the major part of Palestine. The *Yishuv* has never conceded the legality of this restriction any more than of the one on immigration. Since Arabs are willing to sell land in the forbidden zones, the Jewish National Fund has been buying large tracts of arid soil to be reclaimed by Jewish workers. One such tract is Birya, in Upper Galilee near Safed. The decision to "ascend" to Birya was taken. The colonization of a new point under such circumstances follows a technique developed during the Arab riots. A procession of trucks starts out in the middle of the night. By dawn, the *halutzim* are already at work on the hill pitching tents, removing stones, building barracks and surrounding the settlement with a wire fence. The work is completed within one day and is a communal enterprise in which workers from the whole vicinity take part; it is also a rite — another one of Palestine's typical "triumphs."

At the close of the day, when even the ceremony of tree planting had been completed, British soldiers appeared with tanks. The settlers were ordered to leave at once, otherwise physical force would be used. One of the settlers at Birya gave an eyewitness account of the scene:

> We refused, and heard again that familiar refrain: "Very sorry." We were surrounded. Into the circle formed around us rushed British soldiers and policemen armed with clubs and shields (as in the days of King David!). We squatted down on the ground in one pile, each one of us holding another's hand, and started singing *Hatikva*.
>
> The soldiers went to work. Four soldiers to a man. One would use his club with all he had in him till the man being tackled would stand up. Those that would not stand on their feet were dragged to the trucks.
>
> The "battle" lasted all of two hours. The British suffered no casualties. We had two men slightly wounded. The soldiers tore up the tents, demolished the barracks and dragged us to their trucks. All the way we sang and shouted: "We will climb up to Birya a third time." As we were being dragged away, a new group of four hundred men arrived at the ruined camp and, singing, started to build anew. We were taken to Tiberias and set free. But on the morrow, Jews of the old *Yishuv* came with food from Tiberias and Safed. One thousand men and women again set up the camp at Birya. The military again surrounded it, and not till Saturday did they leave. The government gave its permission for the settlement at Birya.

The coming of the old bearded Jews of ultra-orthodox Safed was particularly precious to the young settlers. That the old men, with their earlocks and traditional robes, should have joined the *halutzim* whose "godless" ways they deplored, was a token of unity. The old men could not take part in the struggle, but by their presence they had blessed the effort. Another verse had been added to the poetry of Palestine.

3

Ha'apalah: Illegal Immigration

THE most dramatic form which the resistance movement in Palestine has assumed is *Ha'apalah*, the term used to designate unauthorized immigration. Like *Ma'apil*, the name stems from a root meaning the storming of obstacles.

How this immigration was organized on the European continent, during the war years, by such centers as Istanbul has already been discussed. To complete the picture one must trace the development of the movement in Palestine proper.

Illegal Jewish immigration into Palestine is not a new phenomenon. Throughout the centuries since the dispersion, Jews have entered Palestine as individuals or in small groups, whether or not they could get legal permits from whatever government happened to be in power.

When Palestine was under Turkish rule, the government did not sanction Jewish immigration. Nevertheless, between 1897 and 1917, several thousand young Jews, driven from Eastern Europe by the periodic persecutions and pogroms, made their way to Palestine. The corrupt

Turkish regime of the period put no serious obstacles in the way of entry when adequate bribes were offered.

At the conclusion of World War I, after the Balfour Declaration and the granting of the Mandate, the situation altered radically. A mass exodus began from Eastern Europe, where a wave of massacres had broken out. However, despite the international decision that Palestine was to be recreated as a Jewish homeland to which Jews would come "as of right, not as of sufferance," free Jewish immigration continued to be blocked by the British by quotas and restrictions on the allocation of immigration certificates. Consequently, "illegal" entry again became the only solution for Jews persecuted in Europe. Over 50,000 "illegal" Jewish immigrants entered Palestine in the period between World Wars I and II.

Particularly after the rise of Hitler in 1933, the urgent need of Jews for entry into Palestine became something beyond the pale of discussion. '*Aliyah Beth*, as illegal immigration was then called, came into being.

Something of the mounting tempo of the anguished drive to scale the shores of Palestine even before the outbreak of war can be gathered from the history of the ships which failed in their object and consequently became a matter of public record: On May 19, 1939, three hundred and eight Jewish "illegals" were arrested near Askalon; on May 28, four hundred and one were seized by a British warship near Nathanya; on June 1, the S. S. *Leisel* with nine hundred and six aboard was caught; on June 7, five hundred and five "illegals" were arrested near Naharia — two hundred and sixty of these, according to the laconic announcement made at the time of seizure, had been trying to enter for the second time within two months. They had been passengers on the ill-fated S. S. *Assimi* which had been turned back from Palestine on April 21. So the catalogue went: ships from Constantza, from Bulgaria, from Athens — a modern odyssey shrouded in terror and darkness.

Not all these ships were organized by Zionist groups. "Illegal" immigration unfortunately became a racket for private entrepreneurs concerned only with squeezing the maximum of profit out of the agony of European Jewry. Ships that foundered, ships that wandered for weeks and even for months without reaching shore because of the ignorance or incompetence of the crew, could be chalked up to the credit of the private speculator in human misery. Many of the refugees who finally waded to land were stripped of everything they owned by captain and crew before being thrown into the small boats which brought them close to the coast.

A typical account of the experience of the survivors of one such "private" journey appeared in the *Davar*. The writer relates that he paid $400 for passage with a party of seven hundred and fifty who were to sail to Palestine. In addition, he was directed to bring food for three weeks and not more than twenty-two pounds of luggage. At the port of embarkation, the original group was told that that they would be permitted to leave only if they took with them some fifty Jewish refugees who were being held in the local prison. Finally they boarded a 2,000 ton ship. In the words of the narrator:

> The ship was old and in bad repair; it was filthy and its deficiencies were obvious. Into this floating grave there entered seven hundred and fifty people,

among them two hundred and fifty women and fifteen children. In its hold, sleeping bunks were arranged several tiers high. Sacks filled with straw served as mattresses. We were so crowded that once one lay down on the mattress it was very difficult to turn. But worst of all was the air. This was during the rainy season; all entrances were closed and the atmosphere was suffocating. Two temporary latrines were set up on the deck. At one end of the ship there were two huge kettles, but shortly after sailing it became obvious that they were in bad repair.

The writer goes on to tell how an epidemic of meningitis broke out on board the ship. It cruised along the coast of Palestine unable to land and unable to stop long enough at any Mediterranean harbor to secure food, fuel or medicine. The passengers were without food or water for four days before a port permitted them to anchor temporarily. Periodically, they would have to remain below deck for two days at a time so as to be out of sight of passing ships: they had been booked as a cargo of cement. This meant that the latrines on deck could not be reached and, to use the words of the writer again, "the suffocation was unbearable, the filth indescribable, yet no one could leave his place." During the journey, this boat encountered another refugee ship which had grounded on a sand-bank, and they had to take on the ship-wrecked passengers. The chief terror of the trip, however, was meningitis.

From this account one gets a notion not of a single voyage only, but the history of innumerable other refugee ships that sailed up and down the Mediterranean, desperately trying to unload their passengers. The fate of many of these ships remains unknown. One can only suspect what measures might have been taken by pirati-

334

cal crews, burdened with dangerous human contraband. Some of the ships were captured and turned back after reaching Palestine. When the *Assimi* was sent back from Haifa, the cries of those on board could be heard as far as Mount Carmel.

Such a situation could not be disregarded by Palestine, but, except for a small persistent nucleus, official Zionist bodies for a long time were not in favor of openly defying the stated policies of the British government. However, after the issuance of the Chamberlain White Paper which broke faith with the Balfour Declaration, most opposition to *'Aliyah Beth* ceased. It began to be viewed, not only as a means of salvation for European Jewry, but as a legitimate political weapon against an illegal British decree. The attempt to crush Zionism by edict had to be effectively challenged. *Haganah* started the organization of unauthorized immigration into Palestine. Within the six months preceding the outbreak of World War II, the rate of unauthorized immigrants entering Palestine began to increase rapidly.

The story of the first "illegal" ship to reach Palestine through responsible channels has a legendary ring. The ship was all of 120 tons. It sailed in midwinter from a Greek harbor, carrying sixty young immigrants, thirty per cent of whom were women. In size the ship resembled an ordinary sailboat with a motor. Living accomodations were of the poorest. A terrible storm broke out during which the ship drifted for eleven days. That under those circumstances the frail boat actually reached Palestine seemed nothing short of miraculous to the Palestinians awaiting it. Despite the difficult physical conditions of the journey, the spirit of the group was good. They were a picked element, psychologically prepared for the dangers before them, and consequently they displayed the necessary stamina.

The techniques of *'Aliyah Beth* as conducted by *Haganah* immediately before the outbreak of the war are worth noting. The immigrants were conducted, not like unfortunates fleeing merely to save their lives, but like individuals with an important national mission. Since a selection had to be made, adequately trained men and women between the ages of 18 and 35 were usually chosen. Life on shipboard would be organized on a cooperative basis, with every task shared by the passengers. This not only reduced expenses and increased the carrying capacity of the ship, but sustained morale. Ample stores of food were put on board.

It gradually became possible to charter vessels of larger tonnage than at first. These would be engaged with Greek, Rumanian or Bulgarian captains, but each boat also carried three or four Palestinians thoroughly familiar with problems of navigation. One of the Palestinians was always a competent sailor able to take control of the ship himself, if need be. Another operated the radio, using a special code so as to be in constant communication with those on shore. Still another was responsible for ship discipline. For the success of the venture it was essential that the ship follow a course determined by those with a thorough knowledge of the Palestinian coastline and the possibilities of landing. The cooperation between the captain and the skilled Palestinians was responsible for the extraordinary record of successful, and therefore unpublished, sailings.

One youth who reached the shore in one of these unpublicized, happy landings, described his first night in Palestine with lyrical enthusiasm:

We were placed on trucks, crowded close together. A heavy damp shoe came down on my naked foot. I bit my lip. One must make no sound. I glanced through the darkness. All along the road I see silent figures guarding, watching. The truck goes along crooked roads. At last we see houses and barracks. We are among Jews.

We are led into a large room. A dark-eyed young girl, with the charm of a young mother, is setting the table. A youth stands on guard near the window with a gun on his shoulder. In the corner we notice a sign. It has the name of the *kvutzah* which we have reached. We read the words *kvutzah* X. I whisper the name to my neighbor. It is a name dear and familiar to us, known from our days in the movement in Poland. The name flies from mouth to mouth, *Kvutzah* X! Can it be true? Our hearts are too full for words.

The clock on the wall shows 3 A. M. The first night in the homeland.

After the outbreak of the war, the opportunities for illegal immigration became slimmer. But as the Nazi extermination program developed, the desire of Palestine to save the Jews of Europe in whatever numbers possible became correspondingly intense. Throughout the war, and since the end of the war, special rescue teams of the *Haganah* were engaged in organizing the escape of Jews from Europe. The task involved three distinct phases:

1. Organizing the immigrants and transporting them through various countries — most of which objected to the passage of Jews across their territories — to small ports from which they could embark.

2. Embarking and transporting them safely to the shores of Palestine.

337

3. Landing them on the shores of Palestine. (This phase of the operation was as risky as the previous two. The immigrants had to be protected from seizure by the British who patrolled the coast.)

The smuggling of refugees across the borders of Nazi Europe during the course of the war has already been described. After the end of the war, when the million and a half surviving Jews of Europe discovered the bitter meaning of "liberation" as far as they were concerned, the surge toward Palestine received a mounting impetus. The *Haganah* did not have to send its representatives to incite Jews to flee from soil drenched with the blood of their parents and children. The desire to leave the vast cemetery of Europe required no outside stimulation. There was nothing to hold those who remained alive. The mourners had no graves at which to weep. No tombstones marked the ashes of their dead. The crematoriums, the incinerators of the Nazis had done their work anonymously as well as efficiently.

And if among any survivors there was a fleeting impulse to make peace with the present, to hope for a better future in a Europe emancipated spiritually as well as physically from the Nazis, that expectation was soon crushed. In the Balkans, Jews could still see soap stamped: "Made of the purest Jewish fat." In Poland, Jews returning to their old homes were in daily peril of their lives. Hundred were assassinated by Polish bandits after the liberation. And in Vienna, a dispute between Jewish and non-Jewish teams in a soccer game, a "good-will" match, gave rise to a demonstration whose meaning could not be mistaken. The Christian audience began to shout: "Put them in the gas, put them in the gas." That was a new cry in Jewish history. There had been the *hep, hep* of mediaeval times; Jews were accustomed to the various abusive epithets which mobs could devise; but "put them in the gas," the mass-approval of mass murder, was a new howl. This baying had never been heard before. The madness had sunk deep, and liberation had not made it less rabid.

The lesson was clear. Central and Eastern Europe were poisoned with Hitler's legacy. Jews could not breathe in its air heavy with hate, any more than they could stand on its blood-soaked soil. And so, without organization or help, the march toward the Mediterranean began. Singly and in groups, Jews kept walking day and night in the direction which might bring them nearer to Palestine. By foot or by rail, they streamed from the villages of Eastern Europe, passing from "station" to "station," usually a farmhouse or a barn off the beaten track. Despoiled by bribe-taking frontier officials as they crossed from land to land, they would arrive destitute either in the shelter of the American zone in Germany, or somewhere on the Italian coast. Munich, in the American zone of occupation, became a huge clearing center for the final lap to the shore of the Mediterranean.

This tragic, chaotic exodus had to be directed and aided. Guides, whose purpose was to help rather than exploit, undertook to lead the migrants along the roads most likely to bode success. A large reception center was established in Bari, Italy, where the travellers could be housed and fed till they could board the little tramp ships which would take them to Palestine.

The role of the Jewish soldiers, who formed the Palestinian units of the British army, in aiding the current of Jewish refugees towards the shore of the Mediterranean must be mentioned. The appearance of the military trucks with the Star of David, manned by soldiers from Palestine, amid the Jewries of Europe and North Africa is one of the epic moments of the Hitler decade. More than one Palestinian soldier has described the ecstatic joy of Jewish communities in Tripoli or Tobruk, and the unbelieving awe of the survivors of the concentration camps at the sight of the Star worn as a sign of strength and pride. Nor did the Palestinians fail to take pleasure in the dark and unbelieving glances cast by German prisoners at the Badge of Shame, now an emblem of glory.

The effect on the Palestinians of the first contact with the Jews of Europe was equally great. It is no secret that the Palestinians did everything in their power to aid the survivors in escaping from the camps in which they were still immured and from the hostile territories in which they found themselves. The soldiers repeatedly gave up their rations to the destitute, and any soldier blind to the obligation of surrendering his meal for the sake of his less lucky brothers was likely to get short shrift. They not only shared what they had, but they undertook the obligation of acting as national representatives. This was purely instinctive, done without direction — the result of Palestinian "conditioning" as well as European conditions.

In every camp of "displaced persons" that soldiers of the Palestinian units entered, they sought to combat demoralization and discouragement by organizing Hebrew classes and children's clubs; they taught songs and dances. This was done by soldiers, not kindergartners. Intuitively these young men, who deprived themselves of the usual barracks amusements in their scant hours of leisure, assumed the Palestinian's classic role of a *shliach* — a messenger.

They gathered up refugees along the roads and mountain passes and organized them into collectives which trained for agricultural work in Palestine. They strove to instill the spirit of cooperative labor into the ragged, chaotic mass. And when the moment came to board the "illegal" boats, more than one soldier felt certain that his uniform lost no luster when he helped lead the *ma'apilim* to the embarkation point. Of whatever technical offence the members of these units may have been guilty, they believed with Thomas Jefferson that rebellion against tyrants, or tyrannical decrees, was obedience to God.

A vivid glimpse into the heart of the Palestinian soldier has been given by Moshe Mosenson in his *Letters from the Desert*.* Perhaps one of the most poignant moments he described was that of a bombardment during the North African campaign. The soldiers lay in a shelter listening to the bombs overhead. It was the First of May, the holiday of Labor. One of the boys took out his harmonica and played, while the soldiers sang the songs of the Palestinian workers: "Today is a holiday of hands, hands building in cities, hands building in villages, hands building the world." The soldiers never forgot that they were fighting a war to build a world.

Wherever the Palestinians went, they were received as the bearers of the tidings of a new life. One of the

---

* Translated from the Hebrew by Hilda Auerbach, edited with an introduction by Shlomo Grodzensky, Sharon Books, 1945.

Jewish soldiers wrote to his little daughter in a *kvutzah*: "We, the Jewish drivers, carry a great dream in our hearts — that we will be able to bring our brothers from Europe to Palestine in our trucks."

Another Jewish soldier told me of an encounter in Italy. One evening he was driving an army truck when he came upon a huddle of crying women, old men and children. They were Jews who had been trudging along the road trying to find a place of shelter. All had grown exhausted; a mass hysteria was beginning to develop. Then they saw the truck with the Star of David. They surrounded it and climbed aboard, piling in as best they could. No questions were asked, and no remonstrances availed. This was the magic chariot for which they had been waiting. And as the truck started, they began to sing the partisan chant: "Never say that this road is your last." The Palestinian soldier, like the partisans, had won the right to join in the refrain: *Mir seinen doh* ("we are here").

Whatever was done by the Palestinian soldiers for Jewish survivors was accomplished in scant periods of free time or during occasional precious furloughs. I have refrained from discussing the brilliant role of the Jewish units and the Jewish Brigade in North Africa and Europe because the story of Jewish heroism in the general war effort does not belong to this account. But it should be remembered that the help to the refugees rendered by the Palestinians was given in addition to full and gallant participation in some of the fiercest campaigns of the war.

This almost religious dedication is common to the youth of Palestine. A young Jewish seaman, addressing a group who had assumed the task of bringing Jewish refugees to the Promised Land, concluded his practical advice on conduct aboard ship with the words: "I want each one of you fellows to think of himself as a Moses." Had these words been uttered by an orator trying to rouse a comfortably lethargic audience, they would have been stereotyped and insincere. But the speaker was a tough young chap, the first mate of an "illegal" boat which was setting out, addressing other seamen. Palestine was again giving a metaphor the kind of literal application which transformed it from verbiage to an inspired reality.

As the need increased, *Ha'apalah's* original emphasis on individuals suitable for pioneering had to be abandoned. It became a case of saving whomever possible. Frequently, the boats were overcrowded and the physical conditions, especially if the loading was delayed beyond the expected time, bad. But the morale of the voyagers became proportionately higher as *Ha'apalah* developed. The number of Palestinian seamen on each ship kept increasing as more and more young men received the training required. This gave assurance and dignity to the refugees. They were not at the mercy of a hired crew but in the hands of those who viewed them as allies in a common national struggle. Never were they allowed to forget that they were landing as of right, so that even when a boat was caught by British patrols, the *ma'apilim* would disembark not as cowed, beaten creatures, but would march proudly into the port singing *Hatikvah*.

The courage of Palestine reinspirited the battered remnants of the concentration camps. When the *Transylvania* arrived with a load of legal entrants with certificates, one hundred and fifty "illegals" were discovered

343

on board. The eight hundred properly certified passengers, who came from Dachau, Treblinka or Maidanek, refused to leave the ship without the hundred and fifty *ma'apilim*. They watched the Jewish port workers of Haifa gathering on the shore to prevent the seizure of those without the official right of entry, and they declared a hunger strike — men, women and children. If there were a few faltering souls aboard, who felt that after what they had endured they were entitled to a peaceful reunion with waiting relatives, they were quickly outvoted. Finally, all were permitted to land, and the whole port of Haifa rang with the strains of *Hatikvah* as "legals" and "illegals" came on the soil of Palestine.

Some of these landings are already a part of the folklore of modern Palestine — so quickly is history made. The most famous of these, perhaps because it became the subject of an immensely popular poem, was the arrival of the *Hanna Senesch* in the winter of 1945. When the small ship approached the coast of Naharya, a terrific storm broke out. The rowboats used to bring the *ma'apilim* ashore capsized. It was then that the young men waiting on the shore leapt into the waves and swam to the ship, each returning with a *ma'apil* on his back. A wave brought the ship nearer to the shore. A human chain was formed, and the rest of those aboard were passed along till every person had been saved. The empty *Hanna Senesch* capsized on a sand-bank where it was found the next morning by the British. On the overturned ship was planted a blue-and-white flag with the declaration that the *Haganah* would bring Israel to its home.

After the "illegals" were safely scattered in the settlements, a secret reception was held for the Italian captain and crew of the ship. The captain's speech was recorded and publicized:

> We thank you for your invitation. Take our blessing, a brotherly blessing in the name of the new Italy, though even in the old there was little anti-Semitism. True, we did our job for money, but such work cannot be done for money alone. It needs conviction. Our conviction grew stronger when we saw the refugees we carried, literally saved from death . . . . You, too, have the right to be a small independent people along the large Mediterranean, which should be a quiet sea.
>
> I hope I shall return to you many times, and not in small, broken boats, but in great ships full of *ma'apilim*.

The words of the captain moved all Palestine. In response, Nathan Alterman, whose weekly column of verse in *Davar* has been called the sharpest political comment in Palestine, wrote a poem whose publication was not permitted by the British censor. As a result the poem acquired an immediate *sub rosa* fame. It was circulated from hand to hand and widely recited. The ban on the poem was then lifted.

The mood and sense of the verses, if not their deftness and eloquence, are indicated by the following translation of the Hebrew original:

TO THE CAPTAIN OF THE *Hanna Senesh*

The wind lashed the sea, and the sea
    lashed the ship;
You steered through the tempest's
    commotion.
We drink to you, Captain, and lift
    the glass high;
We'll meet again on this ocean.

345

No Lloyds would insure your small,
    secret craft,
Nor the perilous struggle it
    wages;
But though in the ship's log no
    record be kept,
We'll chart it in history's
    pages.

This frail, hidden fleet, grey and silent, will
    be
The subject of song and of story;
And many a captain, who hears of the
    tale,
Will envy you, Captain, your glory.

The night hid the battle with
    wave and with tide,
But our lads than the storm-wind
    were stronger;
Oh, Captain, you saw how from ship
    to the shore
Each swam with a man on his
    shoulder.

A toast to the darkness that swooped
    on the ship,
And crouched on the long lights
    that sought her;
Oh, Captain, God-speed to the
    small wooden boats,
God-speed to these ships on the water!

A toast to the lads that took
    up the fight
And made it their people's
    Trafalgar;
They turn each frail ship to a
    mailed man-of-war;
The ship is of steel — it will conquer.

346

Years to come — you'll be sipping
    a glass of mulled wine,
Or quaffing a draught that is
    stronger;
Then you'll smile, smoke your pipe,
    and shake your grey head,
And think of the days you were
    younger.

You'll remember past deeds, and say to your
    friends:
"I've seen much, but, by Santa Maria!
I'll never forget the night of the
    chase
When we sped on towards Naharya."

Then you'll hear an answering message
    from us:
"The gates of the land are flung
    wide;
This was done by the lads who
    clambered aboard
In that storm, that terror, that tide."

Then you'll chuckle and whisper: "So
    nothing availed:
Neither radar, nor giant lights beaming;
Not even the cruisers . . . ." You'll finish
    your glass
And fall again to your dreaming.

That's how it will be; so, comrades,
    plunge bold
To the heart of the tempest's commotion;
Oh, Captain, God-speed to the
    small wooden boats,
God-speed to these ships on the ocean!

Another expression of the same sentiment is to be found in the lyric of *Ha'apalah* which is sung to a good, rousing tune by the very "lads" whom Alterman toasted:

SONG OF THE "ILLEGAL" IMMIGRATION

We do not ask you whence you came nor where-
    fore;
You step aboard the ship on which we sail;
If firm your heart about the way we're
    heading,
Then, comrade, mount the deck; we bid you
    hail!

From lowest deck up to the highest
    mast-head
She has no cannon nor machine-guns
    now;
But though her hull has neither bombs
    nor armor,
The boat's a battleship from stern
    to prow.

She carries stalwart, resolute battalions —
An army with no weapon in each
    hand,
But with the will to build and firmly
    fashion
A future for our people and its
    land!

The seriousness with which poetry is taken in Palestine is worth noting. In the general press it is viewed as a political force rather than as a filler, and its appreciation is restricted neither to small literary cliques nor to the devotees of the rhymed adage. Particularly now, when the mood of the people is both tense and high, poems and songs of the resistance are read with an interest usually accorded to the pronunciamentos of statesmen and the edicts of legislatures. The earnestness with which a new lyric is quoted is something like that which Americans lavish on the Gettysburg Address or the Declaration of Independence when they feel democracy threatened.

Alterman's latest epigram, or his most recent paean to the *Haganah*, immediately becomes a part of the spiritual equipment of the Jewish community. New immigrants, whose knowledge of Hebrew is too slight for an understanding of Alterman's brilliant and passionate rhymes, are subjected to the efforts of volunteer translators into German, English or Yiddish. He is truly a people's poet in the sense that he expresses and molds national sentiment in a moment of great national crisis. His poems are as good a key as any as to what is activating Palestine.

Alterman's satirical answer to Bevin's complaint that Jews should not attack the "innocent British Tommy" was widely quoted. The overwhelming majority of Jews in Palestine oppose indiscriminate terrorist acts such as the bombing of the King David Hotel, but their views as to the guilelessness of the British army's role in the Middle East would probably coincide with those expressed by Alterman in his anecdote:

> The minister's plaint is a just one, I guess;
> What has the young Tommy to do with this mess?
> But as the grieved statesman indignantly spoke,
> I thought of an old tragi-comical joke.

To her grandson once grandma unburdened her
    heart,
As she plied him with tea and an apricot tart:
"I hear, my dear child, that again you must roam
To war on the Turks in lands far from home.
So pay strict attention and heed what I say,
And follow your grandmother's counsel straight-
    way."

"Do your duty and fearlessly battle the Turk,
But, my son, make sure that you don't overwork.
Shoot a Turk; then lie down for a nap free from
    care;
Shoot a Turk; then go out for a breath of fresh air;
Shoot a Turk; eat and drink; have plenty of rest.
Remember, of blessings, good health is the best."

The grandson smiled wanly and answered his
    granny:
"Many thanks for your counsel so kind and so
    canny;
But I'd like to know what would happen should he,
This Turk, whom you mention, start shooting at
    me?"

The elderly woman wrung both her frail hands;
"My child, God forbid! But the Turk understands.
Who would do such a thing? For what reason?
    Speak true:
What could the Turk ever have against you?"

Still another characteristic note is struck by Alterman
in *D. P. Lullaby*, which voices Palestine's absolute identification with the tragedy of the Jewish survivors.
Unless one appreciates the intensity of this feeling, the
whole drama of the "illegal" boats cannot be under-

stood. The first line of *D. P. Lullaby*: "Yes, little one, yes, you may cry," refers to another one of those poignant incidents which have become part of the folklore of Palestine. A newly-arrived partisan told a large meeting in Tel Aviv how a child of the Vilna ghetto had reacted in the hour of liberation. The little girl's first words had been: "Mother, may I cry now?" In the bunkers and secret cells where they were hidden even very small Jewish children learned early that the relief of crying was not for them. Those that could not learn were sometimes choked into silence to save a large group from detection by the Nazis.

The Jewish child's tragic question in the moment of jubilee provides Alterman with material for a literary *tour de force*. In phraseology and meter the poem has the lilt and tenderness of a lullaby, which serves to intensify the grimness of the contents. The contrast between the airy grace of the vocabulary and rhythm and the sardonic undertone makes the poem extremely effective in the original. Alterman's great talent as a satirical poet can only be savored in Hebrew, but as the spokesman of the bitterness and anguish of Jewish Palestine he can be followed even in translation.

The theme of the poem, which is too long for complete quotation, is the world's treatment of the Jewish survivors. The atrocities have been made public with only one result:

> So now to climax it all
> There's a long and detailed protocol;
> The case is ended thereby,
> And you have permission to cry.

351

From your bed of rags you may rise
And cry aloud to the skies;
For the world, my darling, is free,
And yours is a rare liberty:
Nowhere on the earth, nowhere,
Will any government dare
To stifle your newly-won right
To cry all you please, all night.
No cabinet since the great peace
Will order: "This crying must cease!"

Therefore, my darling, give thanks
To these statesmen of various ranks,
While the precious four freedoms discreet
Bow very low at your feet,
Declaring: "The powers from on high
Now grant her the freedom to cry."

The poem ends on the characteristic Palestinian note.
The child, the "displaced person," will be saved by
Palestine. The little girl will make her way to the
homeland: "You will come, by the Lord, you will come."
And then,

Lads, hard as a fist in a fight,
Will bear you to shore on their breasts.

For the second time since Moses, the waters will be
divided to let the refugee enter the Promised Land,
despite edicts and White Papers:

The Law will conquer the law,
And the youth in whose bosom she lies,
Will watch with wonder and awe
The first smile dawn in her eyes.

These poems must be read as Palestinian Jews read them, with the cries of Jewish refugees driven by tear-gas and water hose to Cyprus ringing in their ears. Alterman is not the only national poet in Palestine, but his success in his particular *genre* has made him, like *Kol Israel*, a radio of the resistance, one of the most eloquent voices of his people.

But the essence of *Ha'apalah* has been stated in its most succinct form by the "illegals" themselves. When the *Beauharnais* was brought into the harbor of Haifa, a long banner over the deck proclaimed their faith:

We survived Hitler. Death is no stranger to us. Nothing can keep us from our Jewish homeland. The blood be on your head if you fire on this unarmed ship.

4

"The Blood Be On Your Head"

As RECENTLY as April 1945, the platform of the British Labor Party read:

> There is surely neither hope nor meaning in a Jewish National Home unless we are prepared to let the Jews, if they wish, enter this tiny land in such numbers as to become a majority. There was a strong case for this before the war, and there is an irresistible case for it now.

In the same spirit, Winston Churchill was one of the most vitriolic denouncers of the White Paper — before he became Prime Minister.

If the Jews of Palestine were "realistic," perhaps they would resign themselves to the prospect facing them. In the scramble for oil, the game of power politics, the detonations of grand-scale rehearsals for atomic warfare, what chance has the feeble appeal for "justice" and "mercy"? Prudent voices counselling the acceptance of the *status quo* are to be heard even among Jews.

But any genuinely realistic appraisal of the situation has to take into account the fact that Palestinian Jewry lacks just this kind of realism. Only the maddest dreamers could have set out to make the deserts of Judea and the stony crags of Galilee bloom again. The same dreamers, reinforced by the desperate Jewry of Europe, are not likely to renounce the vision for which they have sacrificed so much, and whose partial realization they have so magnificently effected.

The *Haganah* will fight to defend the right of Jews to enter Palestine no matter what that entails. They are prepared to sacrifice their homes for the homeland.

Sir Alan Cunningham, in a statement issued after the British onslaughts, urged the abandoning of further resistance so as to avoid the destruction of "much that has been built with such devotion and skill." The High Commissioner's tribute must have had a sardonic ring for the builders who saw their fields ploughed up, their vineyards uprooted, and their modest houses smashed by British tanks.

Among the factual reports of the damage was a detail which seemed slight besides the assaults, torture, and mass arrests from which the British did not shrink in their enthusiasm for the restoration of tranquility in the Holy Land: the dining-hall of Yagur had been destroyed in the course of a raid.

I find myself thinking of the smashed dining-room. When I visited Yagur, only a few months before the attack, the first place to which I was taken was the large new dining-hall, recently built to accommodate the settlement of over a thousand members. Its erection had meant long and patient self-denial for the members of the cooperative. At last it had been finished, with a modern kitchen, plenty of well-screened windows and the simple long tables and benches customary in the cooperatives. It was a pleasant place in which to serve tea and cake to guests when they arrived to visit the settlement. In the dining-hall, the desert had been pushed back as much as in the surrounding orchards and green field.

After the inevitable tea in the dining-room, I had gone to see Avi, the shepherd of Yagur, who had parachuted into Rumania. Because he was still bed-ridden as the result of his leap, he had been given a sunny room in one of the new cottages, better furnished and with more conveniences than the settlers had at first allowed themselves. All this had been razed in a few noisy hours.

Another settlement which the British invaded was "The House of Aridity." The name is well given, for it lies on the shores of the Dead Sea, far below sea level. There, in the blistering heat of the deep cleft, young pioneers have been leaching the soil — washing it free from salt, foot by foot. As each bit of land is redeemed from the arid salt, they irrigate it, fertilize it and plant it. When I visited the settlement, I saw banana groves and rose-trees blooming on the shores of the Dead Sea, the symbol of utter barrenness since antiquity.

I have been to Manara, a high crag in upper Galilee jutting over Lebanon. Boys and girls rescued from Germany through Youth Aliyah were clearing the mountain rock. I saw vegetables and flowers already on the steep slope and seedlings of trees being nursed on the summit.

In the marsh lands of Huleh, still infested with malaria, I saw young women carefully tucking mosquito nets about their babies before going out to help in draining and reclaiming the soggy soil.

This is familiar stuff. By now every one knows what Jewish energy and toil have accomplished in the wastes of Palestine. I mention this only because in each place some boy or girl said to me bitterly: "And *they* don't want us to do this. Whom are we hurting?" And as we would look at the bare, denuded hills or the long stretches of marsh or desert, I would hear the earnest, angry protest: "There is so much room — room for all of us. If *they* would only let us."

They might be the British, or the Arabs, or the whole crazy world which sought to throttle such creativeness. You cannot persuade a boy who has endured discomfort and braved danger and disease to give life to what has been dead that his sacrifices and labor are of no avail. You cannot persuade a boy who is ready to devote his life to washing salt out of sand, or to transforming mountain rock into fertile farmland, that the rock and the sand must remain untouched. The boy understands something about British imperialism, the baleful influence of the oil interests that are courting Arab favor, the machinations of the Arab League, the possible role of Soviet Russia in her drive towards the Persian Gulf — but the intellectual awareness of the international forces complicating the struggle only serves to make him more desperate and determined. He remembers the classic sentence in one of Bevin's statements: "Considerations not only of equity and of humanity but also of international amity and world peace are thus involved in any search for a solution." Yet that is precisely what the boy in Manara or the House of Aridity demands: "equity" and "humanity." He refuses to be sacrificed again to political opportunism and the imperialist rivalries of the great powers. He knows that a Jew murdered

357

in a post-liberation pogrom in Poland might be alive if he had been allowed to come to Palestine. That is why the boy is a member of the *Haganah* and will do its bidding.

Resistance in Palestine is not based on the fancy that the Jewish community is a match for British tanks and bombers. The very young who offer their lives readily for the most perilous enterprises have no calculations except to resist what they conceive to be gross injustice. Their leaders are motivated by the determination to get a hearing. If Britain needs peace in the Middle East for her designs, let her understand that there will be no quiet as long as the gates of the Jewish homeland remain shut. A world as deeply enmeshed in *realpolitik* as before World War II is faced by the quixotic spectacle of a last flaming appeal for "equity" and "humanity," made by an embattled remnant of the Jewish people.

For those who perish in the unequal struggle, there are tears, but they are not as bitter as those shed for the helpless victims of the extermination centers. The following letter appeared in the underground bulletin of the *Haganah* after four of its members were killed:

To the parents:

Your sons fought for the soil of Palestine with Jewish weapons in their hands.

They fought to open the gates of the homeland, to destroy the decree which choked the Jewish people in its land — and they fell.

In their hearts they bore the agonies of millions of Jews who were burned on pyres, and the suffering of the many thousands who still languish in concentration camps.

They carried the faith in the redemption of the Jewish people and its land.

Your sons were not led helpless to the slaughter; they were volunteer fighters, the volunteers of the Jewish people.

So that no more crematoriums be built for Jews, so that their brothers be liberated from the prison camps, they went of their own will to fight for the existence of the Jewish people.

They were free and they freed. They gave their lives for the redemption of their people.

Be proud, and be blessed in them.

5

The Seventh City

◉

BUT the spirit of Jewish resistance is not truly portrayed if one ends on a note of death, even heroic death. For it is not the mood of Masada that animates those who dash themselves against the apparently impossible. The fury of despair may be a factor, but it is not the decisive one. The banner under which Palestine fights is not Masada. When I seek a fitting symbol I do not think of the suicidal stand at the ancient citadel, but of a new, unknown settlement — Geser.

When I visited Geser on the road between Haifa and Jerusalem, there was nothing as yet to be seen except a few half-finished cottages. The settlers, all of them boys and girls from Youth Aliyah, had still only tents to sleep in. But the plan was complete. The boy with the heavy German accent, who showed me about, pointed to a stretch of hot, untilled earth and said: "Here is the garden; here the eucalyptus." And we both saw the flowers and the tree.

After I had inspected the toolshed, the spot where the barn would be constructed, and had heard of the crops that would be raised, my guide gave me a brief lecture on history. Every place in Palestine is hallowed by historic association; the stretch of bare earth before us also had its shades. On this plain, Joshua had blown his trumpet. From beneath this soil, archaeologists had excavated the remains of six ancient cities.

The boy in the shorts meditated a moment on the six cities on whose ruins his settlement was being built. They, like Joshua, were a part of Geser. And then he turned to me with assurance. He looked at the dry, scorched soil and the few scattered tents and barracks and said proudly: "And this is the seventh city, and the last."

The young pioneer, standing on the earth of his forebears, evoking simultaneously the vision of the past and of the future, had unconsciously voiced the essence of Jewish resistance. Palestinian Jews continue the struggle because they believe that they are building "the seventh city, and the last."

Epilogue: 1976

WHEN I WROTE DOWN in 1946 the proud words of the youth at Geser, that they were building "the seventh city, and the last," neither of us suspected that within two years the struggle against the British would culminate in the establishment of a Jewish state. True, Israel arose in a considerably amputated part of the Jewish homeland, but the compromise Partition Resolution of 1947 was welcomed by the Jews of Palestine and the Diaspora because the major goal of Zionism throughout the forties had been to "open the gates" for whoever could be rescued from Hitler's Europe. Even after the victory, Jewish survivors had continued to languish in the camps for displaced persons benevolently set up by the Allies in the British and American zones of occupied Germany. The survivors who streamed to the camps in the hope of escaping the bloodstained earth of Europe and of reaching Palestine were still held back by British quotas.

Nor were other countries more receptive. As 1946 and 1947 wore on, it seemed for a while that Hitler's victims, sustained by no realistic expectation of escape, would rot indefinitely in Germany. Only the fixation on Palestine maintained morale. In the improvised DP schools, children gathered from every part of Europe and from beyond the Urals studied crudely lettered maps of Palestine and, in recently acquired Hebrew, sang of *Arzenu,* "our land." Their elders sought escape as "illegals," knowing that the first stop on the way to Palestine would be British detention behind the barbed wire of a prison camp on Cyprus.

Only an independent Jewish state, however sorely shrunken from the original promise of the Balfour Declaration (Israel arose in one-fifth of the territory originally encompassed by the British Mandate), could emancipate the survivors from the sterile existence of the DP camps and from bondage on Cyprus. Israel's Law of Return immediately proclaimed to the world that at last there was a state that Jews could enter as of right. The dramatic surge of hundreds of thousands of European and oriental Jews to the shores of Israel was the answer.

However, the rosy expectation that hard-won Jewish independence would be permitted to flourish peaceably in the tiny notch of the Middle East assigned for its expression was to prove illusory. Even after international recognition the young state was from birth engaged in an unremitting struggle for existence against increasingly more powerful foes; but the struggle could never be the bestial carnage of the ghettos and the death camps. More than one survivor whose kin fell in war drew consolation from the fact that the son or husband had fought for freedom; he had not been butchered or gassed; death had meaning.

I began my account with Ud, the baby whose name means "the last brand," the ember plucked from the burning. When I had met his parents in a Galilee kibbutz they had newly come from the ruins of the Warsaw ghetto. A quarter of a century later the father of Ud came to see me in New York. He wanted to tell me about his son. The boy had fought in the Six-Day War of 1967. Since I had written about Ud the baby, the father wanted me to know that all had gone well with the youth. Whether Ud fought again in October 1973 I do not know.

Various individuals whom I encountered thirty years ago were to have important roles in the spectacular development of Israel. Reuben Dafni was to enjoy a distinguished diplomatic career. I have lost track of other parachutists who returned from their missions. The memory of Hanna Senesch has not been obscured by time. On the contrary, her legend grows, and books about her continue to appear. I should like to add one note to her story. In 1950 I attended a meeting of the Overseas Press Club that was addressed by Eliahu Elath, then Israel's ambassador to Washington. At the conclusion of his briefing a young Hungarian woman arose to explain that, though not Jewish, she had been imprisoned by the Germans during the occupation. In prison she had met a marvelous Palestinian girl named Hanna, who kept expounding the ideal of an independent Palestine. The girl had been shot. Now that the dream had been achieved, she could not forget this impassioned, young visionary. Did Israel know of Hanna and her tragic fate? Ambassador Elath was able to assure the questioner that Israel both knew and remembered. The Hungarian woman's unexpected tribute was further evidence that the biographers of Hanna Senesch had not indulged in sentimental hagiography.

The most celebrated of the ghetto heroines, Zivia Lubetkin, did not reach Palestine till the end of 1946. That is why I wrote of her by hearsay. But the coming years were to provide many opportunities for acquaintance. Crawling through the sewers under the flaming ruins of the Warsaw ghetto, Zivia had led the exhausted survivors of the uprising to the dubious safety of a fighting unit in the forest. Even after the German defeat, Zivia had remained for a year in Poland in order to gather whatever members of the youth groups had remained alive.

In Israel with her husband, Yitzhak Zukerman, a commander of the ghetto uprising, Zivia became one of the founders of Kibbutz Lohame Hageta'ot (Ghetto Fighters) in Upper Galilee. An active member of the Labor Zionist movement, she attained political prominence as a member of the World Zionist Executive, at whose sessions I came to know her. During discussions I would find myself watching her. This was how a heroine looked—a slight, quiet woman who rarely spoke during the debates. We would chat after meetings, and she would not disguise her impatience to get back to her kibbutz, where work was to be done. Her two children were, of course, in the army. I could not ask her what tormented me: "After all you have endured, what of them?" The unspoken question answered itself, for one sensed the iron under her simple, unassuming manner. In any discussion of Israeli policy, the notion of retreat from a position she viewed as just, whatever the odds, was alien to her. She had conquered fear in the Nazi house of death; she would not be afraid in Israel. Nor should Jews anywhere be afraid if they had a land to defend and the means to do so. This I understood without words. It was the lesson her life had taught her, and I did not have to ask how it had been learned.

Chaya Grossman, one of the leaders of the Bialystok uprising (I quote her in part IV, chapter 7) also became an active political figure. As fiery as Zivia was withdrawn, she often challenged government decisions from her seat as a member of the Knesset, Israel's parliament. Though in manner, temperament, and party affiliation Chaya and Zivia seemed to provide studies in contrast, strength and courage were equally marked in both women.

Abba Kovner, the ascetic-looking youth who had described his years as a leader of the Vilna partisans, was to fight again in the War of Independence. I saw him once more in 1948, only two years after our first meeting in Tel Aviv. I had gone to Negba, a southern kibbutz overrun by the Egyptian army. Now, with the Egyptians driven back, the children of the settlers were returning to their destroyed dwellings. Abba Kovner, a commander of the southern front, addressed the children sitting in the autumn sunshine on a field still green. He pointed to the ruins of the school and dining hall and promised that a bigger dining hall and new school would be built. In them children would learn how valiantly their parents and grandparents had routed the Egyptian tanks with hand grenades. The children believed him and rejoiced. Since those days Abba Kovner has become one of the best-known poets of Israel; his chief theme is the Holocaust.

Not all the tales have had a happy ending. Joel Brandt, who died in 1964, spent his last years brooding over the failure of his effort to ransom Hungarian Jewry. Subject to

365

the passage of time and political influences seeking to exploit his history for partisan ends, he began to alter his account so as to reflect adversely on the Jewish leaders who had pleaded his case before the Allies. Not enough had been done; the Jewish representatives had yielded too readily to the pressure of the United States, and Great Britain. In view of this changed emphasis, whatever its cause, Brandt's original account, given immediately after the event, is of particular importance. A number of individuals who negotiated with the Germans to ransom Jews were to be charged with collaboration—notably Rudolf (Rezo) Kastner, the Hungarian Zionist leader, whose reputation was finally to be rehabilitated by the Supreme Court in Jerusalem. Such accusations and recriminations were part of the bitter aftermath.

Nor did all the survivors who made their way to Israel find fairy-tale contentment. More than one was to decide, after a period of healing, that life in the United States or Canada was preferable to the arduous task of building a new society in a country beset by enemies. For many the first stark teaching of the Holocaust—that in extremity salvation could only come through Jewish national independence—began to lose its impact. Under the circumstances battle fatigue was natural.

But for most the rebirth of a Jewish state remained as precious and miraculous as their own phoenixlike resurrection from the ashes of the crematoriums. The new anti-Semitism, masking itself as anti-Zionism and raging not only in the Middle East but in the Third World and among the countries of the Communist bloc, was a portent whose meaning they could read all too easily. As in the years immediately before the establishment of the state, Israel became the focus of the Jewish people's will to survive and to resist. The machinations of the Great Powers, oil blackmail, and Arab fanaticism only served to highlight the fierce need to preserve Jewish national independence. On all the borders of Israel a new generation stood watch. Their songs were tougher, less romantically self-sacrificial than those of Hanna Senesch and her peers, but the temper was the same.